FROM NAVAN TO CHINA

The story of a "Chinese Irishman"

Aedan W. McGrath SSC
(1906 – 2000)

Compiled and edited by
Fr. Eamonn McCarthy and Michael Walsh

聖 母 軍

Holy Mother's Army

Note of Gratitude

Sincere thanks to all who have made the publication of this book possible; in particular, Columban Frs. Neil Collins, Michael O'Farrell and Michael Duffy, who were so helpful in the course of the research.

We wish to thank Phyllis McGuinness for supplying valuable personal insights into Fr. McGrath's life.

A special note of appreciation goes to Liam Walsh for his invaluable technical assistance in the project and Fr. John McCarthy for his editorial suggestions.

Original Dedication

To my Brothers and Sisters in the Legion of Mary
who prayed for an Envoy in chains.

Aedan McGrath SSC

2008

ISBN 0-9547831-1-5

CONTENTS

CONTENTS

CHRONOLOGY

1906   Aedan William McGrath born in Drumcondra, Dublin.

1923   Entered religious life in the Society of St. Columban, Navan, Co. Meath.

1929   Ordained Priest in Galway.

1930   Assigned to China Mission in Hanyang.

1933   Appointed Parish Priest of Tsien Kiang.

1937   Starts Legion of Mary at Mission in Hupeh Province; impressed by the spirit and performance of Legionaries which gradually extends to a five Praesidium strong Curia.

1939-45 World War II years - Japanese occupation - mission quarters taken over by Japanese soldiers; forced to leave. On return, after two and a half years, amazed to find that the Legion had continued functioning, often at considerable risk to its members.

1947   Returns home for rest and recuperation. At the behest of Archbishop Antonius Riberi, Internuncio to China, Fr. McGrath makes an intensive study of the Legion system while in Dublin.

1948   February - returns to China and starts Envoy-style organising work, moving rapidly to stay ahead of the advancing Communist forces.

1948-49 Legion now organised in 20 Chinese Dioceses and Apostolic Prefectures, with twenty Curia and 260 Praesidia.

1951   January - Legion of Mary growth to 90 Dioceses, with over 1,000 Praesidia.
Legion labelled "enemy of the Regime" because of the part played in counteracting Communist "Indoctrination" and the "State Church" plan. Severe persecution followed - Legion outlawed - members

arrested, expelled from the country. Many are tortured and executed. The Internuncio, on being expelled, declared: "Even if all the priests are forced out, the Legion of Mary will save the Faith in China."

1951   September 7th - the 30th anniversary of founding of the Legion of Mary - arrested and after lengthy interrogation sent to Lokawei Prison.

1954   April 28th - Feast of St. Louis Marie de Montfort - released from Ward Road Jail and expelled from China. During two years and eight months imprisonment subjected to ceaseless interrogation, and much mental and physical suffering; but refuses to sign any "Confession of guilt", or to betray the faith.

Many Legion Spiritual Directors and great numbers of native Legion members were executed under Communist Rule. Their stories may never be told.

Countless numbers of Christians have suffered religious persecution and still languish in prisons and forced-labour camps throughout China.

PREFACE

Though centred on one heroic Missionary Priest, more than one story is being told in this book. The genesis, rise to strength and ultimate triumph of a spiritually motivated and apostolic army of lay people is what animates this tale. One could almost say that the names Fr. Aedan McGrath and Legion of Mary were synonymous. However, this was not always the case.

As this adventure unfolds it becomes evident that it is the efficacy of the Legion of Mary that is being put on trial. And how it proves victorious! The place of the Legion of Mary in China is unique, from its founding there in 1937 to its attempted suppression from 1949 onwards by the Communist Regime. The great tragedy is that the outstanding heroism of so many Legion members will never be fully known. "This story has to be written up," Frank Duff declared emphatically to Fr. McGrath, "for the edification of the world and for the hope of future generations."

Fr. McGrath made several attempts to complete a written account of his years in China. Up until the date of his death, Christmas Day, 2000, he greatly relished every opportunity of telling his story, especially if it meant the promotion of St. Louis Marie de Montfort's *True Devotion to Mary*. The final motivation for now completing what he had begun sprang from the repeated exhortations of the Servant of God Frank Duff, uncovered in the course of work on his Cause for Canonisation. A number of sources therefore have been collated for this current endeavour:

- An autobiographical account entitled *In Mary's Army*, begun by Fr. McGrath but not brought to fruition.
- Correspondence between Fr. McGrath and his mother; also with Frank Duff and John Nagle (Concilium President 1936-1942) including a detailed diary covering the years of his China endeavours.
- Various published accounts in books and periodicals, detailing the work of the Legion of Mary in China.
- Fr. McGrath's captivity account and his homecoming reception in Dublin's National Stadium in 1954 - the audio recording of which is still extant.
- Other recorded interviews with Fr. McGrath.

These various sources are here blended together and the overall progress of the narrative attempts to follow a chronological unfolding of events, culminating in Fr. McGrath's rousing return-home address.

The letters, which span the narrow time-window of opportunity following Fr. McGrath's return to China in 1948 and the gradual strangulation of missionary activity of the Communist regime, have, for the most part, been reproduced in their original form. They incorporate some references to Legion of Mary operations throughout the world and help the reader to contextualise the events taking place in the China of Fr. Aedan McGrath's labours.

To the man who founded the Legion of Mary, Fr. Aedan McGrath's life is an epic. Frank Duff assures us that, "there is no person whom I know that has made more of his life and done more visible work for God." Fr. McGrath's decision to start the Legion of Mary in his Chinese parish "was the most important event in his life, a step of destiny which was not only going to influence his own life but to change the history of China and to affect the religion of the world."

It always pleased Frank Duff to trace this influence to the African labours of Venerable Edel Quinn (1907-1944). Her courage and example won the heart of Monsignor Antonio Riberi who was to come to China as Papal Internuncio at this crucial time. Archbishop Riberi tells us that, "[W]ithout the astonishing success of Edel Quinn's apostolate, it would have been difficult to find the courage to launch the Legion of Mary amidst the adverse and hazardous conditions which afflicted China in the post-war period."[1] Convinced as to the necessity for the Legion, the newly appointed Papal Internuncio held a meeting among the Bishops of China. He told them it was the will of the Holy See that they would operate through the Legion of Mary; that it was a signal opportunity to mobilise the laity to reach out to the thousand millions of this vast nation. The Bishops agreed. What follows is a portrait of the background and the sequel to that decisive step.

---

[1] *Edel Quinn, A heroine of the Apostolate*, H. E. Mgr. Leon-Joseph Suenens, C. J. Fallon Ltd. Dublin, 1954, p.x

GLOSSARY OF TERMS

Terms used with reference to aspects of Legion of Mary membership throughout this book:

Legion of Mary - "an Association of Catholics who, with the sanction of the Church and under the powerful leadership of Mary Immaculate, Mediatrix of all Graces ... have formed themselves into a Legion for service in the warfare which is perpetually waged by the Church against the world and its evil powers."

Handbook - The official Legion of Mary guidebook for the complete understanding of its spirituality and practice. Until his death in 1980, the Handbook was entirely the composition of Frank Duff, the Legion of Mary founder. A portion is read at each Praesidium meeting to familiarise members with its contents.

Praesidium - the basic unit in the Legion within a parish, comprising if possible, not much more than a dozen members. Senior Praesidia comprise those who are 18 years of age or older; Junior Praesidia comprise those who have not yet reached their 18th birthday.

Curia - a governing body composed of two or more Praesidia.

Comitium - normally governs the Legion in one particular Diocese and serves one or more Curia and Praesidia.

Regia - a Council exercising authority over the Legion of Mary in a large region and ranks next in status to a Senatus.

Senatus - a Council designated by the Concilium to exercise control over the Legion in a country. Two or more Senatus Councils may be approved in larger countries.

Concilium - is the Central Governing Council of the Legion and is based in Dublin, Ireland.

Tessera - printed card or leaflet containing the text of the Legion of Mary Prayers.

Promise - a solemn prayer of commitment made by new members following 12 weeks of probationary membership, formally recited during the meeting. The Legion promise is not a binding undertaking. In invoking the Holy Spirit, and trusting in Our Blessed Lady, the member makes a personal pledge of faith and commitment to the apostolic work.

Work Sheet - annotated list used at a Praesidium meeting to record the work undertaken by the members.

Acies - the annual assembly of all Legionaries for the purpose of renewing their consecration to the Blessed Virgin Mary. It takes place on or around the 25th March. The literal meaning of Acies being – keen/sharp/as a battle line or, in Legion parlance – 'terrible as an Army in battle array'. (cf. Songs 6:10)

Reunion - annual social gathering of Active and Auxiliary members of a Curia incorporating the recitation of the Legion Tessera prayers.

Active member - one who attends the weekly Praesidium meeting and is fully engaged in the work obligation of the Legion.

Officer - an active member with the additional role of President, Vice-President, Secretary or Treasurer.

Auxiliary - praying member of the Legion of Mary who undertakes to recite the rosary and full prayers contained on the Tessera.

Adjutorian - an auxiliary member who undertakes attendance at daily Mass and the recitation of an approved office of the Church.

Praetorian - an active member who undertakes attendance at daily Mass and the recitation of an approved office of the Church.

Tribune - In the early formation of Legion Praesidia, when membership was confined by and large to women only, the Tribune was a male liaison officer whose function was to get people in touch with sources of legal and other material benefits to which they might be entitled. Frank Duff occupied this office in the first Legion Praesidium for some years.

Laureate - a degree of membership created in order to render due honour to those who had helped the Legion in a manner which could be regarded as quite exceptional. In all, 47 Laureates were awarded by the Concilium. This degree no longer exists.

Envoy -   an active Legionary appointed by the Concilium to engage in full
                   time establishment of the Legion of Mary in a territory where it
                   does not as yet exist.

Vexillum -   the Legion of Mary standard or emblem. The model which
                   adorns the Legion altar is 30cm in height.

Standard -   a large representation of the Vexillum, around two metres in
                   height used at the annual Acies Ceremony.

Vexillina -   the Legion Vexillum in miniature, worn as a badge.

Spiritual Director - a priest or religious providing spiritual guidance at the
                   weekly meetings in matters concerning the faith and the works
                   undertaken. Sometimes abbreviated as S.D.

Allocutio -   A short talk given by the Spiritual Director, or in his absence,
                   the Praesidium President midway through the meeting, by way
                   of instruction and spiritual exhortation for the members.

Standing Instruction - the four basic rules of the Legion regarding weekly
                   attendance, prayer, performance of work obligation, and
                   confidentiality of matters learned in connection with the
                   Legionary work - read aloud by the President to the Members
                   from the Handbook at the first Legion meeting of each month.

Maria Legionis - the official Legion of Mary quarterly periodical. First published
                   in 1937, it contains articles of spiritual and Legion interest as
                   well as news of the growth and development of the organisation
                   worldwide. Also referred to as 'The Legion Journal'.

FR AEDAN MCGRATH SSC - TRAVELOGUE

1930
21/08 SETS SAIL FOR CHINA
30/09 HANYANG, HUPEH

1933
    TSIEN KIANG

1942
    HANYANG

1945
    TSIEN KIANG

1947
    IRELAND

1948
16/02 SHANGHAI
06/06 HANYANG
10/06 WUCHANG
11/06 HANKOW
25/06 SHANGHAI
22/08 PEKING
25/10 TIENTSIN
01/11 SHANGHAI
11/11 HONG KONG
12/11 KOWLOON

1949
04/02 CANTON
04/03 KWEILIN VIA LIUCHOW
09/03 CH'UEN HSIEN
14/03 TUNG-AN
15/03 LAI PO
18/03 HONG KONG
22/04 CANTON
03/05 HENYANG – HUNAN
16/05 CANTON
05/06 MACAO
12/06 CHUNGKING
24/07 CHENGTU
04/10 CHUNGKING
13/10 WANHSIEN
16/11 CHUNGKING

1950
26/05 CHUNGKING
04/07 SHANGHAI

1951
18/06 SHANGHAI
07/09 ARREST & DETENTION

1954
28/04 PRISON RELEASE
MAY   HONG KONG
JULY   DUBLIN

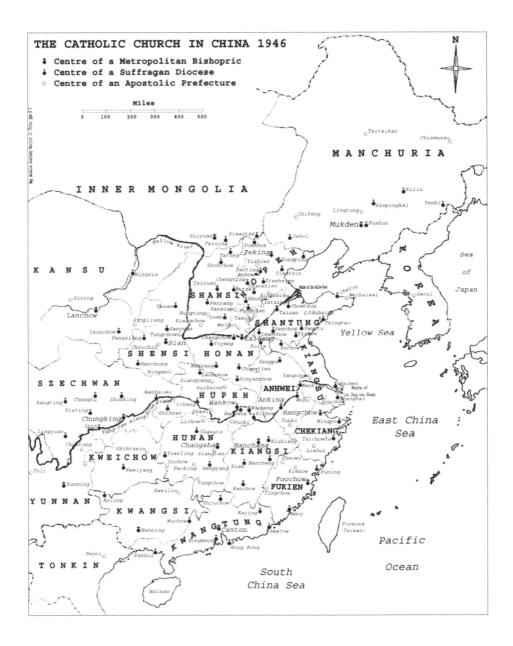

PART ONE

1906 TO 1930

EARLY YEARS

1914-1918 - World War I - Europe in turmoil.

1916 - Easter Rising - Dublin - Irish struggle for independence
        from British Rule.

1917 - Russian Revolution - birth of Communism
        - Our Lady appears at Fatima, Portugal

1921 - Founding of Legion of Mary
        - Establishing of Chinese Communist Party

1922 - Irish Civil War

CHAPTER ONE

DUBLIN

THE MCGRATH FAMILY

On behalf of Christ, therefore, we are acting as ambassadors,
God as it were appealing through us. (2Cor. 5:20)

Four volleys pierced the silence of the night. My father lay dying on the landing. The acrid-smelling smoke of discharged firearms hung in the air. I was in bed, half asleep, when the nightmare scenario erupted. Little did I know that the assassination was to forever change my family.

Lawyers never made big salaries in those days. Even though my father was a Senior Counsel, it was difficult for him to pay all the family bills. Financial pressure was the reason he took on the extra position as a County Court Judge. As such, he had been threatened many times while adjudicating for soldiers and ex-soldiers who were out of work and were entitled to allowances while unemployed. Dublin was under martial law at the time, with British conscripts given free rein in a guerilla war against the 'Old' Irish Republican Army.

William McGrath was a just man and I am quite sure he was very careful about dispensing compensation payments to those who should not by right receive them. Because of this refusal, some military men threatened him, "If you don't give the allowance to us, we'll get you." These soldiers and ex-soldiers were not slow to consort with the Black and Tans.[2]

A short time before my father was murdered, I was sitting at home one evening, looking out onto the front garden, when a Crossley Lorry pulled up outside our house, ominously parking there for half an hour. Guns were protruding on either side of the vehicle and the men wielding them were clad in the black and tan coloured army issue that gave them their nickname. Each man also wore a handkerchief across his nose and mouth to prevent his being

---

[2] The 'Black and Tans' were a mercenary squad of soldiers operating under the British Occupation forces and known for their ruthless tactics.

recognised. Frightened by this act of terrorism, I wondered why they were stopping at my house. I was soon to learn the grim answer to that question.

One week before that fateful day, our home at 129 Altona Terrace, North Circular Road was broken into. My father got up, went downstairs and called out. 'Who's that?' There was no response. The intruders had forced open the front door, gone through to the back and into the garden. Apparently, they were only checking the lay of the land.

The year was 1921. Ireland was at a crucial point in its political history and going through a period of civil unrest. In Dublin, a curfew was imposed at ten o'clock every night. Only the brave or the foolish would risk leaving their home during curfew. I was out with my sister Maeve, who was sixteen at the time, visiting our cousins, the Fitzpatrick's over in Clontarf. We came back at nine o'clock on the tram. At the corner of Aughrim Street, I said to Maeve, "do you notice it's so dark?" The big arc light which normally lit up the five intersecting roads, was switched off. We had never seen this light extinguished at this hour. There was always a Dublin Military Policeman standing at that corner, but he was not to be seen that night. However, we didn't think too much about it and made our way through the streets, arriving home at half past nine.

In the house that night were my parents, Donny my brother who was at that time preparing for his final medical exams, my sister Maeve, the housemaid Maggie and myself. I was alone on the fourth floor. The others were downstairs.

Sometime in the small hours, it must have been about two o'clock, I heard my mother calling. I thought I was dreaming and turned over in the bed to resume my sleep.

She kept crying out, 'Aedan come down, come down!'

Soon afterwards, I realised what had happened. The front door had been jemmied open. My father, fearless as he was, got out of bed, put on the landing light and began to go downstairs calling, 'who's there?' As he turned at the top of the stairs he would have appeared under the light to those below in the hall. Gunfire rang out and my father fell, groaning as he did so, "I'm shot!" Maeve ran to the landing, and with Donny's assistance, picked him up, brought him to his room and laid him on the bed. The assassins fled.

When I came down to the room, Maeve had already gone with Maggie to the telephone downstairs to summon a priest. It was the first thing my mother thought of doing. My father was lying on the bed in a terrible state having taken three bullets to the abdomen and one through the hand.

Fr. Turley, a well-known Dublin Priest in Aughrim Street was brief. He said to Maeve, "You know we are not allowed out. I'll try the Police." He 'phoned the D.M.P. (Dublin Metropolitan Police) - the native constabulary - to be told: 'Father, we're not allowed out either; we can't go out no matter what the situation.' Fr. Turley said, 'Well I don't care, I'm going up to Mr. McGrath.' At that, a kind young policeman then agreed to accompany him. As they made their way along there was still no officer on duty at the corner of Aughrim Street.

All the while, I was standing at the bedside. There was little a young teenage boy could do. I can clearly remember hearing my father say to my mother, "Gertrude, if anything happens to me, it was the out-of-work soldiers who did this."

Fr. Turley arrived before too long. He anointed my father and heard his confession. Even in his wounded condition he was able to receive Holy Communion as Viaticum.

Donny had in the meantime 'phoned up Johnny McArdle, an eminent surgeon. Dr. McArdle gave the familiar answer, 'You know we are not allowed out, even with an ambulance.' My brother then 'phoned up Marlborough Barracks and they, in turn, refused a police escort for the doctor. In the end, the doctor like the priest, showed his heroic commitment to duty, and, getting into the ambulance, risked his life coming across the city to our place at that forbidden hour.

On seeing my father he knew that there was no hope for him. He beckoned to us, saying gnetly, "bring in the children." So we were all called in to say goodbye to my father before he went off in the ambulance to St. Vincent's Hospital.

When we arrived at the Hospital the next morning, my father's body was laid out.

A couple of days later, in a room in St. Vincent's Hospital, the D.M.P. held a sort of investigation of what had happened that night. My brother Donny and some five or six officers were present. Donny was called in and also a soldier who had been up near Ellesmere Avenue that night. The soldier said, "I...saw the lorry down the road." That soldier was not brought back for questioning. All the evidence pointed to the fact that my father was slain with the connivance of the military authorities.

Tim Healy, who was looking after my mother's affairs, wanted to bring a case against the Black and Tans, but my mother refused him reckoning that the important thing was that Maeve and her sons be allowed to live. This also meant that she would be able to receive some compensation towards our continued education.

Aedan McGrath was born on January 22nd 1906 and lived with his family in 'Carraig Uladh', (Rock of Ulster), number 50, Upper Drumcondra Road, Dublin, until he was six years old. He enjoyed a carefree childhood.

Aedan's father had a reputation for being a hard-working man who contributed generously to his family's standard of living. Originating from Portaferry, Co. Down, he studied at the Law Courts and became a Barrister. His wife Gertrude, nee Fitzpatrick, became a teacher in the Kings Inn School. She was one of a family of thirteen and hailed from Downpatrick. Creating a happy family environment for their children and providing for their educational needs was a priority for the McGrath family. Both parents worked hard in those years of widespread poverty and destitution.

From Drumcondra, the family, consisting of brothers Garrett, Donny, Ronan and Aedan and a sister Maeve, moved to the North Circular Road. Another brother, Ivar, the youngest, was to be born to Gertrude in 1913. From this new setting, the family enjoyed summer vacations in Bettystown every year, staying for up to three months at the picturesque seaside resort.

Tragedy would soon strike the family however. Garrett, the eldest, had been seriously injured as a result of a kick inflicted upon him at a football match while at Belvedere College. His bowels were badly impaired as a result of the incident. The doctor prescribed Castor Oil, and, after an operation, Garrett's health rallied for a time, but he suffered thereafter with a delicate stomach and died a short time later from his injuries. Aedan recalls that not long after, Garrett's girlfriend, Allie Mullett, entered religious life.

According to Aedan, his sister Maeve was his mothers' 'pride and joy'. She was a first class pianist, spending as many as six hours a day at the piano. An excellent dancer, the young girl attended Madame Marks/Mr. Byrne's school of dancing in Dublin and was on the stage as part of a dancing show every year. Maeve attended the Sacred Heart School in Leeson Street and studied at Mount Anville in Dublin.

Soon after her husband's brutal killing, the Irish Government granted some compensation to Gertrude, sufficient at any rate to finance the family in the short-term.

They never went back to Altona Terrace after William's death. Gertrude wouldn't hear of it. The family moved to Aedan's grandfathers' house. He lived next door to the old family homestead, Carraig Uladh. A teacher at the Drumcondra, Training College, 'Sutton House', he took them under his stately roof and looked after them in their hour of need.

But, again, tragedy would soon befall the family. Around this time, Aedan's sister Maeve, still at school, began to suffer ill-health. As she was showing no improvement in spite of treatment, her doctor suggested that she should be taken to where she would have the opportunity to rest in rural surroundings. Accordingly, a period of respite was taken in Rhyll, North Wales. Specialists from Liverpool visited, but failed to diagnose her illness. Gertrude purchased a pony for Maeve and her brothers would take her down to the beach every day for two or three months that summer. Recuperation never seemed likely, and sadly, Maeve died there.

Aedan would later opine that they always considered the terrible fright that Maeve received on the occasion of her father's assassination to be the cause of her untimely death in Wales on 15th September 1922.

The remaining members of the McGrath family next moved to London to join Donny who had a medical practice in the capital. From this location Ivar attended Dulwich College to continue his studies.

Aedan attended Kings College on the Strand in London and it was here that his love for the game of rugby was resumed, nurtured as it had been in Belvedere College in his primary school days in Dublin. It was during this period of residence in London that Ronan asked him to make what he later describes as 'a decisive Retreat.' It was in the course of that prayerful time out that Aedan decided on China as his missionary destiny. Following Ronan's example, Aedan entered the Columban Missionary Society at Cahiracon, Co. Mayo in the autumn of 1923 in time for his older brother's ordination on 23rd December that year.

Donny was soon to marry and this brought with it the decision to make a further domestic adjustment - this time, a move to Paris. To give Donny and Isabel their own privacy, Gertrude decided to rent a separate apartment and it was from there that Ivar attended St. Aloysius Gonzaga College run by the Jesuits. Over the course of the next two years of their stay there he became quite proficient in his command of French.

Later, on their return from Paris, Ivar and his mother took up residence in Howth, Co. Dublin. He too, would follow his brothers into the Columban's and was destined to be ordained on 21st December 1935.

Aedan had no doubt imbibed some of the missionary spirit of St. Francis Xavier from his early education at the Jesuit Belvedere College, but it was the newly founded Society of Saint Columban that he chose.[3]

Founded in 1918 by Fr. Ned Galvin from the diocese of Cork and Ross and Fr. John Blowick of Ireland's national seminary in Maynooth, this young and by now thriving order had set its sights on the Missionary work of the Far East. The first pioneering band of sixteen Columban Missionaries had set out for China on March 17th 1920.

Statue of St. Columban – Chapel, Dalgan Park, Navan, Co. Meath

Aedan was not by any means a brilliant student, but what he lacked in intellect he more than made up for by his various natural abilities. Though small of stature, he was good-humoured and spirited, qualities which greatly endeared him to his fellow-students.

1924 was his Novitiate, or spiritual year. In class, we are told that this Novice was serious and attentive, but that he was the first to see and enjoy a joke. His spirit of prayer and recollection were also of note. During free hours he was said to be 'forever lilting songs'. He was blessed with a beautiful tenor voice. A good sportsman, he played a splendid game of rugby, golf, hurling and Gaelic football.

Aedan McGrath was ordained a Priest on the Feast of St. Thomas the Apostle, December 21st 1929. His mother had by this time returned to Dublin when her newly ordained son set sail for China in 1930. His first duty in that vast land was the study of Chinese, which, with its countless ideographs, tones and inflections, was no easy task for a Westerner.

He never became master of the written language, but excelled in the spoken dialect of the man in the street. In time, having an ear for music and

---

[3] The full story of the coming into being of the Columban Missionary Society is colourfully told by Edward Fisher in *Maybe a Second Spring*, Crossroad Publications, New York, 1983, pp.12-18.

being a good mimic, he became as fluent and natural in the spoken word as the Chinese themselves. In fact it was difficult to distinguish his manner of speech from that of the natives. Because of this proficiency in Chinese and due to his affable and jovial dispositions, he became a favourite among his adopted people. A fellow missionary speaks of Aedan's sermons as having an eloquence all their own. Digressing from standard pulpit oratory, he would preach in a simple homely style using his own ingenious examples from everyday life.

It marks a curious retrospect that, although living in proximity to the hub of the early Legion of Mary endeavours, and despite its early prodigious success in Dublin, the young Aedan did not encounter the movement until knowledge of it was brought to him in China.

Three Columban Priests – Ronan, Aedan and Ivar McGrath - 1980's

PART TWO

1930 TO 1946

FIRST MISSIONARY ENDEAVOURS

1927 - Chiang Kai-shek, Chinese Nationalist Party leader strives to eliminate Communism.

1931 - Japanese seize Manchuria - growing threat to China.

1934-1936 - The Long March - Communist forces under Mao Tse-tung pursued by Chiang Kai-shek.

1937 - Japan's all-out invasion of China.

1939-1945 - World War II

1945 - Hiroshima & Nagasaki - Atomic annihilation.

1945-1946 - Communist/Nationalist alliance to fight the occupying Japanese.

CHAPTER TWO

HANYANG/TSIEN KIANG - 1930

For we would not, brethren, have you ignorant of the affliction which came upon us in Asia. We were crushed beyond measure - beyond our strength, so that we were weary even of life. (2Corinthians 1:8)

Following a six week voyage, having set sail on 21st August 1930, Fr. McGrath arrived at his first assignment - the Columban Mission House at Hanyang in the province of Hupeh in Central China.[4] His superior there was Bishop Ned Galvin, the co-founder of what had now become known as 'The Maynooth Mission to China'.

Bishop Ned Galvin with children in Hanyang

---

[4] Father Timothy Leahy describes the journey in his publication, *Beyond Tomorrow*: "I left for the diocese of Hanyang, Hupeh, in Central China in August, 1930. It was a slow journey in those days (more than five weeks) in a P&O liner, via Aden, Port Said, Singapore, Hong Kong, to Shanghai, and finally the last 650 miles in a Jardine steamer up the Yangtse River from Shanghai to Hankow. At Hankow my companion, Fr. Aedan McGrath and I crossed the Han River by sampan to the 100% native Chinese city of Hanyang and from there on, all my journeyings through the Hanyang vicariate were by sampan or Chinese pony or most frequently of all, on foot. There I met for the first time our beloved Bishop Galvin."

Together with his priestly ministry, these early and eventful years of Fr. McGrath's missionary activity were also spent in adapting to the language and customs of his newly adopted country.

In the summer of 1931, a cataclysmic flood of the Yangtse and Han rivers caused widespread devastation. Fr. McGrath recounts how he lost all of his personal property, his books and clothing to the floodwaters and did not regain access to his room in the Columban residence for six months.

Hanyang, like many parts of China, was far from stable, not only because of the Warlords - local dictators who dominated certain territories - but also renegade bandits who created their own mayhem as they robbed indiscriminately from both rich and poor, unscrupulous as to the fate of their victims. The struggle between the Nationalists and Communists was also simmering at this time and sometimes boiled over into open hostilities. The Japanese occupation and the Second World War would further complicate the missionary work, while widespread poverty and the vagaries of the local climate were also a perpetual hindrance to progress.

Worst winter in sixty years as depicted in *The Far East* magazine, June 1930

Fr. McGrath Recalls[5]

In 1933, I was sent by Bishop Ned Galvin to a small parish in which there never had been a resident parish priest. At first, I lived in a small house on the street in the city of Tsien Kiang, one hundred miles north of Hanyang. Later, I stayed in an old converted mill-house which belonged to a lovely traditional Chinese family. My sleep at night was interrupted by the occasional rat scurrying across my bed.

Over a period of time, the patriarch of this domestic community took a real interest in my work such that all three-generations of his family came into the Catholic Church.

It was from this house that I carried out the ordinary duties of a parish priest - looking after the spiritual welfare of the townsfolk and visiting the rural areas to celebrate Mass and administer the sacraments.

I had twenty-five mission stations. There was no electricity, no running water; there were no buses and no cars; I didn't even have a bicycle, so I walked. The twenty five missions would take two months to get round; three days in this little hut, three days in the next one and half a day to walk to the next one and so on.

In the city and surrounding areas, there were no more than 40 Catholics and in the country missions, about 500 in all…

St. Columban's, Tsien Kiang City
August 14th 1934

My dearest Mother,

For a couple of weeks past my news was commonplace, owing to things being normal, which in China is abnormal! A normal spell never lasts long however, and this time proved no exception. I have just had one of the most eventful weeks since I came to China, finishing as it has in another tragedy for the poor people. An unprecedented flood has robbed them of everything - crops, and even houses. I told you sometime ago that the wheat crop was ruined, owing to incessant rains, but it did not rob them of their hope of a rice crop which can always pull them along. Now as the harvest was in sight, having spent all their savings on the fertilising of the land, and delighted at the prospect of a bumper crop, in poured the merciless water, and in one short day wiped out every hope!

---

[5] Fr. McGrath wrote these memories shortly after his return to Ireland in 1954.

15

Only a short week ago, things were settling down. All my smaller schools were closed; students had gone home, so there was no need for me to visit the country districts. I was feeling content, though busy straightening up things, before going down on retreat. Then a report came of rising river waters, which disturbed everyone - from the Magistrate down to the poorest beggar. Business almost came to a standstill, and all conversation circled round the possibility of a flood. The city is very low and has always suffered greatly from floods. As rumours increased and excitement became intense, I walked out to the dykes about one mile from the city, and found the water lapping over the top. Already huge quantities of rice were ruined. The first thing which struck me was the absolute calmness, resignation, and even humour which lit up the faces of everyone. Starvation awaiting the inmate of every house on the dyke, they sat patiently at their doorsteps watching each wave of water coming closer. It made me sad to see such wonderful resignation going without its heavenly reward. No foreigners could have done it. Trouble much less than this would drive any pagan abroad to commit suicide in order to get away from the awful consequences. I took one last look at the dyke and then hurried home to get all my stuff moved upstairs to keep it dry. We knew if the water came over the dykes, the city still had another wall of protection, which was not so good, but a help. Every moment, more alarming reports came and as night fell, the city was properly astir. The people were running about carrying furniture, and useless odds and ends of personal property that they treasured.

We took it in turns to stay up that night and await events. I had not slept half an hour when I was awakened, and told that the dykes had broken below the city, and the water, though not yet so dangerous was in a roaring torrent at the south gate. My ears were sufficient proof! I went down with a teacher to see for myself and the sight was certainly distressing. Pitch dark, and the torrent rushing past the south gate, lapping the steps. Because it had burst the banks below the city, I saw there was no danger - at least for that night - so I went to bed.

Next morning I said Mass and got the Catholics to pray that God might protect the city. The water had risen slowly during the night, and was within a few feet of the top of our protecting dyke. A substantial breach was discovered, and work began feverishly to try and stem it. Hundreds of men, women, and children carried clay doors, old clothes, stones, and anything they could lay their hands on, to try and lessen the flow. Tons of beans were poured into the spaces - so that swelling up in the water, they might fill the opening. Men dived down continuously to feel for the hole, as now the water had well covered it. It was dangerous work too, for often their legs would be sucked in, and only with great effort could they be dragged out again. The poor Magistrate was exhausted with the strain.

Night fell and the flood was worse. All night they worked, yet another day, and as the night of the third day fell, the Magistrate said to me, "all no use, we can't stop it", and he went home and removed his last articles to safety - his prisoners. While he felt no hope, I still felt a strange confidence, although the water lapped near the top of the last dyke. I thought of my Catholics' prayers and the three Masses, greater than all the workmen could think of doing.

To the amusement of many, who were by now convinced that all had failed - a Buddhist priest with his long hair-tied up in a knot together with his assistant, came to the spot "Kao Towed", burned some paper, and prayed over it. During the proceedings some of the crowd, to mock him, said, "Oh the leakage is stopped, 'tis stopped." In fact the water seemed to be flowing all the faster!

That night all returned home disheartened, and did not continue the work. Some of the natives sat at their doors awaiting that awful splash, which would swamp the city and probably tear houses from their foundations.

I slept as usual for I was dead tired, and the sun in the morning awoke me. A boy told me with delight and triumph in his voice, "the waters have ceased to rise." I thanked God from my heart, and said a Mass of thanksgiving. Later on another leakage was discovered after breakfast, more dangerous than the first, but prompt and energetic action by military personnel, hundreds strong, working a whole day and night, strengthened the dyke sufficiently to hold off the waters until they began to recede yesterday morning. Thank God we are dry, but we are the only such place in my district, for some distance around. It was a historic battle, and I firmly believe it was primarily the Masses and prayers which saved us, not without the stupendous efforts of the people (who are partly Catholic).

It was the greatest flood seen for ever-so-long. One mission station of mine, having survived for twenty four years, fell before the waters of this flood. The country people sent up a deputation to me yesterday - all very downhearted and worn out from the fight on their dykes and asked me for aid. You know my reply! For over two months the Bishop's budget is overdrawn, and now the last of my personal resources are going, another week or so of ordinary expenditure will finish me.

Their request was reasonable - in one or two places where the water is deep they cannot hope to sow or reap anything for about a year, and they must starve till then. Their men folk will go out and beg, and this being unbecoming and dangerous for the women and children, they asked me to take care of them in their stead. I had to put them off for a few days to see if the Bishop had any plan. If he has not, may God help them. The city Catholics likewise feeling for their brethren came in last night and begged me to do what I could. All I can do is to trust in Divine Providence.

Some time has elapsed before I could get this letter finished, I have a spare moment and here it is again. The flood did not get into the City, *Deo Gratias*, but nearly all my Missions are washed out, and when the waters receded, the people, with characteristic resignation, again got to work to sow the next crop – this time, millet.

A prolonged dry period followed. The millet still could have stood awhile without water, but not the amount of water that has now come. This repetition of the flood into the very same place, though not in the city, looks set to continue until October, because they have never yet been successful in getting the dykes rebuilt in time before the waters come in again.

The second waters went out, and again my poor people set to work smiling, to set more millet. In the meantime I have been on retreat in Kuling, and I am wondering have the waters come in since? Save that I had to come up for the retreat, I think I would have deserted the place for I had not a penny to help them, and they could not understand why I had not! As I told you, I wrote to the Bishop as my only hope and I waited a long while for the reply, and then it was worse than no reply. I wish I had it to send you. I have tremendous sympathy for the poor Bishop: He began by saying, "Aedan your letter is appalling - and what is worse I am penniless, and have had to turn down every appeal from all over the Vicariate." He continued, "For the past three years I gave generously while I had it, and trusted in God for the days to come -

and now penniless I am faced with this catastrophe - I suppose the Lord has a hand in it somewhere - but at times it is very hard to see Him." Then he spoke of the chances we have had of converts on account of these three years of floods - if we could only open schools. This year, schools will be impossible. The big Catechumenate which he built two years ago, he fears he cannot open, and if no schools, no converts - and yet we have tens of thousands trying to enter the Church. He cannot build for me. I have still to carry on in that Chinese house, which has to be for me school, Chapel, Priests' residence, boys' quarters, kitchen, and stable. He finished his letter by saying, "Aedan it is going to be a terrible year." He remarked too that no money was coming from America, and the Superior General has been unable to send anything.

The Catholics came continually to find out if the reply had come - and this was all I had for them. "No money and no prospects." All I could tell them to do was to go up North where there were no floods - and help the people with the harvest - but now drought has left no harvest and refugees are so many, that I have left my people to go off on their own begging. What can be done in a few months - if things turn out better, remains to be seen.

We are all in the same boat. I have had to dismiss a teacher and a boy already, and generally sit tight and refuse to buy anything. I guess the Lord has His own ideas and will "bring good out of evil", as usual. I am trying to think of a plan to help these poor unfortunates, for nothing gives me greater pleasure than to be able in some way to alleviate their sufferings.

You must dread to open these awful letters lately, but I know that you, and all, will give me and mine a more fervent prayer now, and during the coming year, when you know what we have to face. I hate begging, but this time it is not for myself, it is for the least amongst Christ's Brethren! And as to the reward, it is already promised by the Lord. If you know anyone willing to help please tell them about my flood, and ask the prayers of the Sisters, for my poor people have confidence in them, which must make them efficacious.

Such is life in China, I am happy and well at all events. Aedan[6]

---

[6] The available letters to Fr. Aedan McGrath's mother conclude with the typed spelling 'Aiden'. However, the more popular occurrence of the spelling 'Aedan' is used throughout this book.

CHAPTER THREE

CATHOLIC ACTION - 1935

*I am astonished that you are so promptly turning away from
the one who called you…there are trouble-makers among you
who are seeking to pervert the gospel of Christ. (Galatians 1:6,7)*

Fr. McGrath recalls…After two years of strenuous labours, I realised that
the visitation of all my mission stations, and their proper spiritual care,
plus the work of the propagation of the faith among the pagans was far
too much for one priest. If only I had the support of Religious Sisters to look
after the schools and care for the sick, it might have greatly lightened my burden.
But the Bishop was in no position to give me Sisters, Brothers or even lay helpers.

About this time the Holy Father, Pope Pius XI, was talking and writing
much about Catholic Action. He had completed an Encyclical calling the laity to
participate more fully in the work of the Church and we now see that his
writings were providential and well timed. As Supreme Pontiff he was looking far
ahead and saw clearly the Communist menace approaching. He also foresaw that
the only adequate answer to Communism and its tactics was a fervent lay
Apostolate; that every Catholic must be an apostle.

Not having the haziest notion what Catholic Action meant I bought
books on the subject both in English and Chinese and settled down to study
them carefully. The first thing that struck me was that Catholic Action required
a good deal of office work. It had many divisions and sub-divisions requiring
much clerical activity, a factor which I surmised, would greatly appeal to the
Chinese, who are born organisers and business-people. I had doubts as to its
feasibility but I was prepared to give it a fair trial. Being vague on the matter
myself I suggested that my Catholics have a go at the organisation by themselves;
and so in no time things developed into a monthly meeting. We had
representatives from the town and from many of the country missions, who
would come along regularly each month. At the meeting we would say a prayer to
the Holy Spirit for light and guidance. A president was appointed, and he would
call out the many proposals to be discussed. The Secretary would ring a bell
before each discussion and take the minutes of the proceedings. I wasn't very
clear as to what was happening, but for one thing I knew that there was to be a

subscription from each member, to help to run or defray the expenses of the organisation.

Though there did not initially seem to be much by way of apostolic endeavour, they seemed pleased to hold meetings. It was proposed, seconded and passed that they do some kind of evangelisation. They decided in general that they should help the priest in the salvation of souls. In particular they decided to visit the Catholic houses in the city and try to get people to return to Mass and the practice of religion and especially the reception of the Sacraments...

Catholic Mission,
Tsien Kiang,
4th February 1935

My dearest Mother,

I believe weeks have passed since I wrote, pardon me. I have been busier than I could have imagined. Everything is going nicely *Deo Gratias* and I hope to have a good year of Baptisms. Your most welcome letters have come, as usual bringing news of some kindly soul helping - Cecil Harris, Aileen Mitchell etc. I do not know what to think of you all. I am preaching you all over my district and getting prayers - such as they are...

...I have started Catholic Action here and the enthusiasm is terrific. Everything is going splendidly and all are a great help to me. Their chief duties at present are the baptising of pagan children when opportunities arise, the bringing back to the Sacraments of our lukewarm brethren, and the close study of Doctrine - reading papers or lecturing on Doctrine in my presence with a view to being fit to answer the innumerable questions and difficulties which stubborn pagans propose in the city, in other words, a course of Apologetics. They are a fine crowd and every Priest who visits here is astounded at their knowledge of Doctrine and their earnestness. Every day I am more and more surprised at them. We have our cold ones too - say a prayer for them.

I hope to enclose a photo of our Catholic Action Society on the day of its inauguration. At that time there were not very many members. Every day more are added to their number.

Love to all,

Aedan

...Within months I began to realise that I had little or no control over my fledgling Catholic Action Society. They tended to take on pastoral initiatives without my advice and without an apology. As might be expected, difficulties began to crop up.

Then something happened which made upset me a great deal: they asked permission on Christmas night to give out tickets to those who had been to Confession. I saw they were zealous and meant well, so I agreed. To each penitent who had been to Confession they issued a stamped ticket, which was to be handed back just before receiving Holy Communion. In this way they had hoped to guard against the danger of non-believers receiving the Blessed Sacrament, as sometimes happens when the priest is new in the parish. Then came the Midnight Mass and my bold Catholic Actionists, who liked stewarding in the Church, took their stand in front of the altar rails. As each communicant came forward a ticket was demanded. Now the rank and file of the Catholics had made little or nothing of the tickets, had put them in their pockets, and at the critical moment could not find them. There was some confusion. The girls especially, who with hands joined, heads bowed in reverence, eyes closed and faces veiled, could not for the moment lay their hands on the tickets and became excited and restive and even impatient at the persistent demands for the return of the tickets. Heated words were exchanged and some ladies burst into tears and retreated from the altar rails without receiving Holy Communion.

From the sanctuary I noticed what was happening, the pell-mell and confusion, with tears flowing in streams, so I decided to call a halt to the activities of my apostles. I was very hurt about it all and I wasn't the only one offended. The girls in particular and the school children had been pushed around and returned to their places without having received Our Lord. After Mass I went over to the school to pacify and console them, and to make a thorough enquiry into the strange behaviour of my helpers. I saw immediately that it was outlandish, so the next day I decided to call a meeting of Catholic Action and give them a thorough hauling over the coals. Perhaps I was too severe and strict with them, but if so, it was providential.

The immediate result of my severity was alarming. These disciples were young in years and wisdom and practically all were new Christians. At the meeting they never said a word, but nursed their wounded pride and decided on a sweet revenge. While a number remained humble and faithful to me, the others secretly swore vengeance, and waited for a chance to strike me in the back. They bided their time and before long a glorious opportunity offered itself, and they wasted no time and minced no words.

An employee of the Church had foolishly written a love-letter to a lady of doubtful reputation. This letter, with its suggestive contents, was intercepted by the rebel apostles. They brought it to me and read it aloud, and like the Pharisees with the woman taken in adultery they tried to force me to condemn and dismiss the author there and then. I refused to throw stones or condemn the man just to satisfy their whims and I promptly told them so. "Well," they threatened, "if you don't dismiss that man from the service of the Church within three days, we shall publish this letter with a commentary." I ignored their ultimatum and they swore to report me to the Bishop. My Irish blood boiled up at this challenge, and I threw down the gauntlet. "Publish it if you wish, do as you like. I refuse to dismiss him," I heatedly retorted, and turned on my heels.

Three days later they published the awful letter, and in their preposterous commentary they blackened my own character as well as the unfortunate member of my staff. They wrote to all the Bishops of China and sent them the disgraceful letter, including the commentary which was far more sordid, involving not only the man concerned but myself also, and an aged virgin of 80 odd years, who had been a faithful servant of the Church. The commentary involved us as collaborators in the "crime". It looked, on paper at any rate, a disgraceful affair, a scandal. My character was ruined in their eyes and in the eyes of the unthinking populace.

They printed the letter in the local printing-works, and of course, before the ink had time to dry, everybody in that small city knew what it was all about. Not only that, but copies of the letter were sent or mailed in open envelopes to most of the Parish Priests of China. The Bishops and priests saw through the accusations and promptly consigned the letters to the flames.

Some kind priests wrote to console and sympathise with me. Poor Fr. Grimley, God rest his soul, and Fr. Mackey, came to keep me company, and console me in my dreadful sorrow, for they saw that, as a result of the letter my Church attendance had sunk to a new low. The harm had been done. The Pastor had been struck and the sheep were scattered. The pagan population, the majority of the well-to-do and respectable people, who wanted no relief or help from the Church, were indeed scandalised and shaking their heads. "Is not this the Irishman who presumes to preach the Gospel to us," they taunted. It was simply shocking.

There were five or six of the group who remained faithful to me and their duties to God. The others gave up attending Mass and the Sacraments. They tried to influence against Church attendance, even going so far as to offer the children free breakfasts on Sundays, so that they would not be able to receive

Holy Communion. It was an awful blow to the faith in the community. The devil must have been gloating over his victory.

This storm of persecution had at least one good effect on me, as you will see later, though the following year was a most miserable year for me. Few people attended Church. Those who did attend were subjected to insults, threats, taunts and intimidation and I was very helpless to defend them.

A dark cloud seemd to have descended on Tsien Kiang and I could see little hope for the future.

As soon became evident however, it was that darkest hour of all which was the hour before the dawn.

CHAPTER FOUR

ENTER THE LEGION OF MARY

If past experience is an indication, no branch
of the Legion which is worked faithfully
according to rule, will fail. (Legion Handbook)

In spite of Fr. McGrath's local setback, the heroic efforts of the first Columban
Missionaries in the provision of material relief did much to enhance their
standing among the native people in general.

In July 1936, Bishop Galvin, on a return visit to Ireland, spoke with Frank Duff.
The Bishop stated that it was his daily agonising thought that though the work
of his mission was going ahead rapidly, he realised that his lifetime was not
destined to realise appreciable progress in the spread of Christianity in China.
These two pioneering apostles met that day and spoke together for four hours
little knowing that first seeds were being sown. These seeds began to sprout
when in a November 1936 letter to Joseph Hogan SSC, stationed in Hanyang,
Frank Duff rejoices at the prospect of the establishment of the first Legion
Praesidium in China.

Fr. McGrath recalls... Towards the end of 1936, I went down to Hanyang for a much needed rest. While there I asked Bishop Galvin for permission to start some sodalities. In making my request, I meant strictly only those whose members prayed and sanctified their souls without taking an active part in the work of the apostolate. I was determined to have no more of that in China. I told the Bishop that I thought the Chinese mission-field was not ripe for Catholic Action, and that personally, I was finished with it. Other priests too had bad experiences with Catholic Action. All seemed to agree that its members were inclined to assume the duties of the priest, override his authority and, as it were, confine him to his presbytery. Catholic Action in China seemed doomed to failure.

Thus it was that I was definite with the Bishop. I wanted sodalities, but no external activities in the parish. I was determined to work myself to the bone. I could stay on as long as I liked in China, but I was determined never to try any form of Catholic Action again. In my case it had done more harm than good and had all but ruined my parish. It nearly ruined me.

Having explained my needs, experiences and sorrows to the Bishop, he took me by surprise. He had recently returned from Ireland, where he had spoken to Frank Duff, who had tried to convince him that if he should adopt the Legion of Mary he could convert Christ's teeming millions in arithmetical progression. Now the Bishop had a Handbook of the Legion. He handed it to me with these portentious words: "Father, if you want to start anything, you can start the Legion of Mary." I thought for a while, and then I accepted the book, although reluctantly. What I did not know at the time was that I had received a pearl of great price, a treasure hidden in a field, a book of life.[7]

Before this incident I may have heard passing remarks about the Legion of Mary and possibly I had a vague idea of what it meant, but when the Bishop produced the Handbook that day and suggested I study it carefully, there was a weight on my heart. "Here surely," I said to myself, "is the introduction of another nightmare, a new debacle. Is not this the kind of organisation which has already made me and my parish a laughing stock before the world? It is just hopeless." However, obedience is obedience, and, as Scripture says, it is better than sacrifice, so I brought the book home to Tsien Kiang, and night after night

---

[7] The first Chinese Praesidium of the Legion of Mary was founded in St. Mary's parish, Hanyang city, on January 31st, 1937. Father Joe Hogan SSC, a Dublin man, was its spiritual director. Writing to him in March of that year, Frank Duff rejoices in this raising of the Standard of Mary's Legion and predicts that it will usher in a new era of evangelisation in China.

Priest-journalist Father Patrick O'Connor SSC (yet another Dubliner) was present at one of its early meetings:-
"The men spoke quietly, seriously, but sometimes with a gleam of humour. With neither timidity nor pretence, they talked as if they were discussing a matter of their daily work or business. The oldest of them was Wu, a boat-maker. (Hanyang has the Yangtse river on one side, the Han on the other, and lakes in its neighbourhood). The others around the table were Shu, the cook for the Lorettines' embroidery school; Ch'eng, a fisherman; Li, an employee of the embroidery school (baptised in the early days of St. Columban's mission by Father E. J. O'Doherty). Huang and Kao, two men from Anwei Province, are employed in an industrial plant on the outskirts of the city; this was Kao's first night at the Legion meeting. Dzao, seated beside them, has a small restaurant on the street outside. Miao is a fisherman. A second Wu is an employee of the mission, and Yeh is a peddler. Another member, absent tonight, has a small vegetable garden by which he supports himself. Assuredly they were not the most prominent or best educated people in China or even in Hanyang; but it was from men like them that Our Lord chose His first apostles and the first builders of Christendom. All are 'new' Christians, except two. This is to say, only two were born of Christian parents; the others are more or less recent converts."

read it over carefully. The prospect did not look bright or promising. But there was one remark inserted in a little square on one of the front pages which caught my eye and struck me forcibly. It ran thus: "If experience is any indication, no branch of the Legion of Mary will fail if worked according to rule." I made a bargain with Our Lady there and then, saying: "All right, I'll start your Legion. I'll try it out and keep strictly to the rules and we shall see. But if and when it fails, I will just hand back the book to the Bishop and say: "Thanks very much, Your Excellency. I have tried and failed, and that's that."

Fr. Joseph Hogan pictured with the Sacred Heart Parish Praesidium, Han Yang
Photo Courtesy *Maria Legionis* No.4, 1939

My next move was to call together four or five of those who had remained faithful to me after the collapse of Catholic Action. I reminded them of how we had completely lost face already, but that now we were going to try our hand at a new organisation called "The Legion of Mary." I warned them, that all our proposed attempts must be kept a strict secret lest we should collapse again, and lose face doubly, making our last state worse than the first, and causing onlookers to remark: "this man began to build but could not complete." I asked them to promise me faithfully, that if they should agree to row-in they must maintain this absolute secrecy. They agreed, and so we laid our plans and foundations for the Legion of Mary.

We kept the formation of our first Legion Praesidium under wraps for six months. Its few members used to meet in a little house at midnight. I was still afraid of failure and the harm it might do. But, true to the Handbook injunction, the Legion did not fail. In fact, things began to happen. A second Spring was at hand. Invalid marriages that had defied all efforts at validation were put right. The lapsed returned to their duties. Stray sheep came back to the fold. Catechumens who had been wavering and postponing, came to plead for Baptism. The city was astir. The whole parish was being revitalised by these zealous Legionaries who were working incognito, under the banner of Mary Immaculate, such that, before a year was out there were three Praesidia in Tsien Kiang, a city with only 60 Catholics. By this time we were able to proclaim to the world that the great achievements were due to the zealous work of the members of an organisation known as the Legion of Mary.[8]

---

[8] Independently, Frank Duff and Fr. McGrath had come to the same conclusion: Catholic Action was proving inadequate.

An exchange of letters at this time reveals that Frank looked to Bishop Galvin to be the Legion Standard Bearer in China and to impress its efficacy upon Rome's Apostolic Delegate there as had been done in Africa. Frank Duff predicted that the Legion would open the way for great things in China. However, Bishop Galvin, was at this early stage, taking issue with the Chinese translation of the Tessera, and, occupied with so many other pressing concerns, was not so optimistic.

CHAPTER FIVE

DANGER AVERTED

Lift up O gates your lintels; reach up you ancient portals,
that the King of Glory may come in. (Psalms 23:7)

After a six-month trial with my new group of lay apostles, I announced that a men's Praesidium of the Legion of Mary was operating in the parish. I then permitted the women and children to start also. The same success accompanied their activities, and by the time of the arrival of the Japanese forces to our city, we had five Praesidia working. The Legionaries were able to cope with the situation so well, that hundreds of Catholic converts were made. How this came about is a story worth telling.

The invading army having reached Yokow, the city authorities of Tsein Kiang were evacuating. The people, hearing that I was staying on, turned to me for protection. Many gave in their names to be Christians, but I suspected that this was done more in the interests of obtaining protection than conversion as such. They begged me to save their women and children. I told them that I could not offer them shelter. I had no house. At the time I was living in a poor Chinese shack, which had done duty as house and church during my many years there. They said they would provide premises and also money for food. I agreed to be their "gateman" and to do what I could to protect them from the coming aggressor.

It was a gamble. If I could save them I knew there was potential for further conversions. If I failed, both they and myself were lost. However, I trusted in God and His Blessed Mother to see me through.

Although the Japanese Imperial army had made an all-out invasion of China in 1937,[9] our missionary efforts continued. It was more than a year before the advancing army approached our territory. As they did, conditions became hazardous.

---

[9] On December 12th that year, the Chinese city of Nanking fell to the Japanese. According to a war crimes tribunal convened after the fall of Japan, Japanese soldiers in Nanking perpetrated atrocities of the first rank. Approximately 12,000 civilians were burned alive or bayoneted in mass executions. Vast numbers of women were raped and tortured.

On October 31ˢᵗ 1938, my confrere, Father Tom Tracey had come over from Chang Chieh Kang for the day and as we were chatting after dinner we heard the air-raid alarm and later the roar of engines. I heaped what blankets we had on a few tables, told our Catholics to shelter under them in the event of danger, and then with Father Tom I went out to watch for the 'planes. Before long we heard the noise of bombs exploding some distance away, and five minutes later a telephone message came through from Chang Chieh Kang saying that it had been bombed but that the damage was unknown. We thanked the Lord that Father Tom had not been there, and then we began to think of what we could do to help.

Next morning, after an early Mass, we set out on horseback, accompanied by a small group of locals wearing makeshift red crosses on their arms and carrying what medical supplies we had to hand. We reached the Han River to find it blocked with boats and both banks packed with troops of the Chinese army retreating west from Hankow. There was continuous firing but we very soon got used to that. Our immediate problem was how to get across to Chang Chieh Kang on the further bank, as the military seemed to have commandeered all the boats.

Eventually we succeeded in hailing an empty boat and Father Tom and one of our teachers went across, while I remained to look after our mounts. After an hour they returned to report on what they had found. There was not a soul abroad in the town. Houses had been blown to bits; people lay dead around the streets or were buried under the debris. The wounded lay unattended, their relatives having fled. A bomb had struck the rear of the little church, smashing the kitchen quarters. They were told that the poor old man of seventy who acted as its caretaker had been dragged away to carry supplies for the soldiers. Shops were closed and there was no food to be bought.

Having related their grim tale, we decided that we were doing no good as we stood, so a group of us made our way over to take a look and try to do something to help.

We picked up an old woman on whom a house had fallen and who didn't know where she was, carried her into an empty dwelling, got her a cup of tea from the mission kitchen and then we took a general look round. We had a job getting back, but on the way I met the very person I wanted to meet and made arrangements for the opening of a temporary hospital. We returned to Tsien Kiang on empty stomachs, as did the team who had followed us with the medicines, and next day we started our relief work in earnest, opening two improvised hospitals, one on each bank of the river.

Bomb damage to Church during Sino-Japanese War, 1938.

To encourage the return of the civilian population, which had fled in terror of the soldiers, we tore up Father Tom's sheets and an old red satin placard and made Red Cross armlets. These we distributed among the women-folk to give to their men. Soon we had a stream of men reporting at the church for duty, quite unafraid. The idea of the armlets proved a good one, saving them all from endless vexations and trouble at the hands of the military.

After two days in Chang Chieh Kang, during which we were busy from morning to night, I came back to the city and opened a third hospital there for wounded soldiers. I had no medicines to draw on except my own, but fortunately I had foreseen such a contingency and a few weeks earlier had laid in an extra supply. It proved worth its weight in gold now to those wounded men, some of whom did not have their bandages changed since leaving Hankow.

On December 4th, 1938 I heard confessions in a neighbouring parish, as there would not be a priest there for Christmas. Five or six missionaries had been called to Hanyang to look after property at headquarters in the wake of these military manoeuvers. Catholic refugees were calling frequently at my mission on their way to the west. I considered it a good idea for my new Christians to meet them and so to learn that the Church is well diffused throughout China.

Sunday December 18th, it rained heavily, with a wind that would cut the legs from under you. A snow blizzard was to follow. My diary also notes that we had heard no bombs for two days, but Chinese soldiers were passing through on their way to the front, thirty miles away. We were completely cut off from Hankow and at a loss to know how to raise money. I borrowed from some people and was unable to pay them back, a position I never found myself in before.

By end of the month, the Japanese were advancing nearer every day. Air-raid alarms were incessant but we gave up paying any heed to them after a while. A few days previously we had up to forty wounded soldiers in our hospital. They were easy to deal with and grateful for what we did for them, and from time to time a consoling feature of our work was that we were able to baptise many of them.

31

We had an air-raid alarm early in the New Year, followed by the sound of 'planes and exploding bombs. I got a telephone message to say that Yokow - Father Bob Staple's place - had been hit. Thank God he was not at home. Yokow being only ten miles from us, put our city into a state of alarm.

Air-raid alarms had become the order of the day during the month of January 1939, but we took little heed. No bombs were dropped on the city.

By the end of the month, Tien-Mien, Father McCarthy's place twenty miles from us, had been taken by the Japanese. The news prompted many of the wealthier people to leave for the country. Others began seeking refuge in our Catholic mission.

By March, Yokow, was taken by the Japanese. We expected an incursion in Tsien Kiang at any moment. You can imagine the state of tension we were living under. So many people were looking to the Church for protection. We did our best to ensure that at least the women and children were kept safe. I had not heard how the occupying forces behaved in Yokow, but in Tien Mien I was told that they conducted themselves fairly well. I lived in hope.

A further month passed without military change and I was kept preoccupied with the running of the schools. Being only ten miles distant, the big guns of the Japanese could be plainly heard every day. Chang Chieh Kang was now under occupation. The womenfolk had taken refuge in the church as in Yokow, and Fathers MacNamara and Tracey were able to secure their safety. Here in Tsien Kiang the merchants were willing to lend me a big compound which I hoped would shelter five or six hundred people. My duty was to keep the Japanese out.

The refugees would bring their own food and firewood, and thus be no expense or trouble. While under my care, it was my ambition also that they would attend a course of lectures on Catholic doctrine. It represented a great opportunity to dispel their pagan prejudices against the Faith.

The Japanese overtook us on 1st June, 1939 - a phalanx of 4,000 soldiers. There were by this time over 1,000 women and children in the new compound that had been provided by the city Merchants. We were now occupying a clearly defined area and were surrounded on all sides by a high wall on which the words "Catholic Mission" were written in large letters. The men of our refuge were in two of the houses, both ramshackle places, with a priest to look after each. Providentially, Fathers Tom Tracey and John McNamara, had left their missions and come to Tsien Kiang to offer their assistance and support.

I knew that the Japanese soldiers would soon discover us, so I decided to make the first move. While trying to decide as to the best plan of approach, I was accosted on the street by a soldier. I invited him to join me for a cup of tea and he readily agreed. We chatted for a while and, when I realised that he was an officer, I thought that this was an opportunity to appeal for my people.

Frs. Ivar and Aedan at gateway to Chungsiang Compound

"I am a Catholic priest," I began, and in my church I have some children and women refugees. "What!" he exclaimed. From the look on his face, I almost decided that my hopes were gone. "How many?" he asked. I said, "about 300" hoping to minimise the impression that our compound was worth bothering with. At first he made no reply, and after a few terrifying moments, he told me to wait. He got up and left the tea-house. After what seemed an age, he returned and told me to follow him. I did, and he led the way to the compound. As I called for the door to be opened, I explained to him that I wanted protection for myself and those under my care.

He didn't answer, just gave a nod of his head and smiled. After he had made a survey of the central part of the building and the occupants, he came into my room. I praised his ability to speak Chinese and broken English. He was flattered and at this point became even more affable.[10] He told me to get a large sheet of paper. With a Chinese brush, he wrote two large characters and produced a seal from his pocket. As he stamped the paper, he said, "Put that on your gate and you will have no trouble."

[10] This account is drawn from *Maria Legionis* 1948, No.3, p.5. In his letter to Loretta Young, dated 18th March 1999, Fr. McGrath describes how his conversation with the Japanese soldier moved to the topic of movies and their mutual admiration of this famous Hollywood actress. In that letter, Fr. McGrath gives to her the credit for the sudden affability of the Japanese soldier.

Who was this officer whom I had so providentially met? He was the only man in the 4,000 who could have done that for us that day! God in His own inscrutable way had achieved what seemed, in human terms, impossible. The people, as you can imagine, were very grateful, but it had not yet gone as deep as "Faith." Once again Providence came to my aid. In that time, the Legion of Mary made the necessary impression. After some months of attendance at Mass, Benediction and the other prayers (on account of the smallness of the place, they could not avoid being present), these people came to me saying "Father, now, and only now, do we realise that the calumnies we heard about the Catholic Church were false." They requested doctrine books and were soon asking for baptism. They had been good-living pagans and subsequently made splendid Catholics. Four hundred of these and 200 of the poorer ones in the city whom they helped to convert brought our number 600. Add to that the number we had before and we now have a total Catholic population of 700 in the city of Tsien Kiang. And I credit it all to the Legion of Mary.

During this period of Japanese occupation in Tsien Kiang, the Legionaries of Mary members showed their mettle, helping to restore order out of chaos; they moved among the refugees, telling them about God and giving the necessary instruction to the many new converts.

At the end of the year, the number of Legion Praesidia had increased to six, with a total membership of one hundred. Times were hard in China, but my new Catholics asked me to write to Bishop Galvin and advise him to send no more funds towards the upkeep of the parish, as they decided that he who preaches the Gospel should be maintained. From that day on they bore the burden of my expenses as their finances allowed.

CHAPTER SIX

LIFE UNDER JAPANESE OCCUPATION

Do not lay up for yourselves treasure on earth, where rust and moth consume,
and where thieves break in and steal. (Matthew 6:19)

In a series of letters to his mother written in the latter half of 1939, Fr McGrath continues his tale:

Here at the Catholic Mission, we are getting more familiar with the regular din of pounding guns and the sulphuric smell of war, at least to the point where we no longer lie on the floor paralysed with fear when the firing starts. I am 'playing' the typewriter to the accompaniment of the most ferocious machine-gunning and the thuds of heavy artillery. It started at five o'clock this morning.

Apparently the Chinese soldiers have surrounded Tsien Kiang on three sides. While Father Tom was saying Mass, a bullet hit the roof and I heard other missiles whizzing through the air overhead. Thank God, the city folk have suffered few casualties so far, although I have just seen a number of stretcher-bearers going out to carry back some wounded.

Close to us here, Japanese guns are in position on the mud-constructed defence wall. The Chinese have mounted a siege offensive, but so far they are reluctant to fire their heavy-duty armoury into the city for fear of civilian fatalities.

Battles have been ongoing during July without any significant Chinese advance. Military losses are heavy on both sides.

For ease of movement, the city has been divided. Soldiers and other army activity are confined to the military zone. In the refugee zone, small business outlets are getting back into their stride again, but not the big shops.

The improved behaviour of the Japanese soldiers towards their captors is helping to put the people more at ease.

With the assistance of Father Tom, we performed twenty-nine adult Baptisms on a recent Sunday. That brings our total for the year so far to about two hundred and fifty adults. The number is small compared to other places, bearing in mind that we have over ten thousand Catholics in the Vicariate.

I believe that Cholera has taken root in Hankow. There was one case of the disease here of late. A severe epidemic is likely in present circumstances.

The poor country places are hardest hit at this time. War breaks out at frequent intervals and when the conflict subsides, the people live in dread of bandits who will stop at nothing to force a few coins out of them. The same bandits have many methods of torture, all terrible and inhuman. One such torture is to burn incense on the person's back and legs. We often have to treat such patients here and they are a pitiful sight.

We have had no letters here for a long time, but I have sent my messenger to Hankow and hope to get correspondence soon. Neither have we received any newspapers so that our news is restricted to local events.

Early in August it became apparent that the Chinese were prepared to go ahead and bombard the city in order to rout the enemy. This altered the situation drastically. I urged our refugees to take whatever cover they could during these violent exchanges of firepower. It was terrifying. We heard the sound of Japanese shell flying through the air and exploding outside the walls. Those shells must have found their mark because the incoming fire would invariably dwindle.

We had several nights like that but now we take less notice of the danger as the refugee zone does not seem to be the intended target. However, on the First Friday we had a Holy Hour and we continue to beseech the Lord for protection.

Father Joe Hogan is not doing too well these days. He needs time to recuperate from the strain of the work.

We did our best to celebrate the 15th August in honour of Our Lady despite the persistent shelling. One night, I counted sixteen missiles fired in succession. Then came an ominous silence. We waited a while and then went back to bed. Next morning I discovered that two hundred yards away, a woman had been killed and many wounded. The boys' school and its occupants had a miraculous escape, shells having dropped all around the building.

Even in war, life continues, but in a kind of surreal way. Lately, the local people invited us to a dinner. The Japanese Commander and his officers also attended. To reciprocate the gesture, we arranged a meal in the Mission. They all came. About one hour before the dinner, the Chinese started a bombardment from one mile out. The shells were coming in a direct line for the Church and each one came closer, the last one falling only one hundred yards short. A few Japanese soldiers were on the roof of a nearby house shouting as each shell came over the city wall, while at the same time mapping the exact position of the opposing guns. Father Tracey and myself were standing out at the back watching horrified as children on the street narrowly escaped the falling shells. I must say that we were quite anxious about the situation, but the cooks continued to prepare dinner.

On arrival, the Commander presented me with a gift - six tins of pineapple! The dinner was a great success and he even sang a few songs for us, the first of which was, 'Auld Lang Syne - in English! Then he asked me to sing 'God Save the King'. I presume he meant to say 'Queen'. I explained to him. "That's not my Anthem! I'll sing you the Irish Anthem." Well, I didn't remember all the words, but I sang with gusto. I put in a few German words to fill in the gaps. It must have gone down well as the guests clapped and cheered. The singing continued in various languages, with the Commander intoning in Japanese, English, German and Russian. The whole affair was highly entertaining and the dinner went on for about three hours. This occasion cleared up any doubts the Japanese had about the purpose of our presence in the city.

The regular routine continues. Each morning after a rushed breakfast, I am faced with a crowd of people seeking medical attention of one kind or another. This type of ministry is the one form of 'preaching' that the natives appreciate and understand.

We are in a sort of prison situation here in Tsien Kiang. We cannot get outside the city, except on sick calls. I had such a call recently and, with an assistant, walked on blistered feet to the location. I had to remain the night with the sick person. The place was overrun with bandits, but thankfully they did not bother us. On the way back next morning, the sudden appearance of about fifty Japanese soldiers frightened the life out of us. While we were sitting in a house sipping tea, one of the soldiers aimed his gun at me. I went out to tell him who we were, but he did not understand what I said. In a minute or two, he seemed satisfied that we were not a threat and put down his gun.

We are five months in this condition and the 'visitors' seem to have no notion of moving on. There is still continuous fighting around the city. The poor are suffering most. Our Dispensary has expanded to cater for the increasing number of wounded civilians and soldiers.

We now have around three hundred refugees, many of whom are learning Catholic doctrine. You can imagine how busy that makes us.

I never had better health thank God. This is the first year I was not sick in the summer months - I hadn't time to be sick. The Bishop once said about me 'Don't let that McGrath fellow rest - or if he does, he is sure to be laid up!'

Frs. Aedan and Ivar together in 1940

The events of the intervening years 1940 and 1941 have not been preserved for the purpose of this record.

Fr. McGrath resumes his narrative in his own words:...

By 1942, at the height of the Second World War, I was forced by the Japanese to leave my parish. For two and a half years my fellow Columban Missionaries and I were confined to the City of Hanyang. The Japanese no longer accepted that the Irish Government under Eamon De Valera was sincere in declaring Ireland's neutrality during the war. However, De Valera's subsequent refusal to give the use of the Irish shipping ports to Winston Churchill did finally succeed in convincing them that Ireland was neutral. However, not until then were we allowed to return to our parishes.

It broke my heart that my new parish should be deprived of a priest. A lot of work had gone into establishing the various Legion praesidia. Solid foundations had been laid. The opportunity to build upon them now seemed lost.

Throughout this enforced exile, I endeavoured to busy myself with the more mundane tasks of our missionary headquarters, filling my time by learning to read music and improving my command of the Chinese language. Hopes for an early return to Tsien Kiang were frequently dashed, much to my dismay.

I remember that it was in 1943, that Father Joe Hogan's health really took a turn for the worse. X-rays showed signs of a spot on his lung. Despite this, he still continued with his missionary work. It was impossible to convince him to rest.

In the meantime, life was punctuated by maintaining our Hanyang community, the giving of retreats and seeing after the Columban Sisters stationed here. Occasional excursions to say Mass here and there were also possible.

Visitors from our various mission stations found their way to us from time to time, bearing news of their local hardships. There was an appalling scarcity of food and supplies. Even to acquire a few eggs and a little fish to go with the rations of rice proved difficult.

In November 1944 our banishment came to an end. The day we received our military passes, I was beside myself with joy. I couldn't wait to get back to my people. The seasonal rains had started however, frustrating any early attempt to get underway. When the weather finally cleared up, I made a wild rush over to Hankow one evening after supper. To my delight, a bus had arrived and was due to depart for the country in a day or two. I came back next day and packed my Hanyang belongings. Much to my disgust, the rains began again and I was marooned for a further period.

Then one evening, some schoolgirls came to the compound and announced that a bus was leaving next morning. Just waiting for such an excuse to get moving, Fr. Tom Tracey said he would join me and we said good-bye to all and sundry only to be told that the bus could not leave for two more days. With the help of those same girls, we eventually got across the river and to the bus station only to be told of yet another delay. We went to the Columban Mission in Hankow and waited several days before giving up all hope of travelling by bus. Yet again, we retraced our steps to Hanyang.

Tired of waiting, we decided to travel by river instead. On the first leg of this journey, we covered thirty miles by boat on a sunny morning. We stopped overnight in a Catholic home and, next morning, we walked a mile before finding another boat, which took us in turn to a place near Father Finnegan's parish. After going ashore, we called on the owner of a little bamboo house and there enjoyed a meal, only to afterwards discover that the boat we had just been on had been commandeered, perhaps by bandits.

Seeking out another vessel and five volunteers to paddle it against the strong wind, we made the journey to a point two and a half-miles from Father Finnegan's house, traversing the remaining distance, overland. We were royally replenished there and left after Sunday Mass.

In the afternoon, we boarded yet another boat and, with a favourable wind, arrived at Father Collins' and Shackleton's place quite early. We had to avail of their goodness for two days because the rain came down again in torrents. It was the wettest autumn since my arrival in China.

While on a boat from here, we heard for the first time that there had been terrible fires in Hankow in Father Han's district. I was very anxious for the safety of my own Catholics there and also for the Church. After a hazardous journey, we arrived in Mai T'an, where we anchored because of bad weather.

We eventually left accompanied by the Magistrate of Mai T'an, his secretary and staff, the head of police, military officials and their guards. Between these and the 'carriers', we were like a little army. To reach our destination, we had to walk part of the way along a dyke, which added to the journey. We stopped around halfway and had a meal at the Magistrate's expense.

Next morning, we set out for Tsien Kiang. Fortunately, the telephone wires between the two places were broken and those who tried to send word failed. Entering the city with the Magistrate would not have given a favourable impression, had there been a big reception prepared for us. After walking through water and mud for many miles, we slipped into the city by the back road and into a Catholic household, hoping to get quietly to the Church.

Once our arrival was made known, the people were overjoyed to see us and on Sunday Fr. Tom and I each said Mass. Since our return, we dined out much of the time, such was the welcome we received.

The day after we arrived, we went to see the Japanese Commander and he was very kind, saying that he had been expecting two priests and telling the people about our anticipated arrival.

To my great surprise and admiration, the members of my newly formed Legion Praesidia had continued faithful to their weekly meetings during my absence. They had assembled the Christians, lead the prayers, baptised the children, instructed the Catechumens, witnessed the marriages and looked after the dying. The worth of the Legion had finally been proved to me. The Shepherd was away from the parish but the flock was not dispersed.

With the political situation now starting to clear, many seasoned missionaries had their sights set on a visit home to Irleand. We had heard that about one hundred new missionary priests were ready to make their way to China, having been delayed in setting out because of the war.

I was looking forward to going home myself. I had worked and worried a lot and had become physically run down. Apart from the Prickly Heat which tortured me during the stifling summer weather, I also developed a peculiar complaint, that of sweating on one side of my face. I never heard of this condition before. It became so marked that when I was preaching, a distinct line could be seen on my features, one side perspiring, the other dry. Hot weather aggravated the suffering. I tried all the local cures - steaming my head with this thing and that, drinking the most awful concoctions, even putting big hot cakes on my head. I took them all in good faith, but without result.

It was not until 25th August 1945 that the Japanese received an order to retreat and hand over the city. Upon their dispersal, they were a sorry sight, even pitied by the Chinese after all the years of fighting. They had to give up everything and travel empty-handed. Many went to Hankow, where they were even willing to do work as Coolies.[11] What a change! Mentally and physically shattered, not a few committed suicide along the way.

The Christmas 1946 edition of *Maria Legionis* gives news from the Dublin perspective: "At long last it has been possible to re-establish contact with the Legion in China. The news for which we waited so long is really good news and comes from Rev. Fr. McGrath who is stationed at Tsien Kiang, where a Curia and five excellent Praesidia have functioned during the past six years of severe trials, dangers and difficulties of every sort. Even when Fr. McGrath was forced by the Japanese Army to leave his Mission for 2½ years, the Legion continued to carry out faithfully its weekly round of meetings and of apostolic work. 'Under the most trying circumstances, the Legionaries behaved splendidly in every way,' writes Fr. McGrath. 'On one occasion a drunken Army Official, who was suspicious of the Praesidia meetings, wildly broke into a junior meeting when the young girls were reciting the Rosary. As he strode into the room, swearing vengeance on all and sundry, not one little head turned: the Legionaries continued their prayers uninterrupted under the leadership of the young girl President! As he surveyed the scene, the officer's face changed completely, he removed his cap, bowed his head reverently and quietly left the room - conquered by a group of little Legionaries praying to the Mother of God! How proud I was of the behaviour and spirit of my Legionaries both on this occasion and at other times when bombs and shells were dropping thickly all around the

---

[11] Slang term for a labourer or porter in China.

Mission.' Fr. McGrath states that the American Franciscan Fathers visited his Praesidia and were so impressed with what they saw of the Legion that they have now established a few Praesidia in their Vicariate.

And now for a sad item - the death of Rev. Fr. Hogan, who introduced the Legion to China at Hanyang in 1937. The Concilium expressed its deep regret on hearing this sorrowful news and requested Legionaries everywhere to pray earnestly for the repose of Father Hogan's soul. May this zealous missionary and devoted Spiritual Director rest in peace."

PART THREE

1947 TO 1948

MISSIONARY ON THE MOVE

Political divide of Eurpoe - advent of Super-powers, East v. West.

Chinese Civil War - Nationalists under Chiang Kai-shek v.
	Communists under Mao Tse-tung.

Communist rise to power aided by Russia.

CHAPTER SEVEN

PREPARING FOR EXTENSION THROUGHOUT CHINA

*Among the proud there are always contentions: but they that do
all things with counsel are ruled by wisdom. (Proverbs 13:10)*

The appointment of Archbishop Antonio Riberi as Internuncio to China
on 6th July 1946 marked a new phase in the growth of the Legion of
Mary in this vast land.[12] On that same day, Fr. Joseph Hogan, who had
set up the first Praesidium, went to his eternal reward, having died in Shanghai of
pulmonary tuberculosis.

The Archbishop took up his post, coming from Africa, where he had
encountered Venerable Edel Quinn (1907-1944), that extraordinary heroine of
the Legion apostolate. He had seen in Africa what the Legion could do and had
no doubt that it could play a dynamic part in further propagating the Catholic
faith in China.

Arriving to his new appointment, he summoned the Bishops of China
together and gave them what he described as a message from the Holy Father.
The message was, that they were "to work through the Legion of Mary." He
could not put it in a manner more plain or direct. He said that the Legion was a
tried and tested mechanism in which they could reach out to uncountable
millions.

Then he went on to be prophetic and he said: "You are going to be
expelled sometime and in the meantime it is vital that you build up a framework
which will caretake the Church in your absence, and that instrument lies ready for
you in the Legion." Frank Duff exclaimed, "that was what you would call terrific!

---

[12] The young Riberi had taken up his first diplomatic service in 1929 as secretary to the new
Irish Papal Nuncio, His Excellency Paschal Robinson OFM. Prior to the appointment to his
African post in 1934 at the young age of 37, Riberi had become acquainted with Frank Duff and
the apostolate of the Legion of Mary in Dublin.
Frank had written to Riberi in July 1940 stating that the sending of a Legion Envoy to work in
China was then impossible. Riberi, according to Duff, was in position to exercise his diplomatic
influence to communicate the potential of the Legion among the Chinese hierarchy, now that it
had begun there.

Nothing could be better than that. The Bishops responded in like measure. They said to him that they only wished to do what was suggested to them, but that none of their number had any knowledge of the Legion and they asked Riberi to give them somebody versed in the Legion and who would do the organising. They would help."

Bishops Wang Mu To (Shun Ching), Henry Pinault (Chengtu), Paul Teng (Kiating), Francis Xavier Jantzen (Chungking) and Boisguerin (Shui Fu) – 1949

All the Bishops in China were subsequently to receive a copy of the Legion Journal each quarter. Bearing in mind his dynamic work in Africa, Rev. Riberi was hailed by Concilium Legionis as 'the person who has most spread the Legion over the surface of the earth.' In doing so, he had rendered a mighty service to the Church.

Another key player in the 'China Story,' was soon to enter the arena:

In August, Fr. Joseph Sheng arrived in Dublin for an intensive study of the Legion. Thereafter he returned to Rome to complete his doctorate in theology prior to taking up his post in the Catholic Central Bureau in Shanghai in charge of the Pontifical work for the Proagation of the Faith. While in Dublin, Fr. Sheng also began his Chinese translation of the Handbook.

Archbishop Riberi, shortly after his appointment to China,
meets with Chiang Kai-shek and his Nationalist party.

Fr. McGrath continues his narrative for us…

…In 1947, I was appointed as delegate to the Apostolic Nuncio to undertake the work of spreading the Legion throughout China. "Have you realised the impossibility of the situation?" the Internuncio asked me: "Five hundred million people and only five thousand priests? Even if I doubled and trebled that number, the conversion of China is still impossible."

Archbishop Riberi strongly advocated the Legion because as he said himself, "The Legion of Mary is one of the best things for the Church in our times. It is one of the greatest gifts of Our Lady to the modern world. I am very deeply convinced of that - it brings out the inner essence of Catholic action." When Our Lord said, "Go teach all nations," he did not say it to the twelve apostles only, but to some hundreds of his lay followers as well. "In the early Church," said the Archbishop, "the laity were actively engaged in an apostolate which eventually converted the then known world. The laity would help to convert China too."[13]

---

[13] cf. *The Legion in China*, Father Aedan McGrath, Capuchin Annual, Dublin, 1956, pp.364, 5.

Frank Duff and Fr. Aedan McGrath,
pictured in later years

Frank Duff tells us that in early 1947, "Fr. Aedan McGrath arrived home to Ireland and I cannot give you the exact length of his stay. I've an idea it was about eight or nine months but he certainly did work very thoroughly at learning the Legion System. Then he returned to China."

The insightful exchange of 'news' between Fr. Aedan McGrath and his associates now follows.[14]

Ad Jesum per Mariam[15]

Cunard White Star,
R. M. S. Mauretania,
22nd November 1947

My dear Mr. Duff,

Just a few lines to express my gratitude to yourself, Mr. Nagle, Mr. Murray, Miss Shaw and the other good Legionaries who went to so much trouble and gave up so much precious time to stand in the rain at North Wall to see me off. I felt very much ashamed that they would not allow everyone up to the boat - but I hope you understand. I am treasuring your Vexillina as a token. Please pray always for the success of the Legion in China and for poor me, despite my unworthiness to do such a work for Our Lady.

...I shall always treasure my year's association with the Legion of Mary - a happy year indeed it was, most inspiring and uplifting.

---

[14] Becausee his Cause for Canonisation is in progress, it is not possible to quote directly from Frank Duff's letters. The letters are not an exhaustive compilation. Some have not been traced.

[15] To Jesus through Mary - this invocation is handwritten on the top of each of Fr. McGrath's original letters.

May the members ever increase in their sanctification from which will flow naturally an abundance of good, solid and tactful work.

May God and His Holy Mother ever bless you and all the members of this great organisation. Pray for me. Very gratefully yours in Christ,

Aedan McGrath

CHAPTER EIGHT

OUR LADY'S SALESMAN

I stretch out my hands to you;
My soul thirsts for you like parched land.
(Psalms 142:6)

Fr. McGrath maintained a detailed diary of his activities, consecutive pages of which accompanied many of his letters to Ireland. This precious manuscript provides additional information on his day-to-day missionary work. His new centre of activity was to be the Catholic Bureau in Shanghai.

Diary: The day after my second arrival in China - February 16ᵗʰ 1948 - following on my stay in Dublin to closely study the Legion System, I went to announce myself to the Apostolic Nuncio who was attending the Educational Congress in Shanghai. We talked about the Legion for about an hour and I found that all I had heard about his enthusiasm for the Legion was true, but probably underestimated. He has big plans, but much to my relief I discovered that he knows the Legion must go slowly and be built up on a spiritual basis. He listened with much attention to what I had to say about my experience with the Legion in China following the collapse of a vague form of Catholic Action.

One of his principles I liked was: "Give others all the credit and you do all the work." He wants me to go to the Catholic Bureau as my official headquarters (but I need not appear there often) and to work around Shanghai starting different Praesidia. "Travel is quick by plane and you can do other places too," he said. He thinks that China is ripe for the Legion as Catholic Action has not proved a success. He intends to change the name to 'Lay Apostolate'.

> St. Columban's,
> 287 Rue Maresca,
> Shanghai
> 5ᵗʰ March 1948

Dear Frank,

Just after my arrival I cabled you about the translation of the Handbook never having come and I wrote a letter too. I sincerely hope they got to Ireland. I have had no reply from you as yet and I am hoping every day to hear something about it as the Nuncio and Fr. Chen, who wrote the other half are very anxious.

...[T]he Nuncio...is really enthusiastic about the Legion and confident of its success in China...At the moment I am awaiting his letter to introduce me to the Bishops and then I shall start in Shanghai.

As you may not know, we have a parish here in our Procuration and we are preparing to start a Praesidium when we get the letter. I have every hope of success. Then the Columban Sisters, who have charge of a school in the Slavonic Rite are keen to start too, but they have some difficulties. To begin with, Rome has stipulated that no attempt is to be made to change anything from the Slavonic Rite, so that the use of statues is out of the question. However, their Icons, which are little framed pictures of the Blessed Virgin would be in order. The more difficult question is that of the Rosary. They do not say the Rosary in our form. They use about ten decades and on each bead they have an aspiration addressing the Mother of God and asking Her to pray for us. I think that it would take about the same time. Before I send this, I hope to have more information about it. Please give me your opinion. I think some change will have to be made, as Rome has spoken...

I have just been to see Fr. Wilcock the English priest, who met you in Ireland and who changed to the Slavonic Rite so as to look after Russian Catholics. He is interested in the Legion and saw much of it in England.

Aedan

Diary: March 5th. I went to Mother Duff of the Sisters of the Sacred Heart and had a long chat with her on the Legion. Apparently a Chinese priest under instruction from the Bishop of Shanghai had told them of it and they had prepared to start. They probably do not know much about it so I am going to instruct them. They were thrilled by the story of the Legion in Dublin and hearing about Frank Duff.

March 8th. At Mother Thornton's request, I went down to the Sacred Heart Convent (same as the Mount Anville Sisters in Dublin) to talk about the Legion.

She wanted to start a Praesidium among the University students - the Internuncio had spoken to her about it. She heard that I had been appointed to try and spread the Legion, so she asked me to go. We talked for two and a half hours and she wants to begin after Easter. She had seen the movement in action in England and was enthusiastic about it. The Sacred Heart school is the largest and best in Shanghai. Also today, we have made preparation for a Praesidium in the house parish. There is so much work that they cannot cope with it. The two priests are keen to get started.

A little boy kisses the ring of Most Rev. Antonio Riberi while Mother Thornton looks on

I went to Nanking to see the Internuncio. I had two days there, enjoyed dinner with him each day and we talked about the Legion for hours. Frank Duff is his ideal Catholic; he could talk of him forever. He wants his secretaries to read the story of the Beginning of the Legion.[16] I am to travel to any place possible and begin the Legion. I am here for the present - working around the town. He wants to introduce me officially while here. He is to come to Shanghai soon. We started a Praesidium in my own parish last week - for foreigners, and are beginning one for Chinese next week.

---

[16] As serialised in the early editions of *Maria Legionis* and later published as *Miracles on Tap*, Montfort Publications, 1961.

St. Columban's,
287 Rue Maresca, Shanghai
25th March 1948

My dear Frank,

I received your very kind letter full of encouragement and sound doctrine last evening; many thanks. This is just a brief reply to inform you that the translation (Handbook) has been found - or rather was never lost!

...I am going to see the Internuncio in a day or two and we will get down to work.

...We expect to start four Praesidia in Shanghai after Easter: Two in our own parish: One in the Catholic Women's University and one in St Peter's Chinese Parish. In all, it will mean three Chinese and one foreign Praesidium.

As to possible envoys, I have my eyes open for them and shall give you information as soon as I can.

Aedan

St. Columban's,
287 Rue Maresca, Shanghai
2nd April 1948

My dear Mr. Nagle,

Your letter of March 22nd to hand: many thanks. This is just a brief reply. I am properly up to my neck now!! You will have heard from Mr. Duff of my getting the translation - and you will be relieved. Yes, I received the Italian books and brought them here. What I lost in my other trunk were some Handbooks in English - the Auxiliary leaflets and the Tesserae blanks. However, this need not hold up the work. I am getting others printed on ordinary paper for the present.

We started our first Praesidium last night in our parish here with six members - I wanted to start small and increase slowly. They are a fine bunch of Europeans. We are starting the Chinese one soon. When they make their promises after three months, I shall send on the forms. I was up in Nanking with the Internuncio for two days...he is putting me in charge of the Lay Apostolate (with a Chinese priest) - the Legion is to be my chief work. It is an aspect I had not anticipated, but I think it will give me a very good opening everywhere. As he says, he cannot send me out directly on the Legion work - and has done this to facilitate everything. I am to go straight ahead with the Legion. The Chinese priest will remain in Shanghai and when I have got things going well, I shall go elsewhere - travelling about. I mean to go to Peking soon. I have had an appeal from the Vincentians in Kiangsi for information and I have sent it to them.

You will be interested to hear that Fr. Sheng has been appointed to look after the Propagation of the Faith...which will necessitate his coming back to Shanghai to work. I am delighted, as he will have time and opportunity to deal with Legion problems. He is to do some translating too. I proposed to the Internuncio that the Australian book[17] be translated immediately. It will be more useful presently for Chinese who might not plough through the Handbook. The latter will need some correcting anyway.

Very sincerely yours in Christ,

Aedan McGrath

...P.S. The group of young priests from St. Columban's who came out to China with me have been reallocated to Japan on account of the state of that country. I have introduced them to the Legion here and they are taking it up. Your Envoy, Pacita Santos should contact these Missionaries on their eventual arrival in Japan.

---

[17] Most likely referring to *The Legion of Mary*, The Australian Catholic Truth Society Record, Melbourne, June 28th 1940, (no. 211) - a 25 page booklet summarising the history and explaining the apostolate of the Legion.

CHAPTER NINE

FROM SHANGHAI TO HANYANG

The patient man is better than the valiant: and he that rules his spirit, than he that takes cities. (Proverbs 16:32)

Diary: April 2nd 1948. In St. Columban's parish, Shanghai, we started Sancta Maria Praesidium; six Europeans to deal with the foreigners in this place - expect to increase the members week by week. We already had two meetings and the members are thrilled by the joy of doing apostolic work where there was fear before. They are getting many Auxiliaries and do hospital work.

April 5th. On the Feast of the Annunciation, Mother Thornton of the Sacred Heart Sisters began her Praesidium with six University girls - all Chinese. I was present at the second meeting and found a very capable and keen bunch. They are to work on the students in the University. Title of the group: Our Lady Queen of China.

Aurora University Students - 1948

April 15th. We began our Chinese Praesidium (Our Lady Queen of Peace) in the parish today with nine members - all speak English - so it is easy for the young Pastor to conduct. The parish has no register of its Chinese Catholics and the poor Pastor is badly handicapped. These young people are going to go from door to door with the view to making a parish register.

On April 19th, the American Sisters of Loreto started a Junior Praesidium in their High School. They took the title: Our Lady of Loreto. There were eleven members present. On the first week they enrolled 23 Auxiliary members - mostly people who had not been saying the Rosary at all. As some of the members are fit to be Senior members, they are going to split into a Senior and Junior Praesidium. Before their second meeting one of their members had been killed by a passing motor car. Her companions all went to the funeral and said the Legion Prayers around the coffin; they also had a Mass said for the repose of her soul - fulfilling their obligation. These children are mostly Filipino or Portuguese.

Note to Frank Duff: …'I had a letter from Fr. Victorini who is up in his Mission above Shasi. He has a Praesidium and there are two in Shasi itself. One is Senior (S.D. Fr. O'Reilly OFM) and the other Junior, conducted by Fr. Joyce. Msgr. Bishop Dillon has adopted the Legion as his official form of Catholic Action - as a result of Archbishop Riberi's visit'…

Also I had a letter from an Australian Father in Japan, who had Praesidia at home - looking for information about the Legion - chiefly re the translation of the Handbook into Japanese. He has been permitted by the Bishop of Nagasaki to start in the parish of Urakami - which got a bad time from the atom bomb.

Fr. Wang has arrived to see me and attended the meetings in Shanghai and has shown great enthusiasm. He told me some wonderful stories of what his Legionaries had done for him in his district - Ningpo.

Some days ago a letter was sent to my confrere Paddy O'Connor for publication in his Newspaper (which he has just started by order of the Internuncio). It told of four Praesidia in Kaifeng, which are doing very well; they had held an Acies with over 70 members present. The letter mentioned that they specialised in four branches - music, art, printing a Catholic newspaper and something else - besides doing apostolic work. As the Sisters are down from Kaifeng, I am going to visit them and find out exactly what they are doing. It is so easy to go on wrong lines.

I am delighted with the four Praesidia in Shanghai; they are keen and docile to the rules. I attend them all - I think they are getting into the right methods. When I go away they will be able to give information to others.

I was asked by the Jesuits to give a radio talk on the Legion of Mary. I did so on April 25th and I hope it did some good. It will at least make my going around Shanghai much easier.

Diary: May 10th. Two Praesidia, Sancta Maria and Queen of Peace made their Pilgrimage yesterday to China's famous shrine of Our Lady at Zose - about 25 miles outside Shanghai - a two-hour run. The eclipse of the sun kept the day cool. It was a most ideal day - especially as it had been raining most of the week before and only began again as we entered the buses to return home. We climbed to the top of the hill in the morning to attend Mass - then had breakfast. After that we made the Stations, which are on the hillside.

May 21st. The Internuncio arrived in Shanghai last week and I had a long chat with him. He told me I could start my tour for the Legion any time I was ready. The following day when I was attending a meeting in Aurora University (for women - Our Lady of China Praesidium), Msgr. Riberi walked in and talked to the girls for quite a while. He gave them a pep talk on the Legion and expressed his hopes that they would help to propagate it when they went home on holidays. As I had two flash-bulbs and a camera in my bag, I decided to take a picture. He was easily persuaded. After a first successful flash, I decided to take another. When I had finished I saw that I had forgotten to turn the film, thus spoiling the effort. I was really annoyed with myself. However, he said: "Don't worry - if it does not turn out, I shall come again." Next day when we were having our meeting in St. Columban's, His Excellency walked in again. This time I wasn't taking any chances and I sent out for a professional photographer. He took three splendid photos.

Archbishop Riberi and Fr. McGrath pictured with the Aurora Legionaries.

His Excellency arranged to meet myself and Fr. Sheng who is in charge of the Lay Apostolate. After our talk in which the Archbishop continually expressed his wish that the Legion spread everywhere and that both of us do all we can to foster it. He told me that he would be saying Mass next morning in the Aurora University and that I would have the opportunity to make good my photographic mistake. I lost no time in letting the Sacred Heart Mothers know about it and asked them to let the Legion girls know too. Next morning three of us with cameras, plus a professional photographer went to the Mass and after it - before his breakfast, His Excellency came in full pontificals to have his picture taken with the Legion group. We again got two good pictures, and many with our own cameras. I hope to send them home soon.

Archbishop Antonio Riberi posing with Fr. McGrath and Shanghai Legionaries.

I will soon be on my way to Hankow where I hope to get the Legion started. I intend to leave again for Shanghai when the time for the making of the Promise arrives - when I also hope to set up the Curia, which should be able to look after things while I am away.

St. Columban's,
Hanyang
24th May 1948

Dear Frank,

I arrived in Hanyang and for the first few days met the Catholics from my own parish in Tsein Kiang. They have come to the city in their hundreds and it was distressing to see them as refugees crushed into little rooms and trying to live on their sparse savings. They had been forced to move out of their homes by the arrival of the Communists. I felt very helpless with such numbers and only hoped I was in a position to help them. Those who could remain at home - namely the older ones, are still continuing their weekly Legion meetings and even have some people under instruction in the faith. It speaks well for the Legion, which can carry on under such difficulties. All I am asking from the others here is that they act as Auxiliaries until they can return to their parish.

After a few days I went to Wuchang. The Prelate here is Bishop Rombert Kowalski OFM, from California. We chatted about the Legion of Mary for a couple of hours. He had heard about the organisation from an American Legionary and was delighted to meet someone who was just back from Ireland, where the Legion had started. He had two Praesidia up and running - one for men and one for women and had translated part of the Handbook into Chinese …I returned in a couple of days to attend these meetings and instructed the members in the Legion System. Bishop Rombert showed a great docility to follow all detail. The Legion is safe in his hands. He wants his Sisters to start Praesidia in September with their Middle School. On this matter, I later spoke to the Sisters and their chaplain for a couple of hours...   Aedan

Most Rev. Rombert C. Kowalski O.F.M., who later became the Spiritual Director of Wuchang Curia, pictured with junior legionaries.

Diary: 31st May. I went to see the Archbishop of Hankow and gave him the letter from the Internuncio. He was obviously delighted. The Internuncio had told him about the Legion, but he did not know how to get started. He told his Vicar General Fr. Rosato to bring me to the school of the Canossian Sisters. There I spoke to the Catholics and again to the Sisters - all were very pleased and indeed had been looking for something with as definite a program as the Legion has. Our Lady's special patronage of course has universal appeal. This evening I am going there to go through the form of a meeting with a senior and junior group. The Spiritual Director will be there. He is a very zealous man and has already read the Handbook. We are hoping for great results.

Then I was brought to the High School run by the Chinese priests. It is the best boy's school in Hankow - as is the Canossians for girls. I spoke to the boys there and also to the priests; all were very interested. The priests are reading the literature preparatory to beginning. The Rector of the junior Seminary was there too and he took the Handbook and wants me to go and help him set the Legion going. I doubt if I shall have time these days.

The Archbishop had a group of young men who had just started on some form of Catholic Action - but as he said himself, there was not enough detail. He asked me to talk to them and get them to adapt the Legion. I have already spoken to them twice and they are enthusiastic to change and willing to give the time necessary for the meeting and work. They are a fine bunch. Tonight I am going through the form of a meeting with them. Their Spiritual Director, a Chinese priest, is one in a thousand and has great hopes.

Cardinal Spellman during his visit to China flanked on his right by Bishop Ned Galvin.

Cardinal Spellman arrived here with his entourage for a three-hour visit, especially to meet Msgr. Galvin. I was introduced to Msgr. Fulton Sheen, who spoke over the radio in Nanking. In that speech he said: "Mary is going to pierce China." I believe Mary and her instruments will be the Legion.

I received word of a young Chinese girl who used to be in the Legion in my parish. She has gone to Wan Hsien and there persuaded the Bishop to adopt the Legion. I am writing to her to hear about it.

6th June 1948

Dear Frank,

Your long and interesting letter of May 7th received. Many thanks. It is consoling to read letters from you especially as you write so much helpful material. You will be glad to know that I am not the only one who is convinced that the Legion is the great need in China today. Almost everywhere I speak, Our Lady seems to have given my listeners the sense of such need; it makes work very easy and thrilling. I have such little time to write, especially in this great heat - and one side of my face sweating - that I have resorted to a system of Diary, which I enclose…For Heaven's sake don't look at my English - I never was good at it - and now I have no time to do it well. I hope just to convey facts and a few 'photos. What I enclose is the follow-up to what I sent Mr. Nagle. Tell me if it will do you.

The diary will tell you where I am and what I am doing. The photos' will tell you that I tell no lie. Bigger photos' with Msgr. Riberi will follow by ordinary mail.

Thanks for your suggestions on the Russian-Slav. problem. I shall have to wait until I return to Shanghai at the end of the month to see Fr. Wilcock and give you a report. I imagine that all should be well. I must show your letter to the Internuncio.

As to Envoys - do not think I am lying down on the job? I want to get two committed Legionaries to start. I meant to get to Peking before returning to Shanghai to set up a Curia; but there is such a demand here for the Legion that I doubt if I shall be able to do so until later. However, the then Spiritual Director, Fr. Fuchs SVD is now a visitor to all his missions and is expected here in Hankow soon - so I may meet him and discuss it with him.

We got a beautiful Standard, exactly made to scale in the Jesuit Orphanage in Shanghai - brass covered with oxidised silver; it cost only two U.S. dollars and has the map in relief on the world. I was told by another firm in Shanghai that they could not do it for less than $20.

Fr. Sheng has a new post in Shanghai under the Internuncio and will be able to give us his assistance. He is working on the Handbook translation and I hope to get it printed when I go down to that city...

Aedan

Diary: June 8th. Yesterday was the Octave of Our Lady Mediatrix of all graces and Bishop Galvin told me that he was going to try and set up a Praesidium in Hanyang. Previously he had decided to wait, as the condition of that City is at present very bad; it is full of refugees and most of the priests who can speak Chinese have gone home for a rest. The others cannot go to the country on account of the Communists. He is thinking of putting a Chinese Sister in charge - to explain the Legion.

The Reds are pretty close to us now.[18]

---

[18] A reference to the Communists based on the background colour to the Communist flag and the cover of their manual - the Communist Manifesto.

CHAPTER TEN

APOSTOLATE BEARING FRUIT

*All that the Lord wills, He does in heaven and
on earth, in the seas and in all the deeps.*
(Psalms 134:6)

Diary: June 12th. Attended the first Legion meeting of the teachers of St. Joseph's middle school for girls under the Canossian Sisters in Hankow. There were eight members, including two men, under the direction of the German priest Fr. Ludwig. The teachers went to the houses - as appointed, meeting the parents and becoming friendly with them with a view to getting the children to attend doctrine classes. Two of the more timid teachers coped bravely with a rebuff from the gate-man of a house visited.

June 13th. Attended the first meeting of Queen of Apostles in the Cathedral Parish under Chinese priest Fr. Yang - very zealous[19]; the Praesidium is made up of eleven young men who were formerly a Catholic Action group, meeting once a month. I had spoken to them three times in the past about turning the group into a Legion Praesidium. At first they thought a weekly meeting would be very hard on them, but now they are enthusiastic beyond words and the weekly

---

[19] Fr. Yang was martyred for the faith by the Communists in December 1954.

63

meeting does not cost them a thought. At the moment they are assisting their priest in making a census of his Catholics.

June 15th. Attended the first meeting of Queen of Peace Junior Praesidium in St. Joseph's Middle school for girls under the Canossian Sisters. Their work is chiefly within the school and the Sisters are delighted with the awakening of an apostolic spirit. It is a school of 600 - mostly non-believers. The Legionaries teach Catechism to children in the evening and they also look after the library. I am satisfied they are on the right Legion lines.

June 20th. Having been a couple of times each to the Rev. Mother of the Franciscan Missionaries of Mary (whose rules are bound up with the 'Secret of Mary'[20]), and the Chaplain of the Hospital which they look after, I yesterday gave a talk on the Legion to the Sisters, Chaplain and nurses. The Sisters said that they were just waiting for some such organisation to spiritually assist their staff. While they are always busy, the Sisters told the Chaplain that they will certainly give any time necessary for the meetings to those concerned. Fr. Avidillo, the Spanish priest who is Chaplain is equally keen and intends to gather the students together to discuss the Legion in a few days time.
Mother Virginia who is in charge of the St. Joseph's school told me that she would now die happy as she has seen the day that the Legion entered her school.

On June 25th I flew east from Hankow back to Shanghai in two hours (the boat takes four days - sometimes more). I immediately started into a visitation of the seven Praesidia - and was charmed to see that they were doing splendidly *Deo Gratias.* They have begun to undertake work which is very much against the grain. Up to this they were visiting the Catholics in their homes - and the Hospitals. Now they have begun to visit from house to house. In this city, where the people tend to open the door about half an inch to callers and then close it again, this is heroic work.
One man in a Chinese Praesidium came across about 30 Catholic men in a factory, who knew nothing about religion. He spoke to them and found very willing listeners. When he went next time, they had gathered their wives and children; and the third time, he brought them to the Church for instruction. A

---

[20] St. Louis Marie De Montfort's pamphlet, exhorting a deeper understanding of the practice of the True Devotion to Mary.

couple of invalid marriages have been rectified by another Praesidium. Two Orthodox people have been received into into the Catholic Church.

Shanghai: Our Lady of Sorrows Praesidium at the Good Shepherd Convent. Included are Fr. Aedan McGrath and Sister M. St. Francis of Assisi.

The Good Shepherd Sisters are delighted with their two internal Praesidia; they have changed the spirit of the girls and much good has been done. The members have no pocket money and the secret bag has nothing in it but slips of paper with sacrifices etc. written on them.

At one Junior Praesidium of girls I noticed a little wilting. The Sister had gone away and the young President was giving the members too little work. I suggested that work be assigned to the girl's own home. Next week one of the membersl reported that she had got her mother to the Sacraments after an absence of 20 years! The little girl went first to confession and told the priest that her mother was coming and her circumstances. The same girl told us that her mother was delighted and had received only her First Communion up to that time. An older sister of the Legionary is returning to the Sacraments this week - after five years away; and she got the priest to promise to go and talk to her father, who had not been inside a Church since his marriage. This gift from Our Lady had a glorious effect on the Praesidium as a whole and all are enthusiastic now about solving family disorders - which are many in Shanghai.

Shanghai Junior Legionaries, members of Immaculate Heart of Mary Praesidium
at the Good Shepherd Convent with their Spiritual Director, Sister Mary of the Sacred Heart.

The Jesuits asked the Aurora University girls Praesidium to help them to make a census of their Catholics. It was opportune as the term had come to an end and the members had to find Legion work anyway. We are hoping that this is the thin edge of the wedge for that Jesuit parish.

Fr. Fuchs SVD has been appointed Visitator - and hence is not now in Peking. I met him here and discussed his two Praesidia; they are doing very well. I asked him about the possibility of finding Envoys. He told me of one splendid girl who had finished her University course and was Principal of the Sister's school in Peking. He said she would be ideal and was willing to give up the job. I hope to meet her myself and tell you more later on.

The Dean of the Aurora University for women suggested another prospective Legion Envoy. She has just finished her Sociology course. When I spoke to her, she was delighted with the idea. She assured me that her family would not object to anything she decides.

Fr. Sheng is here in Shanghai. The Internuncio asked him to give any spare time to the Legion and he is only too willing. We are working at translating the prayers and other literature into Chinese. We hope to have something printed soon. Mr. Duff will be pleased that we have decided to retain the Latin terms as much as possible, while giving the Chinese names in brackets.

July 25th. I have been busy visiting the various Praesidia with a view to building them up. I can foresee many people coming to study their methods. I have been satisfied with the way they are working

A couple of months ago when I was downtown, I ran into several priests who looked like Americans. I spoke to them and found one to be a Dominican Superior from Fukien Province. I asked him where he lived and enquired about the Rosary Confraternity. I rang him up later and he came to see me. When I had finished talking about the Rosary Confraternity I began to speak of the Legion. He was interested and took literature. When he returned to his Mission, I believe he handed the book I had given him to Fr. Sheerar OP who is Procurator saying: "You and Fr. Dominic Chang OP will look after the Legion in this Province." I can see Mr. Nagle jumping!! Yes, that is the Fr. Chang for whom he has been searching. Apparently when he returned from the Philippine Islands his former Superior told him to rest and not bother about the Legion. Now he can do as he pleases; it was a lucky coincidence.

Again, another peculiar thing happened: Some time ago I met for a couple of minutes a Fr. Wm. O'Hara CM and I spoke of the Legion. He was on his way to Japan to give a Retreat. Later he returned and wrote to me thus: *If you remember, I met you for a few minutes in our Procure. You spoke to me very earnestly about the Legio Mariae and gave me a Handbook. Your fleeting visit was to me 'another sign'. Let me explain: Within the past twelve months I have received letters from unknown-to-me persons in England, stating that my name had been indicated to them as a possible promoter of the Legion. On the other hand, years ago with my best friend, then a Seminarian, now Father Gou - who wrote to me from Shanghai about the Legion he had started - we had solemnly vowed ourselves to do something for the Diocese when he was ordained. Somewhat contrary to our hopes, he was appointed to a remote parish - but where he unexpectedly came across a local Praesidium. (Spiritual Director, Fr. Wang!)*[21] *All these truly Providential signs have set me, as I should say, agog with the fervent hope of establishing the Legion in every parish all over the Diocese. Our Bishop is interested, his Coat of Arms being 'Ad Jesum per Mariam'.*

That was the letter. I wrote to him inviting him to come up and see things for himself. He replied that he is coming. I have great hopes; he is pointed out as one of the best priests there, if not the best.

---

[21] cf. Diary entry for April 19th 1948.

The Cardinal is here in Shanghai at present on sick leave.[22] I went to see him the other day with the Internuncio's letter of introduction. He received me kindly; while he had not heard of the Legion, or at least very little, he listened attentively. He suggested my going to Peking[23] while the priests there were not too busy and organising a course on the Legion - but that would not the ideal way of introducing it. The Legion must be seen in operation to be believed, and a course without Praesidia demonstrating would be futile. However, his suggesting the idea was kind and he showed a keen interest. He promised me a letter introducing me when I go, which was quite unsolicited.

As to the Curia that we propose to set up this week in Shanghai, I went to see the Vicar General as the Bishop has been quite ill. My purpose was twofold: One, to ask that Fr. Joseph Sheng be appointed as Spiritual Director. My reasons were that he is keen to have something to do with the Legion - also he has received instruction to give his spare time to the Legion. We are working together in the same Bureau. He has translated the Handbook and is available for the job. The Vicar General gave him faculties and the appointment. He should be a great help to the Officers when I am away. My second request was for an Imprimatur on the three translations: Prayers, Auxiliary Leaflet and Victory pamphlet. They should be printed this week.

On July 29th, the Curia was set up. The meeting held in the Sacred Heart Convent was chiefly to do with election of officers and as there were many visitors, including two Jesuits, there was not much business done. I spent the succeeding days training the Officers in their work and handing over of things I had to deal with single-handedly up to this. Their office is in the Catholic Central Bureau, where I have been up to now. It is the Bureau set up by the Internuncio for various activities and is going to be very convenient. Fr. Sheng is upstairs in his office for Pontifical works. Work for me is too much and letter writing will have to be cut down. The Curia is sending you a photo of the Acies-event, with names.

August 22nd. I am now in Peking. Since setting up the Curia in Shanghai three weeks ago, I have been busy visiting some Praesidia with Fr. O'Hara and a Chinese priest, both of whom are now in a position to spread the Legion all over

---

[22] Thomas Cardinal T'ien Ken-sin SVD (1890-1967).

[23] i.e. known today as Beijing.

their Diocese, as they are in charge of Catholic Welfare activities. An added bonus is that they have a jeep - and the roads are good.

All the Chinese priests in the circuit were under Fr. O'Hara in the Seminary, so he expects complete co-operation. While they were going around the Praesidia, two Jesuit Fathers from near Nanking joined in the venture. They were so delighted that they planned to start immediately in their place. They brought the Legion Standard back with them.

Bishop Cleary of Kiangsi (of our Mission) had such disappointment with Catholic Action that his priests did not expect him to agree to the Legion. The last news from there indicates that after receiving a letter from the Internuncio, he gave permission to start a Praesidium. Another relevant development is that one of the Fathers who witnessed the Legion at work in Shanghai has begun it in his Religious Orders' main house.

In the last issue of the *China Missionary Bulletin,* which is published in the Catholic Central Bureau, there were three articles on the Legion. Fr. Legrand the Editor has promised to publish any details about the Legion work in each issue; it will be very useful.

I am still negotiating about the Envoys. The Shanghai one is still to the good; but I'm afraid that the Peking prospect will not materialise as she has a very good job in the University school and her mother needs her. I went to the Fu Jen Catholic University yesterday to see the Praesidium - only four present. Work being done well but much wrong in methods - very docile to correct. They are making an effort to increase membership.

The Cardinal wrote a splendid letter to the Bishop of Peking - I have a free hand to spread the Legion. The job is going to be colossal - I wish I had Envoys.

CHAPTER ELEVEN

ENTHUSIASM IN PEKING

And the light shines in the darkness;
and the darkness grasped it not. (John I:5)

Dublin,
September 7th 1948

Dear Fr. McGrath,

Your welcome letter and enclosure of August 23rd have come to hand.[24] Many thanks for printed matter in Chinese and snapshots. I see that you have managed to fit in the Prayers in Chinese on the ordinary Tessera. Is this a revised version of the prayers? It is good to know you have found a willing translator in Dr. Fang…

Catena Legionis as printed in the first Chinese Handbook

---

[24] This letter has not been found, although the accompanying diary pages are extant.

I hope that the formation of a Curia in Shanghai will take some work away from you. I am wondering if any one of the Curia Officers reads English; if not we shall correspond through Fr. Sheng. Perhaps you would discuss with the Officers the chances of sending a translated copy of the Curia minutes every month.

What is happening about the affiliation of the Praesidia outside Shanghai? Will it be possible to link them up to Shanghai Curia as a temporary measure? I received a letter from the Bishop of Wuchang - telling us of your visit to him and how you found a Praesidium or two established.

About a name for the Curia: I think it best to call it the 'Shanghai Curia.' We use titles of Our Lady only when there are several Curiae in a city ...

I note that one of your problems is that some places are starting up the Legion and not waiting for your arrival. The territory is too vast for one person to cover. It may be possible to get some of the Shanghai Legionaries to move around during holiday time and nurture young Praesidia.

We are mourning the loss of your great Legion friend in the late Nuncio, who was a Laureate member.[25] I'm sure the Internuncio was grieved at the news.

John Nagle

Diary: September 9th. Quite a while since I wrote, but glad to say I am very busy with the Legion at this time. My opinion is that Peking is going to be even more enthusiastic about the Legion than Shanghai. The city is full of priests of all Societies and all are looking for something that is going to waken up the people. That state of mind makes the promoting of the Legion easy.
I gave a radio talk on the Legion this evening.
The Jesuit Bishop of Peking, Xavier T'chao (taking Cardinal T'ien's place) has been very kind to me, offering to call all the Parish Priests together to hear a talk on the Legion. As I thought there might be an element of compulsion involved for the priests, I suggested waiting for the conference for Priests, Sisters and Brothers, which was due shortly. He agreed. At the conference he introduced me and I got a chance to address them briefly.

---

[25] His Excellency Archbishop Paschal Robinson OFM, Apostolic Nuncio to Ireland since 1929.

The Bishop suggested I attend the monthly meeting of the Parish Priests. There he introduced me again and said I could talk for as long as I liked. As a result I have been invited to many places to dine and speak with them. I have spoken to all the Chinese priests in the Collegium Sinicum (Post Graduate College), also to groups of Sisters and again to students from different Universities during a Retreat. I've also been in touch with the Catholic students of Peking University.

To mention a little fruit from these connections: Five Praesidia were set up. I expect to start up many more before I leave and hope to start a Curia to look after them. The enthusiasm of those who wanted to start the Legion makes me not at all fear for the speed of things. There are priests from most of the Northern Provinces here and if they get well introduced to the Legion there will be very little trouble for them to start in their respective places.

Strange to say, many Jesuits are keenly interested. Fr. Bernard who was doing much in France about the 'Grand Retour' went to the Bishop (a Jesuit also) to know what he could do in Peking and the good Bishop referred him to me. He thinks the Legion can be the means of organising permanently *Le Grand Retour*, and he is thrilled by the Handbook.

The Franciscan Missionaries of Mary have started a Praesidium for their past pupils and Fr. McGoldrick is their S.D. and a zealous one too. Two Praesidia have been started in our own parish here under Fr. Kelly. Last night at 6pm, I went over to the famous East Church here in Peking where so many martyrs offered their lives during the 'Boxer Revolution' of 1900. The Church was destroyed then, but has since been rebuilt. After the 1914-1918 war, when the French Missionaries had to leave, Irish Vincentians went to take their place. Among them was one Fr. Kavanagh CM from Wexford. He is now Pastor of that Church - has a grand congregation and the finest school in Peking. He began to translate the Handbook last year but had to leave it off. He needed little persuasion to begin the Legion in his parish. When he did begin, he wanted to do so on the 7th September the date of the founding of the Legion in Ireland. I spoke to his Catholic Action group last Sunday and from that group he selected ten men and twelve women - and on that night we set up two Praesidia. He is a very zealous Spiritual Director and I have no doubt as to the success of his venture and the eventual spread of the Legion to his school and other parishes.

I had a letter from the Hankow Cathedral Praesidium. The young Chinese priest is delighted with his results. He wanted me to go for the taking of the Promise after three months, but I had to excuse myself. To begin with, travelling is expensive and this Peking chance must not be thrown away. I must stay at least until I have a Curia set up - then it will be its worry.

11th. I was invited to the well-known South Church, where Fr. Ricci SJ first served. The ground on which it stands is also covered with martyrs' blood. When I entered the beautiful building during Benediction, with a wonderful picture of the Immaculate Conception over the High Altar, the boy and girl choir singing the Ave Maria in Chinese (translation by Chiang Wen Yeh), I felt very happy indeed. It seemed a good augury for the Legion. I spoke afterwards to the Catholic Action group (about 50) and they invited me to come back soon to set up a Praesidium.

13th: I attended the Junior Praesidium of Fu Jen, which has been there for a year or so. It went off line and this week I am going to put them through the meeting again.

On the 14th, I had a visit from a Fr. De Kart CM (Dutch), requesting information for the Bishop of Tientsin - he wants one of his priests to spread the Legion there. I intend to go there some day soon to see the Bishop. As the Internuncio is expected here any day, I must wait on him. It will be good to have him here while I am on the job elsewhere.

The following day, Fr. Meiners SVD (who thought the Legion just a pious Sodality) had his first Legion meeting with 12 Catholic University students last night. I put them through the order of the meeting and they are all very keen - but none more so than their Spiritual Director, who has the highest hopes to fulfil all his wishes through the Legion.
In the morning I went to see the Belgian Scheut Fathers who have a club for the Catholic students of other Universities and to whom I spoke during their Retreat. They too are going to begin the Legion among these boys and girls. With the Catholic students rounded up from the different Universities - working for the Legion, I imagine that quite a lot can be done.

18th. I gave a talk to the Jesuits who are here from every part of the country learning Chinese; this came about after they had read the article I wrote in the *China Missionary Bulletin* - all very interested and keen to learn more. On that day too, the Legionaries from the school (past pupils), on their first week's duty were turned away from the door of a Catholic Hospital. I though it might upset them, but far from it; they are now visiting people of all faiths in other Hospitals.

22nd. I went to see the Internuncio who is visiting Peking. Salutation: "Now father, quickly - what about the Legion?" He was very pleased with the prospects and told me to stay as along as there was fruit. He is keen to organise Praesidia amongst the Chinese priests who are studying in the Collegium Sinicum.

Msgr. Riberi approved the idea of sending copies of *Maria Legionis* to the Bishops of China. He suggested sending them together to the Catholic Bureau, in Shanghai, from where they can be distributed - in English, 110 copies; in French, 30 copies.

24th. On my annual Retreat.

CHAPTER TWELVE

"BY THEIR FRUITS YOU SHALL KNOW THEM"

*In Him we have redemption through His blood, the remission of
sins, according to the riches of His grace. (Ephesians 1:7)*

Diary: October 1st 1948. I am off my Retreat. There is much interest in the Legion with all priests here. The Austrian Jesuits are outstanding as are the local French Jesuits. I was invited to speak to their seminarians and priests. Within a few days I was astonished to get a note from one of them saying: "I want Tesserae cards; we have started five Praesidia." That is in the parish where Fr. Joliet, the French Jesuit is Pastor. His five Curates had each begun Praesidia in their own areas. I went to attend two of them and found things in good order for such a fast beginning. While there I heard they had started a sixth group under Fr. Kronthaler SJ who had been the first to begin. He had two Praesidia, one for women. Their enthusiasm is genuine and I cannot see them fail. That brings the number of Peking Praesidia up to fifteen.

2nd. Instructed by the Internuncio, I went to the Major Seminary, which is for all of North China - to speak to the Rector, Fr. Cartier CM He was very keen and asked me to speak to his Theology and Philosophy Students. He intends to start a Praesidium soon and his members will be able to do parish work. The Pastor is a very old man.
I just got word from the Pastor of my old Mission in Tsien Kiang that the place is temporarily peaceful. The priest could not return, but many students did and immediately began their Legion meeting again.

6th. Met Archbishop Riberi at a reception in his honour. He told me to go with him to Tientsin.

8th. Went with Internuncio and Msgr. Caprio, his secretary, to Tientsin and had plenty of time to discuss things. When I met him at the Nunciature before leaving, I said: "What a wonderful morning." He replied: "Don't mind the weather - what about the Legion?" He even discussed organising a Congress, when things get going - perhaps next year. He wants the Legion everywhere, even in schools. He never heard of Cecily Hallack's book; he would like a copy - as there is a lot of splendid material in the book.[26]

The Internuncio's welcome at the station in Tientsin was impressive. Bishop de Vienne CM was there with many priests and lay folk. Msgr. Riberi used the opportunity to show his interest in the Legion. I deliberately delayed on the train so as not to get mixed up with the high-ranking clergy and meant to go to my own destination by rickshaw. No, the Monsignor would not have it. Before everyone he called me out of hiding, there and then introducing me to the Bishop and others. He insisted later that I go with him to the Bishop's house where we had a reception and were given lunch. After the meal I remained to talk with those priests who were keen to learn about the Legion. One of them, was Fr. Buenen CM a young Dutch priest who had been specially appointed by the Bishop to organise the Legion in Tientsin - so my work is half done. This latter priest is a specialist in Boy Scouts and Girl Guides and he was just looking for something to spiritualise his officers - and here it is. There is terrific enthusiasm here among the young Dutch priests who have just come to take over. The older French missionaries are finding the work too heavy. I have been kept going meeting people since I arrived. There is no Catholic Action here, so we hope to see the Legion leading a great example.

Fr. McGrath with Fr. Buenen CM in Tientsin

---

[26] Cecily Hallack died in 1938. Her book *The Legion of Mary*, was published posthumously in several editions.

I visited the French Jesuit Fr. Jarry, who wanted me to instruct him in the Legion. He has charge of Tientsin University students and wants to set up two or three Praesidia. I go for the first talk this evening.

A letter arrived the other day from the man who is translating the Handbook, Dr. Fang. He said: *Your letter not only scared me, but almost suffocated me. As a result, I have given up my lectures in the University so as to give more time to the book.* The poor man! I had told him I was waiting for him to finish the translation. I must go down to Shanghai at the end of the month to arrange about printing blocks for pictures. A model book-barrow has to be made and then stocked with books so that a picture may be taken for inclusion in the Handbook. I shall have to leave the forming of the Peking Curia until I return. This will be so much for the better as the members will have completed their three-month probation period.

13th. Last evening I went through a form of meeting with Fr. Jarry's Middle Boys School - fourteen attended, all very keen; most of them are over 18 years of age.

14th. I attended a meeting with the girls from the University with Fr. Jarry SJ as Spiritual Director. The German Sisters of the Immaculate Conception were present.

15th. I went to Sheng Kung Middle School for girls, looked after by the Sisters of the Immaculate Conception (German). I had promised to go through the form of a meeting with the Catholic girls. They had the room nicely arranged; the Legion table was as it should be and fifteen of the Senior girls sat around it. All the Sisters attended and about thirty other Catholic girls from other classes.

16th. I visited the Italian parish of Tientsin with Fr. Beunen. We were cordially received. I had an Italian Handbook with me. Fr. Alibrandi is the P.P. and Superior. The Italian priests are of the Missions of Parma. I met Fr. Castelli who speaks English. They were very interested in the Legion. Bishop de Vienne has asked them to do the parish work, starting with the making of a census.

This evening Fr. Hermans CM (the Dutch priest who had started the Praesidium for boys in his school), came to see me. As a result of their Legion efforts, thirteen people had turned up to Christian Doctrine class.

I gave talks to two communities of Marist Brother in charge of a school for both foreigners and Chinese. The Chinese Brothers too in their Marist School want me to give them a sample meeting.

17th. We had our first sample meeting at the Cathedral - with twelve men attending and their Spiritual Director, Fr. Li. This is a fine parish, but there is endless work to be done. Fr. Buenen CM had his first formal meeting. It wasn't very well run, but I'm sure things will improve.

18th. Fr. Hermans CM had his first meeting with reports in his school; well run meeting and plenty of spirit among the seven members.

Tientsin Cathedral Parish Boys' High School Praesidium, China,
with Rev. Fr. Hermans CM, Spiritual Director.

I went to visit an old French priest who has a parish in the City. I found it difficult to gain admittance, and when I did, I never got to sit down. I said that I had been standing ringing the doorbell for quite a while and then had to go round by the back. He said: "I heard you - but I was about my Father's business." I chuckled to myself and wanted to add (but did not) "I was on that very business myself - with a good introduction from the Mother of Our Saviour." He quoted scripture to me at every opportunity but was not enthusiastic about starting the Legion. He said amongst other things: "By their fruits you shall know them - if the Legion shows fruits, I shall have it." That was enough for me - I felt confident and presented him with a copy of the Legion Handbook.

That same day Msgr. de Vienne CM invited me to talk to the Chinese priests of the Cathedral and Seminary. I was glad of the chance. The Bishop who has shown a child-like pleasure in the early first fruits of the Legion, attended. In my first discussions with him he had said smiling: "Father, I have seen so many come and go. However, we can try." Then seeing surprise in my eyes, he added: "Oh yes, I know you don't think trying is necessary - you think success is certain." "Yes," I said. "Everywhere that the priest is enthusiastic and follows the rules, there is no question of failure." He replied: "We shall see."

19th. I attended Fr. Jarry's first formal meeting with his boys in the Middle School. There were eighteen present, including a Chinese Jesuit.
Fr. Crotti of Kaifeng was in touch with me. He remarked how effective the Work Sheet had proved. He said: "All five Presidents now use it and it is a wonderful way to make members interested in their work." He added that at the last Curia meeting, which was attended by the Archbishop, they had succeeded in launching a weekly Catholic newpaper. A team of thirteen Legionaries, plus two others shall run it. "This paper opens a wide road to our work," he said. "Some Legionaries will be in charge of writing and editing articles ... some shall bring the paper to homes; students can also offer the paper to their classmates. In this way it will be useful for Christians, non-Christians and the Legionaries themselves."
I have just come from Fr. Jarry's first formal meeting with the University girls. There were sixteen present and all are keen on the Legion. The young president said to me after the meeting: "This place is crying out for some activity to get people into the Church."

21st. Another French priest is interested in starting the Legion. He wants to begin with only a few of the best prospects and hopes to get a Praesidium going by the Feast of Christ the King. On Monday next he wants me to go with him to the local jail where there are over one thousand prisoners and quite a few Catholics. His idea is to organise the Catholics (who were interned for collaborating with the Japanese) into a Praesidium and then get them to work amongst the other prisoners. I encouraged him, despite the fact that it can be difficult to make contact with prisoners.

This evening we had our first meeting of the Sheng Kung Middle School for girls - run by the German Sisters of the Immaculate Conception. Fr. Steenstra is S.D.[27]

22nd. I left for Peking on the morning train. I wanted to see a couple of Praesidia and also to collect my bags preparatory to leaving for Shanghai. Even though there are four of the Jesuit Praesidia I have not seen, I am happy with the reports from all. One Father from the Catholic University said over the 'phone: "The miracle has happened." I said: "What miracle?" He replied: "I did not believe that the Legion was possible, or that such high ideals could be aimed at by lay folk - and now I see it is possible." Fr. Kavanagh CM (a native of Wexford) in charge of the East Church, who had started two Praesidia and got them working on the census told me: "They have done more in two months than Catholic Action in the last ten years." Previously he could not prevail on them to go to the houses - now they have made a complete survey of the Catholic families and have unearthed fifteen families who were not on the parish register, five of whom never went to Mass. Also they have encountered invalid marriages, unbaptised children and other cases for follow up.

Three thousand students have been evacuated from the Province of Shansi. Having no other place to live, they are sleeping on the white marble slabs of the Temple of Heaven about half an hour's bicycle run from the city of Peking. Their food is inadequate and their young lives have been disrupted. The girls in the University Praesidium have tackled the problem, spending hours there every week, looking for Catholics and bringing them to the nearest Church. The priest there is also taking steps to deal with the difficulty. The Legionaries were delighted and said to their Spiritual Director: "Father, we should always have hard work to do!"

While they were working among the students a young Chinese priest who was sightseeing noticed them and started to ask if they were members of the Legion of Mary. Guess who he was? Fr. Wu, whom I met at Sancta Maria Hostel in Dublin, the night I was treated to a tea party during my visit home. He cannot get back to his Northern District now and is going to Nanking to teach.

Bishop Tchao of Peking started a Rosary Crusade and was greatly aided by Legionaries, who promoted it in their visitation. They took names of those willing to say the Rosary every day and these they also enrolled as Auxiliary Legion members.

---

[27] Cf. Appendix IV.

Scheut Missions,
209 Ling Sen Road,
Tientsin, Hopeh
October 25th 1948

My dear Frank,

Your most welcome letter of September 25th arrived some days ago…I have two letters of John Nagle's still unanswered. I hope that the few pages of the diary which I enclose will partly explain my delay. I really have been rushed and still am. As you see, I am in Tientsin where so many were martyred in 1900. I hope to leave for Shanghai before the end of the month and get after the printing of the Handbook, though there is still plenty of work to be done here. The situation is getting worse every day. The Reds are closing in by degrees and we don't know what will be the end of it. We are used to these situations in China and it does not worry people anymore than they were worried for the past twenty years - although it was never so bad before.

I have sent you by Airmail a painting of the Immaculate Conception done on raw-silk by the famous Chinese artist Lou Hung Nien in the Fu-jen Catholic University.

The Curia in Shanghai has selected the name "Queen of Apostles". I see by a letter from Kaifeng that their Curia has also selected the same name. John Nagle can mention it to them in a letter - whether the name is to stay or not. As to the Prayer Card there was no trouble getting it all on one sheet, it is the revised version by Dr. Fang. We used ordinary newspaper print and that did the trick. You know that Chinese is more concise than English?

I refer in the Diary to the Internuncio's wish about the *Maria Legionis* being sent to the Bishops here - through us in the Catholic Central Bureau. I hope that is satisfactory. People I have met are very happy to see it. You will read also in the Diary about the enthusiasm of the different groups of Jesuits. One Jesuit priest told me there has not been in the past, any Children of Mary[28] in Peking or Tientsin.

A letter from Fr. Crotti in Kaifeng gives great reports of the Legion. I have been invited to attend their first anniversary of the Curia on December 8th. I shall try to be there if things are peaceful.

---

[28] The Jesuit-run Sodality.

They look bad in that direction; in fact the Reds are again threatening the city of Kaifeng.

Bad news has come from my old mission. The Reds have cut the dykes and flooded the city; all had to flee again. The people had just gone back and started a school. You have no notion of the tragedies being enacted in these places. Naturally these people who were so generous to me during the war, have nothing to do now but look to the priest. The priest who took my place has gone to rock bottom to keep them alive. I have given them all I can, but this new tragedy is distressing beyond words. The boys and girls Legion Praesidia so heroically begun again, are probably disbanded once more.

The new currency in China, which began only a month ago, has shown signs of going out of control also.[29] Some days ago it was only a quarter the value it was supposed to be. Prices of course go up sky-high - the Government try to control prices to save face and the result is that the shops won't sell and the people starve. It's the same all over China. Add to that the scare of the Reds closing in and you have a terrible picture. Thousands of refugees come here every day from the country part.

That is typical of China - floods, bandits, Red and not least, bad Government - the most long-suffering people you could imagine. In all these difficulties, I consider that China has some of the most heroic Catholics in the world. I don't think any country has had such constant disasters - and in the midst of them, such patient sufferers.

As regards the Envoys, I have not been successful. The Peking girl still wants to go but the University authorities cannot see their way to let her off until next September. She is the Principal of their Primary School and has stood up against many attacks of the Educational Board (which wants to get the Catholics out) and also broadcasts regularly on the Catholic Hour. If she resigns this year, it would be impossible to get another Catholic in. She is Secretary of the Legion and a splendid one. Also she is now President of their Junior group...

---

[29] The Chinese Renminbi is abbreviated as R.M.B. and is also known as the Yuan, abbreviated C.N.Y.

You know Frank, that in China up to now, we do not get religious vocations from the High Schools or Universities - not many anyway. One of my great hopes is that the Legion will begin that phenomenon...

As yet, the kind of members we would normally look to as potential Envoys are not in the Legion and we just have to wait. We have wonderful workers there - spending hours in Legion work - but they also have other obligations. Perhaps we could find Europeans who speak Chinese and other languages and are willing to go as Envoys, but I don't know how that might appeal to you.

Supposing I do get suitable persons as Envoys, what is the next step? I did write and ask once, but I suppose in the confusion of my questions it was forgotten.

With every good wish to yourself and all in the Sancta Maria, Morning Star and Regina Coeli Hostels.[30]

Aedan

---

[30] These Dublin Hostels, begun in 1922, 1927 and 1930 respectively, are staffed by members of the Legion of Mary on a voluntary basis. Both the Morning Star and Regina Coeli are in operation catering for the homeless of the city to this day.

CHAPTER THIRTEEN

"THE APOSTOLIC CATHOLIC WILL
ALWAYS BE ON DUTY"

*The eyes of the Lord preserve knowledge: and the words of the
unjust are overthrown. (Proverbs 22:12)*

Diary: 10th November 1948: I helped Mother Lewis, a Sacred Heart nun, to set up a Praesidium in her Chinese Middle School. She said after the first day: "These children would never before agree to do the things they have now been asked to do." Next day I went to visit Bishop Noël Gubbels OFM of Ichang (known as the 'Mission of Blood' on account of all the martyrs there). Elderly as he is and dangerous as is his location, he was going back to his station. I had a little difficulty in making an impression on him, for he did not know what the Legion was; but before I left he was all for the Legion and accepted the Handbook with delight.

> c/o Catholic Central Bureau,
> 197 Yoyang Lu, Shanghai
> 11th November 1948

My dear Frank,

I flew back from Tientsin just eleven days ago and have been busy ever since. As you know, just after that date - or rather before I left - things were very bleak. Mukden had fallen to the Communists and troops were beginning to appear on the streets. I had intended to leave anyway, but it was lucky I did so as travel is getting more difficult every day. I am happy that I went to Peking and Tientsin and set up things there. I am convinced that things will run smoothly under Our Lady's guidance. I believe that all the priests concerned will remain.

I am delighted with the various Praesidia I have been visiting in Shanghai. They have improved much since my departure, which proves the Legion system once again and Our Lady's blessing being with them all the time. It was unfortunate that I had to leave so soon after the start of the Curia - it is doing very well, but under difficulties. Soon after I left, the President had to resign due to illness.

Now to business! I have found an Envoy - and I believe an ideal one. Her name is Teresa Su and she is attending the Aurora University. A graduate of English, she is now doing a post-graduate course in Sociology. She has a wealthy background and hails from Hong Kong. Her father lets her do as she pleases, and she has travelled quite a bit in China to study. She is Cantonese and knows that language as well as Mandarin. Before I went to Peking, I could tell she had potential as a Legion Envoy and because I did not know how she would take to the work, I asked her to join a Praesidium. Now, her fellow members say that her work is splendid and she herself loves it. It has brought her out of herself, and it appears now that she had always wanted to do something like that, but had not the courage or the opportunity.

When I asked her if she would consider Envoyship, her only worry was that she would be a financial burden on the Concilium - this generous spirit is a very good sign.

Teresa Su

She told me that she doesn't intend getting married and though she had considered religious life, she feels called to do apostolic work as a lay person. She had intended to leave Shanghai in the present bad circumstances and complete her studies in Hong Kong, but when I suggested going to Manila for Envoy training, she was delighted. After a few days deliberation she has now confirmed her decision to me.

If she goes to Hong Kong she will have an opportunity to see her father before she leaves for the Philippines. She is determined to carry on even in the event of his trying to stop her. I am writing to the Internuncio tonight to ask him to get a passport for her. I don't know how long that will take. She can wait for the passport there and be sure of being out of the mainland should the political situation worsen. Meantime, she hopes to be able to do a little Legion work in Hong Kong.

Please write and tell me what arrangements are in place in Manila?

Now I must stop and get this off. Please realise the tightness of our position and the necessity to act quickly, and give me a reply and directions immediately.

I have just received a package of Tesserae in French, Portuguese and German. Many thanks to whoever sent them. We can get them printed here when we want them. The Orphanage, which made the Legion Standard for us can also print the Tesserae covers. They will be cheaper here - and that is necessary for China.

Aedan

The Immaculate Conception
by Lou Hung Nien

Diary: November 30th: Attended Shanghai Curia meeting and it was a great success. However, the resignation of two Officers was unfortunate.
The new Officers elected are giving much of their time to Curia work. The President is a European, the Vice President is Chinese - from Mother Thornton's Praesidium. The Curia is to have its Reunion in the Aurora College for women on December 18th.

Monday December 6th: I attended the first Junior Praesidium in the Slavonic Rite ever held in China. Sr. Columban and Sr. Emmanuel (S.D.) were also present. The Russian Jesuit priest, Fr. Andrea, has made a Russian translation of the prayers, the *Akathistos* providing the substitute for the Rosary. The result is a Litany of prerogatives of Our Lady which is most uplifting. According to custom, the prayers are recited standing and take the same time as the Rosary. On the table instead of a statue there is an Icon of Our Lady.

Fr. McGrath attends Slavnoic Rite Praesidium, Shanghai

11th. Hong Kong: I came here by plane. I am staying with the Irish Jesuit Fathers. It is interesting that many of these men were either students with me or taught me in Belvedere College, Dublin. Many of them are enthusiastic. Others do not know about the Legion. Fr. Sheridan was S.D. to a Praesidium concerned with the blind in Dublin and he could talk for hours on the work they did. Fr. Cronin SJ was S.D. to five Praesidia in the army and was also S.D. to the Curia - he set up the first Praesidium in Chaldean. He is just as keen as myself. Fr. Tom Ryan, as you know is a Superior. Having no parish, he asked me to get the Legion going in the parishes. In Hong Kong amongst the different parishes there is a certain amount of jealousy - and I suppose an old fear that the Jesuits might take over. All the Jesuit Fathers here are doing fine work and have boosted the image and understanding of the Church and its mission. Fr. Ryan has been a marvellous leader, even for a couple of years running several departments in the Government. He has proved himself an authority in every line. He even gives talks over the radio on music. When these priests take up the Legion it will increase the value of their work immensely. Regarding the new decree on Sodalities, one of the

Jesuit priests said: "I would still prefer the Legion for it is better; it is new and thus has greater force."

Of all the places I have been, Hong Kong seems the most unfavourable for beginning the Legion. The reasons are these: The priests had already established many organisations of Catholics, which were working splendidly and showing no signs of getting tired. It was clear that while some apostolate was being done, much more could be achieved and with less time wasted on talking and social activities.

The Bishop was willing to try the Legion but he thought that as there was so much activity already, it might not fit in. Many priests were of the same opinion, but all I wanted was a chance to speak to them collectively and let them know what the Legion could do working in conjunction with already-established organisations. The Bishop gave me this chance, having heard of the Legion from Msgr. Riberi, who had never failed to impress it on any Bishop he met.

A day was fixed to meet the Bishop, priests and Heads of schools. When I had spoken for three-quarters of an hour, I turned to the Bishop and asked if I could continue. He nodded to me and I spoke for another half-hour. When I was finished several of the priests invited me to their parishes to talk to their Catholic Action groups. Fr. Maestrini, who in the beginning had said that the Legion was unsuitable, and who said the priests were going to excuse themselves, said to me after the meeting: "Well, you were right Father. There is going to be no trouble." The Bishop stood up and said: "I want to see at least one Praesidium in every parish and school." This was all most encouraging!

After the Bishop's meeting I gave a series of talks to Parish Organisations, and religious communities, explaining the Legion System and tried to make everyone realise that the Legion was not just another organisation, but something very different. As usual there was a small number who afterwards thought they would like to undertake the Legion.

I visited several Convents - one in Kowloon, in which Sr. Imelda is Superior. She was interested in the Legion and told me that Bishop Ford wanted to begin it many years ago. Although he had not started it, he took many ideas from the Handbook. I gave her literature and she set off to spread the idea of the Legion.

In St. Teresa's Parish, I arranged for a day to put the prospective Legionaries through a meeting. After appointing the officers, I explained in detail their obligations to ensure the smooth running of meetings. Twenty people attended the first regular meeting. Their Chinese President was magnificent. He is a student of Engineering just returned from England.

Some officers of the military vessel H.M.S. Tamar attended this Praesidium and were so impressed with its efficient working that they now wish to operate their own Praesidium along the same lines. One of the officers is an ex-Legionary from Malta and another is a young doctor from Rathgar in Dublin. Fr. Corbally SJ is their spiritual director.

The Portuguese are in the majority in St. Teresa's and I am hoping they will be able to spare someone to start the Legion in Macao.

One of the first things the Legionaries tackled was visiting domestics in Catholic homes. The Protestants are doing much for them and have made converts, while the Catholics have up to now done nothing. Now the Legionaries are giving Catholic instruction to these workers with the permission of the host families.

It was Fr. Cranelli who invited me to St. Teresa's. He has now gone to the U.S. His assistant, Fr. Orlando, was not keen on the Legion at first, saying there were already too many such organisations in the parish. Later on as Pastor, he was pleased with the work done. He agreed to divide the Praesidium into two groups - with about fifteen in each. He now has three Praesidia - two English-speaking and one Chinese-speaking, run by the Franciscan Missionaries of Mary.

The Handbook has been eagerly sought after and no copies are left. It is common to see these young men and women going about at lunchtime reading from it. It is good to watch their enthusiasm - ample reward for my labours.

New Junior Legion members in the schools are now visiting those children who should be coming to instruction in preparation for Holy Communion and Confirmation. Fr. Maestrini's group (he is the Editor of *The Sunday Examiner*) is concentrating on bringing Catholic literature to the Catholic homes and also the doing of convert work.

During my stay in Hong Kong I had an opportunity to speak to the Maryknoll Fathers who were visiting for their Retreat. Besides these men there were others who were duly impressed with the idea of the Legion, of which they had known nothing before, or had wrong ideas. Many took Handbooks and intended to start up Praesidia on their Missions. One priest from Korea was definite about bringing the idea back home with him. Also, one of our Columban Fathers from Korea whom I met in Hong Kong and who had been a Legion S.D. in Australia, decided to begin the Legion when he returned to Korea.

Seventeen Praesidia were formed in Hong Kong before I left. This came about by that intitial series of talks, followed by the sample meetings. Before long it was possible to send prospective members, to such meetings to see how the established Praesidia worked. Some of the priests were cautious and did not believe until they experienced the first fruits. What did attract them was the fact that there would be a Curia meeting every month at which they would hear the reports from other parishes and also from their own schools - something which they had always wanted up to this, but had failed to do, was to co-ordinate the groups of their own Catholic Action

First Praesidium established in Hong Kong, Fr. McGrath on left.

Bishop Valtorta came to visit some of the Praesidia in the Cathedral Parish. He was delighted and said after one meeting: "It has come to stay!"

I intend going to Kweilin soon to set things in motion. Msgr. Romaniello and Fr. McCabe MM, whom I met in Shanghai have invited me. I am hoping to seek permission for Fr. McCabe to look after the Legion in his Vicariate. The organisation has appealed to him from the start as a means of spreading devotion to the Rosary.

After Kweilin, I mean to return to Hong Kong to start the Curia and then back to Canton to do the same. Beyond that, my plans are uncertain. I am expecting my brother Ivar soon from the U.S. and he will be going to Hanyang. I want him to check up on the Praesidia in Hankow and Wuchang where I've not had recent contacts.

Hong Kong
15th December, 1948

Dear Frank,

Your letter of November 27th and Mr. Nagle's[31] of November 16th both to hand. Many thanks to you both for such encouraging letters. I was delighted to hear all the good Legion news, especially that things had begun in Algiers. May it be the means of breaking down old barriers. I am pleased to note that you appreciated the picture of the Immaculate Conception. I was more than rewarded for any trouble I went to in getting it done. Your letter to the painter did not arrive as yet - and may now be too late, as Peking is in imminent danger. If you are writing to him, please put one thing straight - the painting was not exactly a gift from him. He went to much trouble to paint it in the time given, but I paid him for it.

As to my brother taking such an interest in the Legion - I had a letter from him and his change of attitude was evident...

My move to Hong Kong might make you wonder. I intended to come here anyway - especially after His Excellency's visit here when he told me of his hopes - but things were hurried up by the political situation. Shanghai is going to fall unless something extraordinary happens. Now if I was caught in Shanghai - even though we might be allowed to work, we would not be able to move about for the present at least. Again, letters would not be allowed to go through. That would mean the end of my mission to China. I would be forced to become Spiritual Director of one of the Praesidia and remain there. Again, the work of the Curia as regards all of China would finish. They would have to confine themselves to individual Praesidia. Seeing this situation, I consulted the Internuncio and told him my plan. He agreed. I have come to Hong Kong and brought a certain amount of literature with me. I intend to start Praesidia here and if Shanghai is cut off, then we can communicate with those in free China from here.

The French Jesuit in Peking, who had six curates and eight Praesidia has lately come down to Shanghai and has praised the Legion system to the heights. He has spoken it to all the Jesuits in Shanghai, with wonderful effect. As I said in the Diary, they are all

---

[31] This letter is not on file.

91

touched by the work done and want to start the Legion. Shanghai is a place where the French Jesuits have been in control for hundreds of years. The Sodality is flourishing and even though the priests are conservative, they are astonished by what the Legion is doing and, the day I left the city, they started a Praesidium in one of their most important Churches.

That Californian Jesuit of whom I spoke in the past and who went around Shanghai studying the Legion, has done wonderful work with his Praesidium. The priest who is with him came here lately and said that his lethargic school had been wakened up - and while it had been anti-Catholic, is now pro-Catholic. Again, the Jesuit Fr. Jarry of Tientsin could not have been more genuine in his enthusiasm.

…Teresa Su is on her way to Hong Kong. Fr. Gracia has written in anticipation of her visit to the Philippines. She expects to leave for Manila after Chinese New Year. Her Visa has not yet come.

…Regarding refunding the Internuncio: Teresa bought all her own clothes, so no refund is needed. I shall tell her to keep account of her expenses from there on. The Internuncio pays for my travel and expenses by way of a loan to the Legion.

I have just received a letter from the Apostolic Administrator of Canton inviting me to start the Legion.

I received several letters from Tientsin (from now on they may be cut off), one from Fr. Beunen who expressed wonder at the success of the Legion.

…I have just received a letter form the Aposotolic Administrator of Canton inviting me to start the Legion.

Very sincerely yours in 'The Legion',

Aedan

PART FOUR

1949 TO 1950

OBSTACLES MULTIPLY

July 1st 1949 - Mao Tse-tung's essay, On the Dictatorship of the People's Democracy published

Compulsory reading for prisoners in Chinese Jails.

The essay strove to justify a number of political campaigns and large-scale arrests of people suspected of being against the New Regime in China.

Communist Triple Independence Movement set-up: Self-support; Self-propagation; Self-rule.

CHAPTER FOURTEEN

CANTON - JANUARY 1949
KWANGTUNG PROVINCE

To you I lift up my soul O Lord, my God.
In you I trust: let me not be put to shame,
let not my enemies exult over me.
(Psalms 24:1-2)

Diary: Monday February 14ᵗʰ 1949: Having been invited to Canton by His Excellency Msgr. Deswaziere, Apostolic Administrator of the Archdiocese of Canton, I arrived on the February 4ᵗʰ. The Bishop had appointed Fr. Charles Daly, an Irish Jesuit to be in charge of the Legion there. He and other Irish Jesuits are in charge of the Sacred Heart school in the Cathedral Parish. Also Fr. Meyer (Maryknoll), who is well known for his Catholic Action work on the cell system and who is won over by the Legion system, is in a parish in Canton district. The latter had formed several groups for active work and while they were good, they were still in the early stages of formation. When I arrived I found groups ready to be turned into the Legion. These priests had decided that it was time to do so. The day after my arrival I addressed the Bishop and priests. Next day I spoke to all the assembled groups and the following day to all the officers. They are all perfectly docile to the move and every day this week I have a meeting to set up according to Legion rules. The Spiritual Directors are so keen on it all that I have no fears. Another Jesuit, Fr. O'Meara (who's mother is a Legionary in the South of Ireland and whose sister is President of a Curia there), will be S.D. of a couple of these groups. In this city of Canton, there are only four thousand Catholics. I can see great strides being made by the Legion and great fruit being reaped through Our Lady.

Yesterday I helped to set up a young men's Praesidium in a place called Shameen (where last year the British Consulate was burned down). It is the parish of Fr. Limat, a Swiss priest. They were nervous at the prospect of regular Legion work. They ended up very enthusiastic - the inevitable result of the Rosary and the meeting. Today, I set up the women's group in the same place with the same enthusiasm.

Shameen Praesidium, Canton, with Frs. Limat, Meyer and McGrath

Since the Irish Jesuit Fathers came here and began to teach in the Schools and Universities, things have brightened up a great deal. Also there are two Maryknoll Fathers in one of the Universities, which is predominantly Protestant. However, these priests are so good at their subjects and so friendly with everyone that they have been able to build a Chapel on the Campus, which is a great attraction to the students. They are winning many converts and the Protestants are saying: "If these priests are here much longer they will take control."

20th. We had the first men's Legion meeting of the University. (S.D. Fr. O'Meara SJ) They went through it in a very businesslike way and accepted their work willingly. During the meeting the members asked many pertinent questions.

21st. Started up the women's Praesidium of the local schoolteachers under Fr. Daly SJ. I have no doubt that the starting of these several Praesidia will have a very good effect on the members as they have seldom done anything Apostolic.

22nd. Attended Fr. Meyer's Family Group and set it up as a Praesidium. They are mostly made up of married couples. They too were keen to get down to work and love the business-like method of the meeting. Some of the work assignments consisted of husbands and wives working together. It is the first time I have seen the like.

> Cathedral, Shek Shat,
> Canton,
> 22nd February 1949

Dear John,

My lapse in answering your letters is terrible - but I can't do much about it if the Legion will insist on going ahead so fast. Your two letters of December 31st and January 21st arrived.[32] You are as careful as ever in answering my questions; many thanks. I had a letter from Frank written on January 9th and I must get down to write to him too. I mean to enclose a sort of back-diary, which will bring you up to date with events here - but it is not very detailed ...

You will see that Fr. Cronin and Fr. Corbally have started their Praesidia with Fr. Ryan's blessing. Fr. Ryan told me that he helped to start many Legion groups at home and that in Kweilin (where I am going) during the war he bought the Handbooks and got the group together ready to begin. Then the Japanese chased them out. He told me how efficient the Legion was in Dublin and how he only had to ring up Mary Duffy on Youth Delinquency work and the case would be looked after. They are free to start the Legion in Hong Kong if they wish - I mean individual Jesuit Fathers. Where the Sodality is in action, progress is going to be slow. Most of the priests hold that the Legion is far ahead of the Sodality. It will all come right now that the Legion is sweeping other parts of the Colony.

As to our Envoy - she has had very bad luck. It took four months to get her Visa, and that with help from Fr. Gracia in Manila. Now that it has come, it states that she must wait on her turn - which would not let her off until July. In the meantime, Teresa may come down here with her father for a couple of weeks; and if she does,

---

[32] Neither of these two letters are on file.

she can help me to explain things in Cantonese (her native tongue), which can be understood by the majority.

Regarding the translation of the Handbook - there is no question of changing anything in the book itself but just the Chinese characters. Fr. Sheng says that it is very good. The Chinese title for 'Legion of Mary', literally 'Holy Mother's Army', is the same as we have used for some years. It was selected by Bishop Yu Pin of Nanking and is the title used on those first Tesserae sent to you by Fr. Joe Hogan. The Internuncio has done everything possible to facilitate the printing and has got many priests to help. He has even borrowed paper from one of the Catholic magazines.

News came to me recently that the Reds have entered Kaifeng. The Catholic newspaper published by Legionaries there has had to stop publication.

It looks like Canton, is going to beat all records in setting up Praesidia. Fr. Meyer and the Jesuits are responsible for their preparation.

Aedan

Diary: 23rd. The men's Praesidium of the Sacred Heart schoolteachers began under Fr. Leo Donnelly SJ. Their chief work will be to contact the parents of the pupils of this big school.

24th. A Praesidium has been formed among the nurses in the big Hospital (S.D. Fr. O'Meara SJ), where Catholic Sisters are helping with administration. The Sisters have between three hundred and seven hundred Baptisms per month, mostly children and adults in danger of death. Now the nurses who are Legionaries are going to contact patients and do the baptising if necessary.

26th. I spoke to the Sisters in a more remote section of Canton. Most had never heard of the Legion. It thrilled them to realise what they could do with a Praesidium. Two of them said they had been Adjutorian members in Canada and were recruited by the local Bishop but they had no contact since with the Legion. This part of Canton is without a Church. I spoke to the local priest and he is going to let the past pupils of the local Sisters school start a Praesidium.

27th. The Chinese Pastor of this Cathedral is elderly, but interested in the Legion. He attended many preliminary meetings and prepared a group of parishioners to start a Praesidium. I attended his first meeting; it was devastating! About thirty-five members walked into the room. There was a young Secretary of about fifty years old. The average age after him was about sixty and running to over eighty in many cases. There was pandemonium in the prayers! They said their own when it suited them. The print on the Tessera was too small for them to bother reading it. The numbers were too high for a single meeting. In the middle of the meeting, a Church bell (which was presented by Napoleon III!) rang, indicating that it was a half an hour before Benediction. They all blessed themselves and began to walk out. The Parish Priest saved the situation by calling them back. By this time I had decided to let them carry on to the end and then speak to him. However, he took the situation in hand and suggested that the younger ones be active members and the less active be Auxiliary members. They were all pleased with this arrangment. By this time the President (aged eighty) had gone into a trance and felt like taking a nap. I would have suggested it to him earlier! I think it is possible to get the makings of a first-rate Praesidium out of the best of them.

7p.m. Second meeting of young women of Fr. Limat's parish - splendid. All had good reports. Frs. Meyer and Limat are highly optimistic.

Between the Jesuits and the Maryknoll Fathers they have Legion representatives in every University here. They all intend to start Praesidia. As the Colleges have only opened, I am waiting until the Curiae in Hong Kong and Canton are set up, to begin these new Praesidia.

February 28th. A most promising meeting has just concluded with the men teachers group of the Sacred Heart School (S.D. Fr. Donnelly SJ). Many good contacts were made and duly noted.

March 1st. Attended Fr. Meyer's 'Family Group'. All the members made useful contacts and were pleased with the way they had been greeted in the various houses. Fr. Meyer did not expect so much and showed his joy. He expressed high hopes for the Legion in Canton. "We can now sit back and smoke our pipes and have our work done for us," he said jokingly.

March 2nd. First reports at meeting of teachers under Fr. Donnelly SJ. They have all got into the spirit of the work.

March 3ʳᵈ. Went with Fr. O' Meara to the venue of the Hospital nurses meeting, which could not be held due to a terrible accident on a ship. Many casualties had to be treated.

March 4ᵗʰ. Set out for Kweilin yesterday, which is the Prefecture of Msgr. Romaniello. He had invited me to start the Legion there. The weather was so bad that the aeroplane could not finish the journey. We landed in Liuchow, to be told we would have to go on to Kweilin by train next day.

It was all Providential. I was delighted to have a chance to meet the local priests, who happened to be of the Paris Foreign Missions Society. The Pastor Fr. Madiore is well known for his zeal in the Prison Apostolate. He was glad to have the chance to hear about the Legion. He invited me to go with him to visit the local prison to see how he dealt with the Catechumens. He has been successful with all of them - even winning over the Warden to Catholicism. With him converted, it was easy to organise the men inside. Fr. Madiore gives instructions three days per week. The Maryknoll Sisters go with him to instruct the women. He has already baptised eighty of the inmates and proof that they are genuine is that they have brought their wives and children to instruction after their release. I was impressed by the way the prisoners answered the priests' questions. He treats them like children. He introduced me by saying he had good news for them. At hearing this they all brightened up and I am sure they must have thought that I was going to get them out of prison! Then he told them briefly what I was doing and asked me to speak.

Thus I had my first chance to speak of the Legion of Mary in Liuchow - to prisoners. They were very attentive and seemed interested. The great thing was that Fr. Madiore was there and he caught on to the idea and is determined to start a Praesidium.

So, it is an ill wind that blows nobody any good!

Fr. Aedan visiting with Maryknoll sisters in Kweilin

March 5th. It was a long day on a very slow train. I travelled with a Maryknoll priest whom I had met on the plane and we arrived in Kweilin at 11 p.m. where Msgr. Romaniello and Fr. McCabe were on the platform with their Jeep ready to take me to the Mission. Next morning after a good night's rest. Msgr. Romaniello rejoiced my heart by telling me that he had appointed Fr. McCabe to look after the spread of the Legion in the District. The following day we set about marking out a route around the Mission, which would enable me to pinpoint and speak to the priests in charge of the various areas. Fr. McCabe could follow up and get the Legion started. Already he had been speaking to the local priests and had even prepared two Praesidia. We attended a meeting of young men that night in the Parish Church under Fr. Daubert MM He and his co-worked Fr. Gillick became intensely interested.

March 7th. I spoke to the local Maryknoll Sisters. Their group assembled and I put them through a meeting.

CHAPTER FIFTEEN

KWEILIN - MARCH 1949
KWANGSI PROVINCE

"FATHER, I NOW SEE THE DIFFERENCE ..."

The heart of a man disposes his way:
but the Lord must direct his steps.
(Proverbs 16:9)

Diary: March 8th 1949. Fr. McCabe and myself started out on our tour of the Missions in Msgr. Romaniello's Jeep (given to him by friends in the U.S.). Fr. McCabe drove. It took us four hours to cross three rivers on rafts just to get to the first Mission Station in Hsin Hsien. Fr. Jacques MM, who had to leave the North of China on account of the Reds, was in charge. He is an indefatigable worker and already within the last year has baptised about one hundred people. Many of the townspeople seem to have already come to him for instruction in the faith. The day before I came, natives from six villages arrived also seeking to be received into the Church.

Fr. Jacques has brought many of his Catechists down from the North. They are well trained to give religious instruction and, having come in close contact with the advancing Communists, are aware of the urgency of the work.

This priest lives in a ramshackle house on the main street. From morning until night the house is full of people, and from 5pm to 8pm it is a beehive of activity. All available rooms are occupied with people learning their catechism.

He has a training school there also. The student teachers live like religious. They study all day and in the evening watch the experienced Catechists at work.

The best Catechist there is a young girl whose methods are an inspiration to all. I was thrilled to discover that I knew her. She had been a Legion President in the Fu Jen University Parish in Peking when I was there and is a striking example of what a President should be. Many priests in Peking had gone to see the Legion meeting conducted by her. She had to leave the place and was invited by Fr. Jacques to help him in his new work. She spends much of her time helping the poor and the needy. Many people have been won over by her kindness and from this kindness it is a small step to religion, especially in these parts where such caring is not evident. Her Northern dialect is not well understood, but she has set about correcting that and has begun to teach the people Legion methods. Fr. Jacques is so overwhelmed with work that he is now going to set up a Praesidium.

On the 9th, I moved on to Ch'uen Hsien, a compound of not too many houses. This Mission had been set up by Fr. McCabe incorporating a 'Boys Town', for orphans. There are three priests here - Frs. Glass, Quirke and Murphy. The inrush of Catechumens is even greater than in Hsin Hsien. Already the priests have instructed five hundred and have still six hundred to come before Easter. Here too, the idea of the Legion appealed greatly. Fr. McCabe is willing to help with the work of formation. It is wonderful to see such activity here. In other places the Church is at a standstill.

12th. I set out with Fr. McCabe in the Msgr.'s Jeep for Yang Shoh and the Western Missions. The road we took today provided panoramic views. They have a saying here: "Yang Shoh is even more beautiful than Kweilin." Well, that is where we went. Fr. McCabe was continually stopping the car so that I could take photographs. It was a delightful trip and he proved a great travelling companion. I have never met anyone with such sanctity and humour combined. He has tremendous devotion to Our Blessed Mother and seeks at every opportunity to speak about Her. We are lucky indeed in having him to look after the Legion in the Kweilin Vicariate.

I arrived in Lai Po and found a large compound incorporating a Church, presbytery, Minor Seminary and Catechist's School with four priests in charge. Across the road is the Maryknoll Convent with a congregation of mostly Chinese Sisters. The Fathers are often away during the week and come back to a busy Sunday, beginning with hearing between two hundred to three hundred Confessions. I saw the same activity here, with many conversions. The instructors receive no payment in any of these places. They come in their spare time: women during the day and men at night. The Pastor, Fr. Reegan had written to me for books and information. He received the books but I had not the time to answer his letter. I apologised and promised to make amends while in Lai Po. All there were interested in the Legion.

A strange thing - in the Convent there was a St. Louis Nun named Sr. Rose Victor, who used to be a Legionary in the U.S. and about whom Mr. Nagle wrote to me several times, in an effort to contact her. I wrote to her about the

Legion, but she had not the chance to introduce it herself. She was present when I talked to the Sisters who all became enthusiastic immediately. We set up a women's Praesidium next day. Fr. Reegan and the Sisters had been preparing for this event. Sr. Rose, the Superior, told me she was finding it hard to convince the Chinese Sisters of the effectiveness of the Legion. They thought that no one would keep the rules or do the work. As Sr. Rose had to move on to another Mission to visit some native Sisters, she came with us in the Jeep and I had a chance to answer her questions on many points en route.

14th. I went on to Tung-an to visit Fr. Greene[33] and Fr. Nugent. They too have native Sisters helping and all are busy with new converts. On the way there we stopped to pick up a Fr. P'ing Lo. When he came out of the house, we looked at each other in surprise. We had spent five weeks together on the SS General Meigs coming from the U.S. in 1948.
Fr. McCabe and I spent one night in Tung-an. All are determined to establish Praesidia to help them in their immense work.
Next day we returned to Fr. Reegan's disrict in Lai Po and spent another day there and today came back to Msgr. Romaniello's place in Kweilin.
I intend to get a plane back from here to Hong Kong on March 18th, if there is no fog. I want to meet my brother Ivar, who is coming from the U.S. on the 'General Gordon'. I also want to set up the Curia in Hong Kong.

16th. I found that the first Legion meeting of the women here in Kweilin took place two days ago and had been a great success. Msgr. Romaniello was delighted to see the way Our Lady was helping everyone. He was surprised to find that all the work assigned was done successfully, some after much inconvenience to members. The Maryknoll Sister, who had initially written for information, said my arrival solved everything.

18th. Back in Hong Kong: I heard from Legionaries that everything was doing extremely well. The enthusiasm was evident. Next day when I met Fr. Maestrini he told me that the Parish Priests were more than satisfied, and not a few quite dumbfounded at the work done. They had not expected such results.

---

[33] Fr. Robert Greene's book, *Calvary in China*, G. P. Putman, New York, 1953, gives a detailed account of life as a missionary in Tung-an under Communist Rule. An extract from this volume was originally published in the Legion periodical *Maria Legionis* in December 1953 and is included as Appendix III.

20th. I met my brother Ivar at the boat. He is looking well and has returned to China a fully-fledged Legionary, having left here not just so sure about it all. I brought him to a couple of meetings and he was surprised to find such efficiency. I am perfectly happy about the different Praesidia. The Catholic Centre group under Fr. Maestrini is forming a 'Poor-Girls' club. Two other Praesidia are taking, as part of their work the running of a night school. Half of the time will be given to Doctrine, with a view to the making of converts. They will visit the families of the children. The University Praesidium has begun visiting the Reformatory School on a weekly basis. They will call on the boys in their homes when they leave this institution.

26th. Bishop Valtorta rang to say that the Archbishop of Changsha, Hunan Province was staying with him and would like to see me. He had heard of the Legion activities and wanted to know more. I spoke with him and that night he came with Bishop Valtorta to the women's branch meeting in the Cathedral. He was very surprised at its efficiency. He is a great advocate of Catholic Action. When the meeting ended he came to me and said: "Father, I now see the difference. Our Lady is obviously behind this movement. And besides, the definiteness and detail make the Legion effective. I shall certainly organise it in my Vicariate."

28th. Rosary Church Praesidia: The Parish Priest of these groups was one whom I found it hard to convince about the Legion. He held back for quite a while. On my return from Kwangsi I heard that he had begun and was thrilled with the success. I was not disappointed when I went to see for myself. Suffice to say that in the middle of the meeting he said to me: "This is the greatest thrill since my ordination."

29th. I visited the Maryknoll Junior Praesidium in Hong Kong. I had just set it up before leaving. Grand work was being done and the Sisters were enthused.
I am now busy preparing for the first Curia of April 5th. Bishop Valtorta is coming too. This will be the first co-ordinating of Catholic Action here.

30th. On Friday I visited the 'split' Praesidium from St. Teresa's. They had to divide on account of numbers. I was delighted with this one. It is made up of women and the President has a wonderful idea of her duties. She is one of those who devoured the Handbook within the first week!

Ricci Hall,
Hong Kong
30ᵗʰ March 1949

Dear John,

Your welcome letter of March 10ᵗʰ to hand.[34] Many thanks. I am enclosing my latest pages of diary. I am in the middle of preparing for the first Curia here and I am happy about its possibilities. There are now nineteen Praesidia going strong. You need not fear about too rapid a pace. My reason is this: The Spiritual Directors are keen and appreciate that the Legion is helping them in their many tasks. Our Lady is taking China under Her wing and I have confidence in Her protection.

Here in the Hong Kong Curia, the members are just about to make their Legion Promise. I intend to make the Curia Officers do regular visitation of Praesidia soon, so as to keep things in line. There is no need to do extension work here for a while, but the priests are appealing to get the Legion started in new places and it would be a pity to discourage them.

I just had a telephone message from the Rector of the Regional Seminary in Hong Kong, Fr. Harris SJ asking me to go and talk to the students. I have been working for this and hoping for it since I came here. Someone must be praying hard. These priests go all over China and are known for their fine spirit.

Legion members are aware of the restrictions concerning the wearing of the Vexillina. In ordinary work they are certainly better off without it. Where census-work takes Legionaries into dangerous places here in China, I think the emblem may well be a protection.

As to Teresa Su, the Consulate will allow only five Chinese to leave Hong Kong each month. Teresa is on this quota and has to await her turn. There is a chance of a cancellation soon and she may get away. At the moment she is helping in Canton and doing useful work.

You refer to Miss Helen Huekels. She must surely know of the existence of the Curia in Shanghai and of my roving commission. I wrote to her a month ago telling her how delighted I was that she was back and asking her to help the Hankow Praesidia (just across

---

[34] Letter not on file.

the river) to start their Curia, but I got no reply. I have asked my brother Ivar to make it his business to meet her and request the same favour. As you suggest, she will be a great force in Central China and if she consented to be an Envoy it would be wonderful.

I am eager to get away to Central China again, but I think it advisable to set up the Canton Curia first. I would ultimately like to get back to my original base in Shanghai if conditions allow.

The Slavonic Rite Praesidium in Shanghai is doing fine and they are starting another Senior group. They also intend to start a Praesidium in the Latin Rite. Those girls who left for the Argentine brought all the literature with them and intend to get the Slavonic priests to begin the Legion there with their Russian refugees. What is the decision about their alternative prayers? I am anxious to hear.

Now that Hong Kong is established, it will be an invaluable stepping stone to getting the Legion better organised in southern China.

Wishing you all every blessing,

Aedan

Diary: March 31st. I went along to Fr. Cronin's University Praesidium. The Bishop also attended and was impressed. He even hinted that the members might be doing too much, with so much other work to be done in the College. But those young men and women wanted to do it all. Later on as examinations approached, the Spiritual Director asked them if they might like to do lighter work, which would fulfil their obligation and yet take less time - they refused! They wanted to go on as they were. They were trusting in Our Lady for their examinations and she did not let them down. Every one of those students passed their tests, while a great number in the University failed!

April 1st. Today I followed up on Fr. Harris' invitation to speak to the Jesuit Seminarians. Students from Peking and from other Seminaries were there. When they are ordained, these young men will be working in many parts of China. I was glad to find all were interested in the Legion. Fr. Harris bought the Chinese Handbook for the students to study. When I mentioned forming a Praesidium he hesitated and said: "Not for the present - but if those students do not know all about the Legion before they leave here, it will not be my fault." On my speaking of the necessity of seeing the Legion in action, he replied: "I intend to let them go out to the different Praesidia in Hong Kong to see it for themselves."

2nd. The Praesidium I visited today was one of the earliest to be established in Hong Kong. It has done wonderful work. Mother Angelica is in charge, though they get their cases-to-visit from the P.P. They have four Junior Praesidia attached and their activities spread out like a fan to three distant parishes where the members teach Catechism on Sundays. It means that the children offer up their Sundays for the Legion, which in Hong Kong is a big sacrifice, but they seem to love it all.

5th. This was the day of the co-ordinating of all the Hong Kong Praesidia in the Curia. I had taken much trouble to nominate good Officers and ensure that all went well. We had a marvellous attendance, including the Bishop and all, bar one of the Spiritual Directors. The election of Officers went smoothly. The President and Vice-President and Secretary are Chinese. The Treasurer is Portuguese. The Bishop gave the Allocutio and I must say he was not sparing in his praise of the Legion and in expressing his hopes. Amongst other things, he said: "I may count this day as the best of my missionary life in Hong Kong, because I see that something has come which will never disappear." It had always been his ambition to co-ordinate the Catholic Action in Hong Kong - but somehow this had never come about. Now, within two months of the Legion starting, almost all the parishes and schools were represented at a general meeting to inspire each other and to consult on forms of activity. It was decided to have a Curia Reunion to enable the members to get to know each other, and to prepare for an Acies.

CHAPTER SIXTEEN

HUNAN PROVINCE - APRIL 1949

"I WENT BY TRAIN TO HENYANG, A TWENTY TWO-HOUR RUN"

*By wisdom the house shall be built, and by prudence it
shall be strengthened. (Proverbs 24:3)*

Diary: April 6th. One Praesidium visted during this time disappointed me.
I had set it up, but I had not been long enough there to settle it. The
meeting was dull. The President was mostly silent. Reports were asked
for casually and then only a few. Work was hardly dealt with at all. I remained
after the meeting to speak to the President as the S.D. was in a hurry to get away.
She was a capable woman, but had not realised her position. Before I could even
speak, she said, "I know that something is wrong, but I don't know what it is."
As I was hungry, I suggested dinner and a chat. She agreed and over the meal she
listened to all I had to say on the President's role. I suggested she go to see a few
other Praesidia and she was delighted at the idea. Later on when I met her she
had been to two meetings and had made notes on their procedures, which were a
credit to her. She asked me to go to her own meeting next week and so I did.
The change was a revelation. She took things into her own hands, conducting the
meeting beautifully, to the delight of the S.D. who had been a little in the dark
too. She inspired the members by her business-like methods. Those who through
no fault of their own had no reports, resolved not to come without them again.
Within two months, that Praesidium had tackled difficult Hospital work and
started a Poor-Girls Club. It had also taken on endless 'case jobs' for the priest.

From April 9th to the 20th, I continued my visits to the various Praesidia in Hong Kong.

Shek Shat,
Canton,
22nd April 1949

Dear Frank,

I must get this letter off even though it is short. I arrived in Canton yesterday and I am busy preparing to set up the Curia here before I set off for the Interior again. I came down with Msgr. Romaniello, who is on his way back to Kweilin, Kwangsi. He is delighted with the Praesidia, which were set up and, since I was there, other priests have followed suit. Fr. McCabe MM, whom he appointed to look after the Legion there, is on the job.

We had our first Curia meeting in Hong Kong on April 5th and I suggested that they hold an Acies in August.

I suppose you heard about the wonderful Acies they had in Shanghai. The Internuncio came from Nanking and presided. Bishop Walsh gave the sermon. The newspaper said that six hundred and fifty were present, but the Jesuit pastor reckoned that at least one thousand attended, including Auxiliaries.

I have another possible Envoy in view. I am just waiting for her letter, as she wants permission from her father. Let's hope he agrees. She has been a fine Legionary and is also a University Graduate in Shanghai. She has been a very efficient stenographer. She speaks English perfectly, also Mandarin, Shanghai and some Cantonese. I realise more and more the need of Chinese Legionaries to carry on this work, especially if the Reds take over. The native Chinese have greater ease of movement.

I received word from Hankow and the Praesidia are doing well, though they are wrong in some points. I know that Fr. Ludwig's junior Praesidium has over thirty members, which is far too many.

I still wish to go to Shanghai, only that I want to get to visit some other Vicariates before the Reds arrive.

My brother has got back to his Communist occupied parish. He is delighted to be reunited with his flock.

The Legion in Peking is not disturbed, except in the University, where the members have left the city.

Canton is pleased with the Legion. Fr. Donnelly SJ has become highly enthusiastic, saying: "This is a wonderful system."

I shall write soon again. With all best wishes,

Aedan

Diary: April 24th. Fr. Purnam MM, one of the Fathers working in the Ling Nam University in Canton invited me to speak to his Catholic students. He drove me out in his Jeep. The students were very nice and intensely interested in my topic. They were willing to tackle anything and were only afraid that they might not be asked to do enough, or that the work might be that of collecting funds. Many of the students are from overseas.

26th. Msgr. Deswaziere attended the first Curia meeting in Canton, with all the S.D.'s. The President is an architect, who studied in the U.S. He is a former Principle of a Middle-East school. The Vice-President is a very efficient Secretary of the Catholic Welfare Bureau. Both speak fluent English. The Secretary and Treasurer are both principals of schools. Eleven Praesidia are affiliated to this Curia. The Bishop in his talk expressed hope for the Legion in Canton, which up to now has lacked an apostolic spirit among Catholics.

Canton
29th April 1949

Dear Frank,

Just a few lines with enclosures: Extracts from the *Sunday Examiner,* Fr. Maestrini's paper, a photo of Teresa Su and a few others. We had our first Curia here in Canton three days ago, with Bishop Deswaziere present. None of the Praesidia members have made their promise, but will be doing so soon. The Bishop has suggested a Mass, which he will say on May 1st with all Active and Auxiliary members present. It is not an official function, but it ought to help and His Excellency is keen on the Legion.

I was anxious to have the Curia established as I am leaving immediately. As you see from the newspaper, the Reds are moving fast and I want to make contact with other places before the troops arrive. I shall write from my next place, if I can get there before anything happens. Keep us all in your prayers.

Best wishes to all,   Aedan

Diary: 3rd. I went by train to Henyang, a twenty two-hour run. The district is Hunan Province. It is under the Italian Franciscans. They were all very kind to me and next day brought me to see Bishop Angelus Palazzi OFM. He was a little surprised that I should be there at such a time. However, when he heard of the Legion and realised that it was just the time to begin, he gave me his blessing and the chance to talk to the priests and the students in his Middle School.

During the week, I was able to start three Praesidia in the Parish, one for men, one for women and one for the nurses in the Hospital. I met Bishop Kurtz OFM. He has just been appointed to Ling Ling in Hunan, which is not far from Henyang. I had met him in Hong Kong and found him interested in the Legion, having seen it operating in Africa. Five Chinese priests were going to the Bishop's new post in Ling Ling and he asked me to give them all the information possible so that they could start the Legion.

Being a practical Bishop and seeing that he could travel to most places by boat, he bought a small outboard motor that was capable of being attached to any Chinese Barge. While I was in Hunan, he duly bought a boat, but it proved much too heavy for the light motor. However, he would not be put off and one wet morning we waved the Bishop and his priests off. The boat was loaded with their luggage. The boatman who had sold him the boat was so afraid that he felt obliged to warn the Bishop of the dangers, but to no avail. To show how doubtful the boatman was of arriving safely in Ling Ling, he handed me money for two Masses. I presumed this to be for the souls of the passengers in the event of a mishap! His fears were well founded. Next day they all arrived back having had a most harrowing experience. The vessel took one whole day to cover seventy miles. A storm blew up and nearly turned the boat over, sweeping into the water the pot of rice that the cook had just prepared to eat. The passengers were miserable, having to sleep without bedclothes and they were also ravenous with the hunger.

Next day the crest-fallen party made its return journey with the current, in four hours. Now the boatman's Masses can instead go to the Holy Souls. The following day, the Bishop decided to travel by open truck and asked me to go with his party so that I might influence one of his priests towards the Legion. I agreed and we went off in dry weather. We had not gone far when rain began to fall in torrents. We had a most uncomfortable journey. Fortunately, there was a Hospital run by German Nuns at our destination. We retired there and the staff dried our clothes for us.

Later, I made enquiries about starting the Legion there and the Sisters agreed.

112

A day later I returned to Henyang by the same truck. This time I got sunburnt! An evacuation of sorts was taking place from Henyang at that time. When I arrived at the Church, the Father Procurator told me that the planes out of the local airport would not take any foreigners. The aircraft were of the military variety. He told me also that possibly the last trains from the local station would be leaving that day. So I had to hurry to my room, pack my things and rush to the station. The train was supposed to arrive at 4pm, but it arrived instead at four o'clock next morning. What a night!

The station was packed like nothing I had ever seen before, with people hoping to get on the train. We could buy only third-class tickets, which meant it was going to be a struggle to get on at all. Our party consisted of five - two Sisters, two Italian priests and myself. One of the Sisters was elderly. We had to sit on our luggage and try to sleep. In the middle of the mayhem, as we awaited the train, soldiers began to exchange gunfire and we scrambled for cover dragging our baggage with us. Otherwise we would have lost our belongings. The fighting lasted about half an hour and apparently the soldiers shot one of their own men in the leg. When peace came again we settled down on the platform to sleep; at least I did. I could not stand any more.

Around 4am, the train arrived, and then the fun began! Even the roof of the train was packed. People were also sitting on the engine. There were no lights on the train and we had to feel our way aboard amidst the surging crowd.

I certainly would have given up had not one of the Italian priests been so determined. He spurred our party on and then he climbed in through a passage over boxes and firewood. He appeared at a window and shouted to us to pass up the baggage. I don't know where he put it, but he continued to fight his way on board and pile in the stuff.

Then he told us to help the Sisters clamber on. The older one wanted to cry, but she didn't get the opportunity. We just lifted her up and pushed her over a barricade of wood. We don't know where she landed. Later, when I climbed up with the other priest and landed in pitch darkness, I thought I would suffocate. Not knowing where I stood, or on whom I was trampling, the situation was most distressing.

After about an hour, the day kindly dawned and we found ourselves standing in a passageway on the train. Then by pushing our cases about we were able to sit on them. The two Sisters were given seats with the guard and we remained in the passage for the whole twenty-two hour trip. I slept well on the floor of the passageway, not caring who stepped on me.

We were able to buy food at the various stations, but nothing on the train. The country people did good business on account of the crowd. We bought foodstuff from them through the window of our carriage.

I was really annoyed with myself as there was no need for me to be in this situation. I could have been working anywhere else in the vast Chinese territory. At any rate, this was no time or place to start the Legion.

We got into Canton at 2am the next night and fortunately there was a Portuguese woman there who offered to take us to her home until the morning. A curfew prevented us from moving out of the vicinity of the station.

I shall never forget that trip, the only consolation being that I was able to take the occasional photo of the beautiful scenery from the moving train.

May 17th. I visited a Praesidium in Canton and next day moved on to Hong Kong to meet Fr. Dan Corrigan and Fr. Mark Kelly who had just arrived from Peking. That evening I met Fr. Maguire who had failed in his attempt to get to Henyang by train. His experience put mine in the shade. He spent nine days on a train. Bandits held it up and robbed the people, but the robbers stopped and fled before reaching his carriage. At one place the train was held up for so long that he got fed up and decided to walk to the next station! Before he had gone far he heard the train coming behind him. Leave it to Fr. Maguire. He stood in the middle of the tracks and waved his hands. Strange to say, the train stopped and the driver let him into the coal wagon. He was black as soot when the train arrived!

Fr. Corrigan, who hails from my former parish of Tsien Kiang, told me that the two Praesidia are still functioning, but without a priest, in a place which was under Communist control. As the young people had to disperse, the Junior groups closed down.

19th. Today I met a Vincentian from Tientsin and he told me what wonderful work the Legion was doing there. They now have twenty-two Praesidia. You may remember that I established only seven groups in that place. This increase has come about even during the Communist occupation.

CHAPTER SEVENTEEN

HONG KONG - MACAO - CHUNGKING SUMMER 1949

100 CHINESE PRIESTS IN HONG KONG AS REFUGEES

Do me justice O Lord! For I have walked in integrity,
and in the Lord I trust without wavering.
(Psalms 25:1)

Diary: May 20th. I found another University graduate willing to do Envoy work, but there is nothing definite yet. For the next week or so, I am supposed to be resting in Stanley, where the Maryknoll Fathers go on holidays. I want to bring them to see Praesidia in action.

29th. I said Mass in the Carmelite Chapel in Hong Kong today and gave a sermon. It would not be hard to guess my subject, as it was within the octave of the Ascension. The eighteen Sisters in this Convent are Chinese. Most of them are from wealthy native families, many of whom are not Catholic. All are Adjutorian members of the Legion, as also those Carmelites in Shanghai and Chungking. They were the first to give us a helping hand with their prayers.

June 5th. Accompanied by the Internuncio's Secretary, Fr. Martin Gilligan, I went to the island of Macao from Hong Kong by Steamer, a three-hour journey. He was going to see the Bishop and urged me to go along to promote the Legion. Being a Portuguese Colony, Macao is very Catholic.

Many of the natives had wanted to begin the Legion in Macao, but without the Bishop's permission it wasn't possible.

The Bishop, Most Rev. John Romahlo, a Jesuit, lives in a Summer Palace on the highest place on the island. He is the second most important person there in civic life, after the Governor. On arrival he was very kind to us. We stayed there overnight. Next morning he brought us on a tour of the island in his car and we called into all the religious institutions. Later he drove us to the boat.

Someone had already presented him with the Legion Handbook in English, so I offered him one in French. He is hesitant to begin anything new. Fr. Gilligan took the initiative with him as he speaks French. I could understand them speaking. Nothing but Chinese could come from me and as the Bishop spoke only French and Cantonese, that was no good.

Fr. Gilligan pressed hard about the Legion and as a result the Prelate promised to study the French Handbook, while his priests could read the English edition. He told us that he would inform us of his decision. This was as much as we had hoped for.

8th. The Hong Kong Curia meeting was satisfactory. Remote preparations were made for the Acies, which is to be held in August or September.

9th. After months of waiting, our first Chinese Legion representative left for Manila by Pan American Airlines. Teresa Su received her passport many months ago but then could not get her Visa for Manila. The Legionaries there, headed by Fr. Gracia have been doing all in their power, even going to the President of the country. Members of the Hong Kong Curia and her two sisters accompanied her to the airport to wish her bon voyage.

Teresa Su, Envoy to China, on the day of her arrival in the Philippines.
With Teresa, center, are Rev. Fr. Manual A. Gracia, CM, Spiritual Director and officers of the
Senatus of the Philippines; Mrs. A. Decepida, Mr. Andres Decepida, and Mr. Tongga.

10th. A letter just arrived from Bishop Paschang of Kongmoon, which is not far from Hong Kong, asking for fifty Chinese Handbooks and other literature. He is of the Maryknoll Mission and must have heard of the Legion only lately from priests returning from their missions.

12th. I left by plane today for Chungking in the province of Szechwan, arriving after a four-hour flight. We could not land on account of the fog, which is common here in summer. We had flown for about an hour and then the Chinese pilot came down through a cloud just over a large field before landing with a thud. There was nothing but a mat-shed on the field. It was forty-five miles from the town.

I arrived at the Bishop's residence during dinner and the Bishop with his priests received me kindly. Most Rev. Francis Xavier Jantzen, a member of the Paris foreign Missions, has been here for a long while. Despite his age and illness, and being left for dead during the war by an assassin, he is still puts in a long days work.

In this Vicariate there are about sixty Chinese priests, spread over a huge district of mountains and rivers. It is the most difficult Mission I have yet encountered. These priests live a very hard life and on the plainest of diets. In the midst of it all they are able to laugh, not least the Bishop himself.

Just a few days ago, five young French priests arrived from Europe. This has helped to lift the fog, so to speak, as some of the priests here are quite old, one over eighty. They are still carrying on with their work, with no question of going home. They don't seem to consider that there is a war; it seems to make no difference to their schedule. I must say that there is great comraderie among these missionaries.

I spoke with Bishop Jantzen about the Legion. He had been thinking about that sort of organisation all his life. He had considered setting up small groups under Our Lady and with a definite programme and now, here it was being offered to him. He called the Pastors together and let me talk to them. He then arranged a round of places for me to visit and ordered fifty Handbooks to send to his priests. He got the 'Notes for Officers' in Chinese printed within twenty-four hours and also copies of the 'Victory' pamphlet. He runs a small newspaper for Chinese priests and this month it gives much detail about the Legion.

Chen Yuen T'ang,
Wu Ssu Lu,
Chungking,
Szechwan Province
19th June 1949

Dear Frank,

Your letter of May 7th was a wonderful one. I also received a letter from John Nagle, written on May 31st; but as far as I can remember, they both came about the same time.[35] I was travelling about and people did not know where to find me.

I had the pleasure of sending off Teresa Su from the airfield on June 9th. Fr. Gracia did grand work and got her an exemption from the quota at the end of May. He has since wired me to say she arrived safely. Since then I have heard nothing because I am hundreds of miles from Hong Kong now, but I hope to hear soon. Teresa was very happy going away and having met the Secretary of the Manila Curia, Miss Conchita Cuervo, who came to Hong Kong about two months ago, she knew what a welcome was awaiting her and that she was going to live in 'Mary's Cottage', prepared by the Legionaries, even to their painting of the pictures on the walls. Her two sisters saw her off too, one having being brought back to the Sacraments and having being confirmed and the second one is ready for Baptism. Teresa did not waste any time in Hong Kong and Canton, visiting most of the Praesidia in the Curia and between times, looking after her relatives. She has set several people on the right road. She looks a delicate little girl, but she is very determined. I think indeed that the delicate Envoy to Africa gave her courage too.[36] Her rest in Hong Kong did her a lot of good.

There are now one hundred Chinese priests in Hong Kong as refugees, and many more escaping to the free parts of China. It is certainly a time when lay people could do endless good.

A little news before I go on: Lately one of our priests who had two Praesidia in Peking came down to Hong Kong, after enduring six months under Communist control. His report about the ordinary life of the Church is consoling. The chief difficulty is the

---

[35] Neither letter appears on file.
[36] i.e. Venerable Edel Quinn.

118

schools. The Legion continues to do fine work. This priest left his two Praesidia in the care of Fr. McGoldrick. The University Students Praesidium had to disband, because the Catholic students who were in it, left the University. However, they can do work in other places.

I heard about the Tientsin Praesidia from a priest who had just left there. He did not know that I was connected with the Legion and he was expounding what a marvellous work it was doing there. Then I asked him how many Praesidia were there. He said twenty-two. I had left only seven under Fr. Beunen and the numbers have increased since the Reds arrived! I was really delighted to hear this. Be careful of news in that quarter. It might easily be harmful. He said that the native priests were afraid to move about, but that the Legion was fulfilling an important role.

That bit of news bears out my own impression that Our Blessed Lady's protection was evident. I need not fear the Communists.

In Shanghai, all the Sisters in charge of the Slavonic Rite were ordered out before the Reds arrived. They were terribly disappointed. I met them in Hong Kong and their enthusiasm for the Legion could hardly have been greater. They were delighted with the news in your letter. Unfortunately the Sisters did not realise that the Legion should have continued when they left, especially as some of the members who held Soviet passports, were keen to continue. I encouraged them to write immediately to tell those girls to carry on with the Praesidium.

Some Russians from Shanghai who had left previously for the island of Samar, near Manila, have started a Praesidium there.

All the Slavonic priests have now left Shanghai with their parishioners. One of the Loreto School Praesidia had to close because all its members left. You have no idea of the exodus. However, we are contacting Legionaries in Hong Kong and other places and when they return, they can resume their membership.

Your *Formula for Conversion*[37] booklet is wonderful and impressed more persons than myself.

We are all waiting anxiously for the result of the discussion in Rome about the Slavonic Rite and the Orthodox Church. When I

---

[37] A pamphlet written by Frank Duff.

mentioned it to Fr. Wilcock SJ he was thrilled at its possibilities. His work for years has been to try and break down prejudice between the two Churches.

I tried to get some rest in Hong Kong, but there is such Legion activity there that I decided to combine rest with my work here in Chungking, which in these parts is less feverish.

My visit to Henyang was a lesson. Apart from the terrible return journey, I learned that to set up Praesidia in places where soldiers are retreating, is not good practice. Bishop Kurtz will be able to get going, but in Henyang, street activity is taken up with soldiers waiting for battle. Most of the people have left the place and my three young Praesidia probably have been forced to close. The members were imbued with the Legion spirit and promised to join wherever they could.

Canton is now in the same position, but the Curia is so good there that I don't fear for the future. However, as they are expecting the Reds anytime, I decided to get away to where there is still a semblance of peace.

Bishop Jantzen, the grand old Bishop of Chungking has embraced the Legion system. He is instructing his priests everywhere about it and I have already set up two Praesidia here, with two or three more to come. I shall be here for some time to get things going and then there are plenty of other places I can move to where there is comparative peace.

Tomorrow I shall start a Praesidium in the parish of St. Joseph and we have one planned for nurses in the hospital run by the FMM sisters. These Franciscan Missionaries of Mary now have several Legion groups in schools and hospitals.

I have not touched my diary for a long while, but I hope to do some notes here. That may fill gaps in the news.

Aedan

Diary: 25th. Today was marked by the Jubilee of one of the priests, fifty years ordained! We had solemn High Mass, attended by all the Sisters and Pastors. When all were gathered in the common room afterwards, the eighty year old missionary started to greet the new priests in the customary French way, with a kiss on both cheeks. Then he came to me and asked if I was French. One of

them announced that I was. Thereupon he greeted me with two rubs of his beard. Later he apologised and joined in the humour of his mistake
I believe that in Paris before the priests leave for the Missions, all the others kiss their feet. They may be sentimental, but they are tough on the Missions and have given a great example in the present crisis. Many of their men are still up north without any question of leaving. The French Nuns are the same.

27th. I learned that Dominic Chang OP, who was once a Spiritual Director in Manila, has begun a Praesidium in Fukien Province.

28th. I had a talk with the two FMM Sisters who will be in charge of the Praesidia in the Catholic Hospital here, where there are nurses in training. We shall begin the Legion next Tuesday. This week they are doing examinations. The Msgr. has introduced twelve of his Chinese Sisters into Legion membership.

Chen Yuen T'iang,
30th June 1949

Dear Frank,

Just a line to correct a mistake: Msgr. Jantzen is Archbishop of Chungking, not Bishop. Today he showed me his monthly issue, *Inter Nos*, for his clergy and the back page is entirely devoted to the Legion. In it he describes briefly its methods and what has been done here already in terms of the Lay Apostolate. He expresses his wish that all parishes and schools have at least one Praesidium. He also promises to give details in later issues, besides sending priests the 'Officers Notes' and Handbook, both in Chinese.

I had a letter yesterday from Teresa Su, in Manila, plus a photograph of her arrival at the airfield. Fr. Gracia and the other members of the Senatus, including many Chinese were present to meet her. She was charmed with the reception. She loves her cottage and her companion Miss Quenca, the extension worker. Archbishop O'Doherty, who was very ill and had been anointed, wished to see her. She and the President of the Senatus went to meet him. The Prelate was delighted and spoke kindly to her, asking if everything was as she wished, and, if not, she was to be sure to tell him. Teresa has already joined the Praesidium attached to the Senatus and has had her first assignment: to visit the girls in the 'bars'.

I had a letter from Fr. Gilligan, Secretary to the Internuncio today saying that he will probably come to Chungking soon. Speaking of Fr. Gilligan, when I was in Macao with him to see the Portuguese Jesuit Bishop there, the latter remarked that the translation of the Portuguese Tesserae, which I had sent him, was not the best.

Say a special prayer for all of us these days.

Aedan

Diary: July 3rd. Just arrived from Peking is a Belgian Scheut Superior, on his way to his Mission. On the priest's arrival he was asked about Peking. He said the Church is undisturbed and flourishing, with the wonderful aid of the Legion of Mary. He said Tientsin now has twenty-five Praesidia and two Curia. You will remember that Bishop de Vienne CM appointed Fr. Beunen CM to take charge of the Legion there. He has done Trojan work. According to our visitor, he even travelled to Peking to get Fr. Coquyt to help out. I hope that they will now take the necessary steps to form a Curia.

5th. This evening I set up a Praesidium of student nurses in the Franciscan Missionary Hospital. Their work will be mainly within the confines of the building, but they will go to other Hospitals when they get used to the work. Fourteen members attended. This will also prepare them for the work of establishing the Legion further afield.

7th. Today I received a letter from Tubabao, Samar. It was the United Nations authorities who evacuated Russians and some others from Shanghai to this Island, as they had no other place to go. The incident was written up in the newspapers. The conditions under which these people live, is bad: nothing but tents to sleep in and the place is infested with mosquitoes.

The following is the letter I received from the new Praesidium there:

Our Lady of Fatima Praesidium.
Tubabao, Guiuan, Samar
20^h June 1949

Dear Fr. McGrath,
    This is to inform you that the Praesidium of Our Lady of Fatima has been established here in the U.N. Evacuation Center. The

122

inaugural meeting was held on 11th March 1949 with our President Paul Laki and eight other members present. We now have twenty-two members, with Sr. Irene Hartung as President. The work so far has consisted in visits to the Catholics in the camp, then later to keep the Camp Chaplain in touch with them, to inform them of Church services and the Catechism classes. The meetings are held under special conditions. We gather in the Library Tent of the Chaplain, where we take with us benches from the Chapel. Some members are obliged to sit on crates or cots. We have no Statue of Our Lady, no Vexillum, no candles and no Secret Bag collection, the latter because of lack of funds. We do not intend to make the Legionaries take the Promise on account of the special conditions and because most of the members are to scatter to all parts of the world in a short time. Fr. Wilcock is our Spiritual Director. Because of our arrival from Shanghai and our imminent departure from the Phillipine Islands we consider ourselves under your jurisdiction. Therefore, we have not written to Dublin, but submit this as a report to you. We expect further guidance from you. Br. Laki had written to Br. Allan who promised to communicate with you concerning us.

W. Kulik, Secretary

I was delighted to see this spirit, after such suffering. They had only just begun in the Shanghai Praesidium before being forced to leave China. Br. Laki had been the Secretary of the Latin Curia and Sr. Hartung was one of the first members of the Legion in Shanghai. Others were attached to the Slavonic Rite Praesidium. I have written to the Senatus of the Philippines to see if they are aware of the existence of this group.

CHAPTER EIGHTEEN

CHUNGKING TO CHENGTU - JULY 1949

"THIS WILL BE GENUINE WORK"

The harvest indeed is great, but the labourers are few.
Pray therefore the Lord of the harvest
to send forth labourers into His harvest.
(Luke 10:1-2)

Diary: July 8th 1949. Three Chinese priests arrived in Chungking today from Kweilin over in Kwangsi Province. They tell me that there are now four Praesidia in Kweilin city alone and that Bishop Romaniello is so enamoured that he looks after them himself. He had said: "We should have installed this Legion long ago, but it is not too late." A letter from Fr. McCabe MM, my chauffeur during my visit there tells of how the Praesidia have increased in numbers all over the place: four now in Lai Po, four in Tung-an, and about four others besides. He said that he can see several others in the making. That will bring them to a total of over twenty Praesidia.

9th. Today the *Sunday Examiner* carries a column reporting on the Legion in Kwangsi, Kweilin and Tung-an. It is worth repeating the headline: *The Legion Grows in the Interior.*

Fr. Irwin Nugent, the Maryknoll Missionary, from the small market town of Tung-an in Kwangsi Province, dropped in to the Catholic Centre here last week before going back to his Mission. After asking all kinds of questions about the Church in the Interior of China, the conversation inevitably turned to the Legion of Mary. He confessed that after my visit, both he and Fr. Robert Greene were dubious about the workability of the Legion in their town and were not at all convinced by my arguments![38] They thought it was all very well for Shanghai, Peking and Hong Kong, but a bit above the Tung-an natives, who are mostly illiterate. However, these two priests took a step in faith. Together with two

---

[38] Following Fr. McGrath's visit to Tung-an on March 14th last.

native Sisters, they gathered a group of eight women and got into the work right away. Only three out of the eight had enough learning to read the prayers. "We were fortunate," Fr. Nugent said, "in having the wife of a former gambler - who knew everyone in the area - to call with a co-worker to specified Christians. The first work reports at the Praesidium meeting will long remain in my memory."

The results of those first assignments became apparent the next Sunday morning at the Parish Mass, where attendance visibly increased. Encouraged by this, the Missionaries decided to start a Praesidium for men. Fourteen men were approached and twelve readily responded. The steady increase in the numbers of parishioners at Masses each Sunday continued. At first thirty, then thirty-five and so on, and never once dropping back since the Legion started.

Fr. Nugent showed me a letter he had just received from Fr. Greene, referring to the Feast of Pentecost. The letter ran: "We have had the best attendance in Tung-an since my arrival. The Legion of Mary accounted for all the increase and did marvellous work helping us as the Christians are moving in from our remote mission stations."

12th. I had a letter from Teresa Su, the Chinese Envoy studying in the Philippines. She has knuckled down to work very fast. Fr. Gracia is sending her on a month's extension work with another legionary. She finds the climate very hot, but I'm sure she will get used to it.

16th. Today, I went to Sa Ping Pa, a place about an hour from here by bus. It is an ideal place to start a Legion Praesidium with a view to contacting the thousands of University students here. There is a female student in this place who has come from the Aurora University in Shanghai and who had been a Legion President. She has given the Franciscan Missionaries of Mary here a talk on the Legion and they now have two interested Catholic Professors, four Catholic students and another graduate from Peking University, which is plenty to start a Praesidium.

19th. The nurses Praesidium is much improved. The President is going to be very efficient and is creative in giving members their assignments. I may see them for one last time before leaving for Chengtu.

24th. Though suffering an attack of Malaria, I rose at three a.m. in the oppressive heat, and, perspiring heaviliy, I offered Mass. After breakfast I took the airport-bound bus. I decided on Chengtu in Central Szechwan as my next destination because it is cooler. Four of us travelled together, all priests - two young men who belong to the Chengtu Mission, a Scheut Father, returning to Ninghaia in Mongolia and myself. The plane took off on time. One and a half hours flying over the most beautiful countryside brought us to Chengtu, the Peking of Szechwan. I loved the place even on landing, the climate was so cool. As the bus, which bought us from the airfield to the city passed through the streets, I liked it all the more. All the streets were bordered with trees and the old single-storey houses with their turned-up roofs looked pretty. Behind each house there was a courtyard decked with flowers and shrubs. By comparison, the houses in Chungking are made from foreign construction materials and are not as attractive. That fact, plus the heat made me uncomfortable in the Chungking environment. Besides, the latter place is built on hills and when you want to go anywhere you have to climb, or else let a Rickshaw pull you, which is even worse! On arriving at the Mission in Chengtu, we found a big entrance, and a large courtyard decked with flowers, the biggest I have seen in China, with palm and date trees in a central area. During their recreation, the missionaries sit out in this courtyard in the shade of the trees. The French Fathers of this Mission have great taste and go to immense trouble to bring out the best in nature. Inside this lovely setting a single-storey house stands

The Fathers were kind to us on arrival and before long we found there was as much beer as anyone wanted to drink! The priests grow their own hops. The brew is light and makes for a healthy drink. By contrast, the local water is not good. At the table there was plenty of fruit and very tasty food, even finger bowls. This makes for such a pleasant change.

25th. Today I spoke to Fr. Poisson, a charming old man, who will probably be made a Bishop. He had heard of the Legion and received a copy of the Handbook in French. After reading a few pages, he decided the Legion was just 'one other' organisation and too difficult to start up. His Catholic Action Group had failed miserably. When I had finished telling him about my own story on the Legion in the country places and my visits to Dublin, he was interested and saw that Our Lady must be very active in the movement. On explanation, the system seemed simpler and the detail appealed to him. He gave me 'carte blanche' to try and establish the Legion in Chengtu.

Fr. Poisson directed me to speak to the Chinese Pastor of the place. I did so and found a holy old man, not very progressive, but he could see the necessity to get the lay folk working for more converts. Catholic Action had failed and he feared his people would not have the time to give to the Legion, or would not continue the work. This priest got a group together and I spoke to them. They showed an eagerness to keep the rules; one said: "This will be genuine work."

26th. I went today to the Benedictine Priory, a beautiful house in Chinese style and with large grounds. The Italian Prior, Rev. D. Raphael Vinciarelli was kind to me and listened sympathetically. He had never heard of the Legion. He was working a good system with the University students and was making converts. The Catholic and non-denominational students alike went to the Priory. He is now hoping to give the Legion a try with his Catholic students. The same evening I went to see the Redemptorists; they have quite a nice house and a school attached. They have enticed three teachers to come down from Peking University where they had also been in the Legion. They will have lots of work in the school and may start a parish group later. The Chinese Pastor would not like to see a rival Praesidium in the Parish, but he will see the necessity later.

27th. Met with the Superior of the FMM Sisters in the local Hospital. She had not heard of the Legion, but now wants to set up a Praesidium of nurses. My poor French has to come more and more into play.

28th. I encountered two Pastors of Churches in the City. I am going again to their places soon to do something about the Legion. Things look bright here and objections seem to melt away after explanation of the system. The first thing that strikes people is that the Legion system is built on De Montfort's *True Devotion*. The disciplined method clinches the bargain! Success in other parts of China has been a great help and photos' have proved my statements that there are now many Praesidia throughout China.

CHAPTER NINETEEN

CHENGTU/WANHSEIN – AUG/OCT 1949

He that fears the Lord will receive His discipline: and they that will
seek Him early shall find a blessing. (Ecclesiaticus 32:18)

The following statistics quoted from the *Fides Catholic International News Agency* for August 1949 (Maria Legionis, 1949, No.4, p.20) shows that the Legion of Mary now exists in 16 dioceses and numbers 143 Praesidia and 7 Curiae: These official figures were constantly changing - e.g. Fr. McGrath's diary indicates that by April 1948, Shasi had 3 praesidia.

	Praesidia	*Curiae*
Shanghai	17	I
Hanyang	2	I
Hankow	9	?
Wuchan	9	I
Shasi	I	
Nanking (Yangchow)	2	?
Peking	15	?
Tientsin	22	I
Chekiang	4	?
Fukien	I	
Canton	II	I
Hong Kong	20	I
Kweilin (Kwangsi)	20	
Kongmoon	I	
Kaifeng	5	I
Chungking	4	

Diary: August 1st. Today I heard of the nomination of the new Bishop of Chengtu, where I am at present. He is forty-five year old Msgr. Henry Pinault. He is only the third Bishop here in one hundred years. Rome gave the go-ahead for the consecration without the official papers.

Msgr. Paul Teng is the newly nominated Bishop of Kiating. He will be consecrated with Msgr. Pinault.

This evening I went to I Tung Chiao where Fr. Audren is Pastor. He is a zealous man and was wondering what sort of organisation he should establish. He had written for Catholic Action books and was reading one by Fr. Meyer MM, whom you may recall turned over completely to the Legion system. Père Audren has turned out to be a real Legion enthusiast.

3rd We had our first set-up Legion meeting with Fr. Audren and it proved promising. He regularly has priest visitors at his Legion meetings. Even his Auxiliary members are bringing in converts. The three Praesidia already set up are doing census work.

In Kwei Wang Chiao where the old priest, Père Theophile, had said he could not find even one Legionary, they now have a good Praesidium.

17th. I cycled thirteen miles into the country to visit a Trappist Monastery. As I was travelling along a narrow path with rice-paddies on either side, my foot slipped from the pedal and down I went, my bike landing on top of me. I was covered in mud. Picking myself up before three laughing bystanders, I thought how appropriate it all was. The name of the place was 'Mud'! The 'Monastery' was made up of a series of small houses all joined together. The Monks, all Chinese except for one Belgian, wore black and white habits. I was given a grand welcome, got a change of clothes and a fine dinner. Living even more sparsely than usual and being themselves refugees from Peking, they find it hard to make ends meet. They till the land and make their own shoes.

The Monks promised to become Adjutorian members of the Legion and were considering starting a Praesidium within the refugee Monastery. I gave them a talk on the Legion and put them through a sample meeting.

On my way home the rain came down in torrents.

21st. Not feeling well, I spent the next few days in Hospital. There is no one to give medical care here in the compound. The Little Sisters were wonderful and the rest did me good.

30th. I made a journey to Kwei Wang Chiao, where Fr. Audren has his Praesidium. One case he related: The Praesidium President had fallen out with another parishioner. As a result of a Legion visitation the man returned to the Sacraments the following week.

One of the Legion members has a brother whose marriage is irregular. Through the Praesidium, there is every hope of getting the problem sorted, as also is an invalid marriage.

A letter came from Collegio de Propaganda Fide in Rome, signed by a Leo Craig, whether a priest or not I don't know. They are going to hold a Marian Congress next year and they are to have a big Legion stall. They wish to display Chinese Legion literature as well as that from every other country. Rome wants as many facts as possible about the Legion in China. I am preparing something for the Vatican. The statistics are certainly encouraging.

September 4th: Yesterday I attended two Praesidia and found them as good as I could wish, and Our Lady's presence is obvious in the work. All members are experiencing the thrill of bringing people back to Church and are generous with their time. The reports are so interesting that the meeting time of one-and-a-half hours seems too short. Apart from the few students who are in the Legion groups, the rest are for the most part ordinary poor people without any learning. But as usual, Our Lady does not seem to mind what kind of people they are, so long as they 'give their all'. The thrill of these things does not wear off me. The Bishop and priests of this place are beginning to take notice of everything that is happening. I would say that the Legion is destined play a big part in the Diocese, even in the outlying districts.

Lately there was an article in the *Hong Kong Catholic* paper comparing the Legion to Fatima. It was a reprint from *Integrity*, an American paper. Those here who had loved Fatima, were thrilled by the comparison and this article made it all more acceptable. No wonder in Shanghai they used to call the Legion "Fatima in action".

12th. I went to the first-report meeting of the Praesidium at the South Gate. Its work had been done during the Mission given by Redemptorist Fathers and it received a great lift in such an atmosphere. Legion members were instrumental in fixing up nine marriages. One person came back the Sacraments after twenty years; three returned after fifteen years and many others after a lesser time. The Legionaries were pleased with the way Our Lady helped them at the start.

16th. Beginning today, I gave four talks on the Legion to the students of the Chengtu Seminary during their Retreat.

21st. Chengtu has five visiting Bishops and about fifty priests for the Episcopal Consecration ceremony. These days are full of excitement and everyone is busy.

I had a few words with Archbishop Jantzen of Chungking and he told me that the Legion was doing very well since I left. He waited three months before passing this verdict.

On Saturday the Bishop of Shui Fu came to see me to talk about the Legion. He proved a wonderful listener and immediately became enthusiastic. He promised to have a Chinese priest ready to study the system so that he can introduce the Legion all over the Diocese.

25th. Today, visiting Bishop Boisguerin from Shui Fu and Bishop Wang from Shun Ching, along with three priests, came to see a local Praesidium meeting. They were suitably impressed.

27th. I went to hear the first reports of the Redemptorist Praesidium and they were very good. A certain family was visited by the Legionaries. During the visit one legionary spoke to the father regarding the children, the other spoke with the mother. The report at the Praesidium meeting could only be given by one member, her co-worker being absent from the meeting due to illness. When asked for the co-workers element of the work report, she replied: "What about the secrecy rule? We never spoke to each other about the visit on our way home." There was a great laugh amongst the members, but the report spoke well for their idea of keeping things confidential!

October 1st. Today Mao Tse-tung proclaimed China a Communist Republic at the 'Gate of Heavenly Peace' in Peking. He is quoted as saying: "This Government is willing to observe the principles of equality, mutual respect and territorial sovereignty."

4th. Today I flew back to Chungking with Bishop's Boisguerin and Wang. These Bishops are en route to the consecration of Msgr. Tuan who was appointed Bishop of Wanhsien on 9th June by Pope Pius XII.[39]

---

[39] The last Chinese Bishop to be appointed by the Holy See before the Communist takeover. After 20 years spent in forced labour camps he was permitted to return to his diocese in 1979. He died on 10th January 2001.

On arrival I made enquiries about the different Praesidia and got satisfactory reports. One of them has split to form two Praesidia.

9th, 10th & 11th. While in Chungking, I attended three Praesidia and gave my blessing as new members took the Promise. The reports were excellent and they have done a great amount of work.

12th. This date was fixed for the starting of the Curia in Chungking. It was to be at 5.30pm in the Bishop's residence, with the Prelate as Spiritual Director. The boat on which he was travelling to Wanhsien was due to leave at 7pm that evening which left little time for a satisfactory Curia meeting. As Divine Providence would have it, the boat departure was delayed until the next day. As a result we had enough time to conduct all the Curia business successfully and elect the new Officers. I took them out to supper afterwards and gave them detailed instructions about the work.

13th. Eight of us boarded a small Steamer this morning to set out for Wanhsien and Msgr. Tuan's consecration. The journey took most of the day taking us through this region of the Yangtze Rapids. The Steamer vibrated going through whirlpools. The scenery was marvellous. I took many photographs.
On our arrival, the Wanhsien priests had a lunch ready beside the dock. We were escorted with banners and to the accompaniment of cheers. Then there was the blessing in the Church, followed by a welcome dinner.
I discovered that they already had a Praesidium of thirty members here in Wanhsien. A Legionary friend of mine named Kiang whom I had baptised, was here some time ago and started the Legion.
One of the Christians here painted a huge picture of the head of Msgr. Tuan, which looked like Clark Gable, or someone in Hollywood. They paraded the portrait around the town today at the head of a float drawn by about fifty men carrying the presents given by the people, each offering on a table. These included a soft hat, bedspreads, pictures, lengths of satin to make vestments and new shoes of all colours.
About fifty priests came to the ceremony, which was a most impressive event. It gave me a grand chance to spread the Legion. All the local notables were present, including two Anglican ladies. The ceremony was followed by an official reception with long speeches.
The Diocese has a new young Prelate, zealous and popular in Bishop Tuan who has kindly invited me to stay a long time and visit his country Missions, with a

view to starting the Legion in these places. I may not be able to visit many, but I must try to do some. I have to work faster as the war goes on, and I have much yet to do.

20th. Visiting Bishops left for Chungking.

21st. Bishop Tuan asked me to speak to the priests. My talk on the Legion woke them all up, especially the Bishop. They had not realised this form of Catholic Action was such a force for good. Bishop Tuan, who had been wondering what he would do to pep things up, realised the Legion was Providential. He gave a eloquent talk himself to the priests about his ideas on the subject and made it clear that he wanted the Legion all over his Diocese. A sample meeting was arranged for that evening. So after supper with the Legion table set up, the priests sat around as members, filling the room. I asked the Bishop to imagine himself as S.D. and to imagine me as President. I admired his humility and that of the priests. We began with the Rosary and went right through the motions of a meeting, being peppered with questions all the way through. My hopes are high. I suggested to the Bishop that he appoint a priest to study the Legion system and to let him later go through the various country parishes. He consented to my request, appointing Fr. Shu, who was in Peking at the Collegium Sinicum and who had heard my talk on the Legion there last year. He is young and enthusiastic.

26th. I founded a Seminary Praesidium, with sixteen members, possibly the first of its kind in China. The other Seminarians sat around to learn and will later form their own Praesidia, e.g. in Ichang (Hupeh Province). The Prelate there is Bishop Gubbels whom I met in Shanghai last year. Ichang is now in the control of the Communist, but the students will be returning soon.

30th. The Orphanage Praesidium is set up, with twenty young girls plus a President and Vice-president.
At 1pm I set up a Praesidium for the University students, who will work in their own University, contacting and influencing other students.
We had the first report-meeting of the new Seminary Praesidium. The students showed themselves timid in reporting and contacting people. They need to be encouraged. It will prove good formation in preparing them for their priestly work later on. Having been for years in the Seminary, they are inclined to keep to themselves and find it difficult to approach others with a view to the faith.

7pm - Praesidium for nurses in the Hospital set-up. They have a wonderful President whom I guessed might have been in the Legion for years. She had known nothing about it before and has a most impressive manner. The Bishop wants this Praesidium to contact patients after they leave the Hospital. Great enthusiasm was shown and there will be no shortage of work for the members.

November 1st. A second Praesidium was formed in the seminary. The seminarians will thus return to their respective Dioceses with knowledge of the Legion. The group includes students from Ichang, a place I have been unable to visit.

2nd. Set up a mixed-Praesidium in the Town, near the Church; it comprises all sorts of people. They have fourteen members.

To date, there are eight Praesidia here. The reason for this speed is the enthusiasm of the Bishop and his priests, especially the P.P. in the Wanhsien Cathedral.

Lately in one of the Hong Kong Catholic Papers I saw a report of a speech by Bishop Valtorta at the Marian Exhibition. He said: "I was very happy to attend the recent Acies of the Legion of Mary in Hong Kong and to see hundreds of young men and women consecrate themselves to the Blessed Virgin's service in work which entails courage, endurance and strength of will."

Both in Chengtu and here in Wanhsien I met a man who was one of the first members of the Legion in Kaifeng, Honan, under Fr. Crotty. He was a great enthusiast and had in his autograph-book a few lines from the Archbishop of Kaifeng stating that if any Bishop or priest wanted to know anything about the Legion, this individual would be well equipped to inform him.

6th. I attended three Praesidia meetings today, beginning at 10am with the Orphanage meeting. All the work assigned was carried out. Three or four of the Praesidia this week sent members to help a poor dying woman. She had been lying on the ground in filth and was unable to help herself in any way. The Legionaries went to her in turn to bathe her, wash her ragged bedclothes, and to console her. They wanted to give her charity, but on asking me, I told them to give what they wanted to the priest and he could deal with her. One woman gave her a padded-cotton bed cover. The Legion members also got boards, lifted her off the ground and put her into a house. I went myself to see her.

Chapter Twenty

Wanhsein to Chungking – Nov/Dec 1949

"I decided to be 'liberated' there"

O Lord, to you I call: hasten to me;
hearken to my voice when I call upon you.
(Psalms 140:1)

Diary: Saturday November 12th. The Reds are closing in fast on this place and also Chungking. I have been a little doubtful whether I can make Chungking or not. My letters are there and I want to consult Fr. Gilligan, the Internuncio's Secretary as to what to do next. I want to carry on as long as possible and then to be 'liberated', so that I may be able to move about in China again, if the Reds allow me freedom. The Bishop and priests want me to wait until I set up the first Curia here in Wanhsein on Sunday. Last night I went with the old resigned-Bishop to the boat, which was to take him to a country place in case of fighting here. I myself had meant to leave by this boat.
A plane was supposed to come on Friday, but it did not arrive. A crowd of people went to the airport hoping to leave, but their hopes were dashed.

13th. This morning we were staggered to see the old Bishop back again. The boat he travelled on had been commandeered by the military; this leaves things even more doubtful than before. It is possible that I may not be able to get away by boat. In that case I shall have to go by train, which is a slow mode of transport.
Today we set up the first Junior Praesidium in a girl's school. The eight members are to undertake Legion work in their school. The Orphanage meeting was held at about the same time. Then at 1pm we held the University meeting. Some members were absent for one reason or another. At 3pm we held our first Curia meeting. I wanted to see that they knew the right way to go about it. There being eleven Praesidia, we had a great crowd and the Bishop consented to be the Spiritual Director. The four Officers are splendid. The President is a girl of about twenty. She is one of the most active-minded persons I ever met. After the meeting I took the Officers and in the presence of the Bishop and Fr. Chang, put

them through their duties. While we were talking, a letter came in for the Bishop from a priest who had been here for the consecration, saying he had started three Praesidia, with wonderful results. This looks like the awakening of the people. It may all sound very fast, but in the present circumstances and with the priests so enthusiastic, I have no fears.

During the Curia meeting the Bishop gave a talk. I never heard such praise of the Legion. He holds it now as his trump card in his work.

We got a report through a missionary recently that in Tientsin University, they now have Praesidia amongst the Professors, University students, Middle School students and Domestics. All are doing mighty work inside and outside the University. It is wonderful to hear such news, seeing that one of the French priests had undergone a trial before the Student's Court!

On Monday 14th I attended the Praesidium in the parish of St. Joseph. Before we were finished, word came that Martial Law had been declared in Wanhsein. It was not easy for us to get home after the meeting. Everyone was running, including soldiers who wanted to leave the city. That evening a wire came to say that the plane would be at the airfield next morning without fail.

The boat, which should have taken me to Chungking, was commandeered again and rumour has it that the river is closed on account of bandits. So, 'what now?' I asked myself.

The Catholics are to give me a send-off tea today with the priests and Bishop - very kind of them, but I am wondering if I shall be able to get away at all now.

15th. There were more false alarms about the availability of river transport away from here.

16th. Rushed onto the last boat leaving Wanhsien! There were six hundred passengers, all of us relieved to get on board.

Arriving in Chungking three days later, I was undecided as to what to do. I considered travelling by air to Kunming via Hong Kong. But later I heard that Kunming was also in the grip of the Reds, so I decided to be 'liberated' here!

I did not want to be in Hong Kong and then unable to re-enter China. I will have plenty of work in Chungking for a while and I trust that Our Lady will step in and get me moving again.

The Archbishop is pleased to have me here and wants to organise the Legion in as many places as possible in the City. He is very happy about its work.

136

29th. The Red Army approached and met some local resistance in the form of gunfire and shelling. Many of the priests left, and, not a minute too early. There were only five priests and the Bishop remaining and nearly one hundred refugees in their care.

I went to bed at 9pm to the accompaniment of distant gunfire and intermittent volleys in the street. At 11pm I was awakened by a deep booming sound. As the house vibrated, I jumped out of bed and with the help of a flash lamp found my clothes. I discovered that the locked window had burst open and was minus two panes of glass. The room was littered with scraps of debris and I did not know whether we had been hit directly by a bomb, or what was happening. Outside the room I found a door smashed open. Splinters of wood and glass littered the floor, making walking a hazard. Some time later, I met the Bishop and the other priests. They were examining the damage. The refugees were terrified and I was shaking, as I usually do under stress. Ceilings had collapsed in many places, one falling on a priest's bed, but he was not hurt. A window casment was prevented from falling on another priest's bed by the frame of a mosquito net.

The Bishop guessed rightly, that the damage was not from a shell, but the blowing up of the local arsenal.

A few of us gathered in my room and had coffee. We retired after an hour and slept in our clothes. We spent next morning cleaning up the mess and could not venture onto the streets. We didn't know exactly what was going on, but guessed that the resistance had been overcome and the 'Liberation Army' would arrive soon.

The Marist Brothers who conduct a school on the opposite side of the river to the arsenal telephoned to say that all their windows were broken. A huge rock had penetrated the roof of the school and had passed clean through three floors.

30th. It has been fairly quiet today, except for sporadic firing by the police to keep order in the streets. It was a good thing that the police were there. Having nothing much to do, I got down to the study of the Chinese-language characters again; I need it badly. At 7pm there was a 'stop press' saying that the Liberation Army would be welcomed in at 9pm and that's just what happened. We heard the cheering and the firecrackers of their local supporters.

Some time after that, when we were going to bed, there was another terrific explosion and flash. The windows still in place shook again, but none broke. We heard later that the explosion was from a further-away arsenal, destroyed by retreating troops.

December 1st. Communist soldiers are visible all over the city. They are patient with the people, who bustle them and ask questions. This morning's newspaper has plenty of news, including the Liberation Army's policy with foreigners: complete protection to lives and property!

In the evening, a plane machine-gunned the city, but I think only one man was killed.

2nd. Just a small section of the Liberation Army has been left in the city, the rest having gone on to Chengtu, to chase the Nationalist Army.

When I went out into the streets, I spotted only a handful of soldiers, mainly men belonging to the 'Preservation Corps'. Everyone was happy that there was no fighting and the soldiers were so well behaved. They did not seem to bother anyone and were insisting on paying for what they receive. The Officers and men carried the same pack and gun and ate the same food.

Such confidence was felt by the business people that they were re-opening their shops in some places. The only thing that kept the other shops closed was the fact that the money question was not yet settled. There was no new currency in place and therefore little could be bought in the shops.

At 8pm there was a report that forty Nationalist planes had left Kunming to bomb this place here. This rumour had a devastating effect on the people. Everyone ran with blankets over their heads to the nearest bomb shelters. Later, we woke up the old Bishop and suggested evacuation, but he decided to stay at the Mission. So three of us stayed at home, the Bishop, Pastor and myself. All the refugees found their own shelter. We sat talking until 1am and then decided that the bombing-rumour was a false alarm. We said Mass and went to bed. I slept until 10.30 next morning. I needed the rest.

3rd. I went to the Hospital to see the newly formed nurses Praesidium. It could be much better and I am glad I am in Chungking to check up on these things. I think it is Providential that I was left here. This seems to be the place with most difficulties and lacking any priest to take the Legion in hand. I slept in the Hospital the same night, said Mass next morning and gave a sermon. After breakfast, the Bishop came in looking miserable. He wanted to go to an outside parish to visit the Carmelites. The local Consul gave him a Jeep and a few of us bundled in and went along with him. We could see there was great damage in that quarter. Two whole villages had been wiped out by the arsenal-explosion and thousands of people, including Nationalist soldiers were dead; terrible indeed. It was appalling that the people were not warned about the blast. The

138

arsenal was deliberately blown up by retreating troops. The huge granite rock, which fell through three floors of the Marist Brothers School, had been blown three miles. The sound of the impact must have been horrific!

On the night in question, the Carmelite Sisters were at their meditation and the Superioress cut it short, as the Sisters were tired. The last Sister had barely left the Chapel when the place collapsed. Had they remained seconds later, the blast would have killed them all. Our Lady certainly showed her intercession.

4th. I visited the first Praesidium at the Hospital; it was good, but also needs tuning up. I took the Officers of both Praesidia again and gave them another going-over. One can trace the faults to the lack of a Worksheet. They like to trust their memories, with disastrous results.

5th. I went to St. Joseph's parish number one Praesidium. This group, though doing good work, has the seeds of faults, which might pull it down badly. I gave them all a good talking to and hoped to see things improve next week. Apologies from absentees were not being sent in. The minutes did not include any mention of those who failed to report and the Worksheet was not as I would like it. Besides, work which should have been done in pairs, was done by single persons.

I visited St. Joseph's number two Praesidium. Having come from the number one group, it was natural that this one would have the same faults. They got their talking-to also.

8th. Feast of the Immaculate Conception. Last evening I went to the Marist Brother's School and sang Mass for them, followed by Vespers and Benediction. It was all very nice. The Brothers have a fine choir. I spoke to Officers of the established Praesidium and also to Br. Florent, who is beginning a Legion group himself - with past pupils.

10th The Curia meeting was held today. There was a splendid attendance and it was well conducted. The President is also in charge of the number one Legion group in St. Joseph's. Two of the new Praesidia have taken up Hospital visitation. The Curia decided to hold its annual reunion on the following Sunday.

My visits to Praesidia on each of the following three days were satisfactory: worksheets in evidence and a distinct overall improvement.

13th. I began my Retreat. On the last day of the exercise I attended the General Reunion of the local Curia. The Bishop was behind the idea of the Lay Apostolate and had the Chapel beautifully prepared for the big occasion. Over one hundred active members participated. The choir was composed of the boys from St. Paul's School and nurses from the local Hospital. One of the Sisters played the organ and Br. Francis conducted the singing; all very inspiring. The Blessed Sacrament was exposed and we recited the Rosary, which was followed by Benediction. The Bishop consecrated the whole Diocese, Priests, Sisters and Brothers and all Catholics to the Sacred Heart of Jesus and the Immaculate Heart of Mary. He said this was the most appropriate moment to fulfil Our Lady of Fatima's wishes. *Totus Tuus*, the hymn composed by George Dennis, the boot-maker from Dublin, was a fitting finish. In the garden in front of the Chapel refreshments were served.

During the next week I kept going around the different Praesidia, correcting little faults. All have pepped up appreciably and one new group has been formed from St. Paul's School past pupils and two more Praesidia are to start this week.

25th, Christmas Day. I said Mass and heard Confessions in the Catholic Hospital. St. Joseph's Church was filled with people, with Masses going on from daylight until noon. The priests estimated that over one thousand Confessions were heard in that Church alone. Many had come to confess after five to forty years' absence. The Legionaries have tackled so much work that a fourth Praesidium is being set up.

27th. I went to the Marist Brothers Junior Praesidium for the first time in months and was delighted with its efficiency. Bro. Francis, who is Chinese, but trained in France, is a lively Spiritual Director.

29th. Today a Praesidium was formed in the Bishop's residence, with thirteen members. The President is a young girl recently married. She first joined the Legion in the Aurora University in Shanghai. . . .

CHAPTER TWENTY ONE

CHUNGKING - JANUARY TO JUNE 1950

"THE MEMBERS DO ENDLESS OTHER JOBS"

If you lose hope being weary in the day of distress,
your strength shall be diminished. (Proverbs 24:10)

Diary: Sunday January 1ˢᵗ 1950. A New Year has begun and today there are processions on the streets to officially welcome the 'Liberation Army'. History is unfolding before my eyes.

7ᵗʰ. There was a big attendance at the Curia meeting. Immediately afterwards, I left for Sha Ping Pa, which is about an hour's run by bus. I had been invited there by a French priest to help him start the Legion. I wanted to begin there months ago, but the University students were unsure of their tenure so we had to wait. I said Mass and preached there next day and then brought thirteen people in to explain the Legion to them. We started a Praesidium the same day.

10ᵗʰ. I had a letter from Bishop Tuan of Wanhsien. He is charmed with his Legionaries. In the end he said: "May Our Lady bless our Diocese as well as our Legion of Mary, upon which the future of Wanhsien relies." During the changeover, when the Communists took control, two of the Praesidia had no meetings as the members were scattered, but they have begun again.

14ᵗʰ. I went by bus to Sha Ping Pa to assist at the second meeting of the new Praesidium. We discussed the work for next week and the President got it down in fine detail. At fifty years of age, the Legion has given him a new lease of life.

Chungking, Szechwan
18ᵗʰ January 1950

Dear John,
I was delighted to receive your letter of November 30ᵗʰ and to get all the news of other parts of China, such as Peking and

Tientsin. Also today I received your beautiful calendar with the picture of the Immaculate Conception on the cover. Lou Hung Nien would be honoured to see his picture. You got a wonderful print of it. I received also your letter to Fr. Beunen and I have forwarded it...

I had word from Bishop Tuan in Wanhsein. They are enjoying peace and the Legion is continuing to do wonderful work. Bishop Tuan says: "The future of our Diocese rests in their hands." We now have eleven or twelve Praesidia here and I have succeeded in getting rid of the prevailing faults of which I spoke ...

Msgr. Riberi is living in Nanking as far as I know. The Nanking address will get him anyway: 25 Tien Chu Lu. I hope that the various Curiae will still be able to correspond with you.

These letters will be slow, as there is no airmail from here.

Aedan

Dublin
7th March 1950

Dear Fr. McGrath,

We were delighted to receive your letter of January 18th and to know you are in good form. We were looking for news of you from many sources. Delighted to know my letter of November 30th arrived safely, but I am afraid that many of our letters did not reach you. Perhaps they may turn up in due course.

I am glad to see you received the calendar. I hope you are also receiving the Legion journals? On the Christmas issue we reproduced the calendar picture and it was greatly admired. I am delighted you thought so well of the reproduction.

Warmest congratulations on your work in Chungking and many thanks for the enclosed report. Bro. Hegarty, who writes in French, is corresponding with the Curiae in China, which send us their Minutes in French. Hence, he will correspond with Chungking when the Minutes arrive. You will be pleased to learn that I am now hearing regularly from Shanghai, Peking and Canton, while we received the first Minutes from Chengtu and Tientsin. The post has been most irregular and I take it that some mail has probably gone astray. The progress in extension has been so rapid that it is difficult to keep in touch. If we could set up a reliable Senatus or a few regional Senatus, it would be a great thing. In regard to Shanghai, the position has become complicated. The original Curia is now the English-speaking one and is a small body. The Chinese-speaking Curia is now divided into three Curiae, with one of them a Comitium, but they have not made contact with us at all. Fr. Sheng is S.D. of the English-speaking Body and has been appointed Diocesan S.D.

I am hoping you will be able to visit Shanghai and see the situation for yourself. I suppose you know that extension in most areas has been rapid. For example in Peiping there are now about six Curiae and eighty Praesidia, all under a Comitium. The Spiritual Director is most earnest and is an excellent correspondent. Hence, your self-sacrificing and zealous work has borne a very rich harvest and the Legion can never repay you for your invaluable services. However, Our Blessed Lady is never outdone in generosity and she will do what we are unable to accomplish in regard to adequate thanks.

Many thanks for the address of the Internuncio. I hope to write to His Excellency shortly. Do you know that Teresa Su is now finished in the Philippines and will be returning soon to China? I hope she will be able to get in touch with you and discuss her future. She appears to be worried about her father, who, she says was under the impression she had gone away for University studies towards a further Degree. This was a surprise to us, since, if she is to go ahead with the Legion Envoy work her father would have to know about her venture.

We have heard a rumour that you may not perhaps be able to continue your work in China. I do hope that such is not the case; there is no indication of it in your recent letter. If the rumour should turn out to be correct, would it be possible for you to get permission from your Superiors to go to Korea for a while? The Apostolic Delegate there has asked us for a representative to start the Legion. His Excellency is recommending the Legion to the Bishops, but he has nobody with the time and experience to do the job. Should you be unable to continue in China, it would be wonderful if you could transfer to Korea.

Last night we started the first of a series of lectures on the Legion in St. Columban's Navan at the request of the Superior,

Very Rev. Fr. Ganly. We had one hundred and seventy five students and some members of the Community present. All gave us a great reception. We are bringing a Praesidium down to hold its meeting in the College: this will be the best way of demonstrating the working of the System. I was speaking to your brother and was able to give him the news contained in your letter.[40]

Have you heard that we appointed an Envoy to Japan? She is an Australian Legionary, Agnes Orlebar. The Apostolic Delegate there and all the Bishops are greatly interested and anxious to have a Legion ambassador.

You will be very sorry to hear that Brother Duff's mother died last week R.I.P. This is a very great blow to him, particularly since it is the third death in his family within nine months. I know that you will remember to pray for the repose of his mother's soul.

We eagerly look forward to hearing from you soon again and we shall continue to pray for your wellbeing and health. The Concilium again desires me to express its deepest gratitude for your noble work, and we send you our warmest greetings and good wishes.

John Nagle

Diary: March 8th 1950. During the past two months, I have been held up from writing this Diary for many reasons: one excuse was an eight-day Retreat I had to give to the Sisters of Charity: Another was a week or so in Hospital with a heavy cold. The rest of the time, I was visiting Praesidia and doing a lot of letter writing. The visiting of Praesidia was necessary, as during this period, many members could not attend their meetings. They were doing a study-term under the new government and attendance was impossible. However, these things did not stop the others from carrying on.

At the March Curia meeting all was set in readiness for the Acies and we hope to get a good gathering. Just after the meeting we ran up against a new difficulty, namely: the President has been forced to resign from his Curia Officership and also that of his Praesidium. We are constantly running up against these obstacles, but it does not affect the main work.

---

[40] A reference to Fr. Ronan McGrath.

144

Lately, I had a letter from Fr. McGoldrick, one of our Columban Fathers in Peking and it contained wonderful news of the Legion there: over one hundred Praesidia and four Curiae have been set up.

Another letter from Fr. Beunen CM, Tientsin stated that they had over fifty Praesidia there and in another place not far away, they had twenty-four Legion groups. In all they had about seven Curiae. This news staggered me too. It is obvious that Our Lady has taken things into her own hands. Fr. Beunen stressed that everything was being done strictly according to the Handbook.

The Bishop is delighted at the progress in Tientsin.

Thus ends Fr. McGrath's day-to-day Diary entries.

Catholic Mission,
80, Wu Ssu Lu,
Chungking
15th March 1950

Dear John,

Your letter came through Hong Kong...I shall let you know when I am leaving for Shanghai. It was very good of the Concilium to give a loan to Hong Kong for the printing of the Handbook.

I have not heard from Teresa Su. I don't know when she expects to return. I suppose she will do some work in the vicinity of Hong Kong before going on to Shanghai. What do you think? She will be invaluable to the Senatus there in teaching them how to do their correspondence. A letter from Hankow showed great satisfaction on the part of the priests. I don't know if they have their Curia yet. I shall give you more information later. . .

Aedan

P.S. I just received a nice letter from Miss Shiels, written on May 20th 1949! She is willing to help out the Legion in Hankow.

Dublin
13th April 1950

Dear Fr. Aedan,

It was a great pleasure to receive your letter of March 15th and to have such good news regarding yourself and affairs in Chungking.

Our letters appear to keep crossing in the post, but I hope you have received my last letter of March 7th. My letter of November 3rd went astray in the post. You do not appear to have received any of Frank's recent letters of November 25th and January 21st. Perhaps they have turned up since. He has suffered a great blow by the death of his mother, which followed the earlier deaths of his sister and brother. Practically all his family has been wiped out and Frank is now alone in his home on Morning Star Avenue.

In spite of your remarks, I shall have to send this letter by the same postal route as previous letters because the postal route from here to the interior of China is not yet available. You will be glad to know that I have received the Minutes from Hong Kong, where the Legion appears to be doing well. I think they have not started reprinting the Handbook as they are trying to find out the exact position in regard to the first edition.

Yes, the progress in Peking is extraordinary. In my last letter there, I urged the Officers to consolidate and not to think further in terms of going ahead. I was glad to know they had made provision for a number of Councils to look after the various Centres. I also heard recently from Tientsin and it is most encouraging that everyone there is in good form. I have not heard at all from Hankow, but I am glad to know you had a letter from there.

Teresa Su should soon be going to Hong Kong. It seems unlikely she will be able to travel far for some time. I suppose she will find useful work to do in her own locality. I think she said she had written to you.

John Nagle

Chungking,
26th May 1950

Dear John,

I had a letter from Joe Sheng and the Legion appears to be doing well in Shanghai. He told me that Hong Kong had not yet printed the Handbook. They are producing it by themselves and also copies of it in English. It is much cheaper than the former one. Joe suggested that Teresa Su remain where she is for now. She wrote me a note before she left Fr. Gracia.

We were expecting special blessings on the Legion during the month of May and I suppose the Spiritual Directors would say that we got them, but they were in a form hard to recognise: The Legion members and myself were put right into the crucible. I sincerely hope we came out of it much refined. The name of the Legion in Chinese - Holy Mother's Army - caused the authorities to be very suspicious and when they came to investigate they told us to stop operating until they examined the situation. Naturally my heart was nearly broken and the last month has been a time of real trial. We have been hoping and praying that the end of the month would see things cleared. We gave the Communists the Handbook and other literature, to show them that the Legion is in the Church for the good of the members and through their goodness to help others in various ways. There have been endless questionings and we are glad of it, for the more the Reds realise what the Legion is, the more they should be willing to allow it continue the good work.

The azure blue of Mary's Mantle has been clouded for many weeks now. May we see it in all its brightness before many days have gone by.

> Pray for us all.
> Aedan

Dublin
27th June 1950

Dear Aedan,

...You will be pleased to know that Teresa Su has arrived home. I understand that her father is dangerously ill. It seems that he is not expected to recover. Is it not strange how things work out in the end? You remember that we were wondering how matters would be fixed up with her father? Later, Teresa may have the strength to see more friends. She is in touch with Mary Cheng, who told me recently of good progress in her own household...

> John Nagle

Chapter Twenty Two

Update from Shanghai

4th July 1950

How then are they to call upon Him in whom they have not believed?
But how are they to believe Him whom they have not heard?
And how are they to hear, if no one preaches? (Romans 10:14)

Catholic Central Bureau,
197 Yoyang Road,
Shanghai
4th July 1950

Dear Frank,

As you see I am back safely in Shanghai and more or less back on the job...To go back a little: you must have realised that we had our difficulties in Chungking and that the Legion was actually stopped by the authorities until they investigated everything. Naturally my heart was rent in two and I spent the most miserable days of my life during that month of May. We had hoped that the Reds would realise that the Legion was nothing but a beautiful social work, but that it should all be stopped was heartbreaking. In the middle of the consternation, I received my pass to move out. Although things had not righted themselves, I was assured by Msgr. Jantzen that by August 15th he was determined to have all the Praesidia going again. Since the Legion was stopped, very little has been done by way of apostolic work. The priests now understand more clearly what a help the organisation is to the Church.

I was pleased to be leaving a place where my work was stopped and where I had to sit inactive for some months. The trip to here was exquisite beyond words. The little Steamer passed through the Yangtze Rapids, with towering mountains on either side. I had a few hours with Msgr. Tuan of Wanhsien at our first stop. He was just as thrilled with the Legion as ever and his Praesidia were doing first-rate work. He realises more than ever that the Legion was a gift from Our Lady to him on the day of his consecration. He is pressing the Fathers all over the region to start it and in most of the big places it has begun already. Whenever the Fathers return to the Mission they attend the local Praesidium meeting to learn more about the Legion system. He told me that the best group of all was the one I was most fearful about, namely: the orphans whom he allowed to move outside the Orphanage to instruct the children after school hours. Some of the senior ones are going regularly to the Poor Houses to assist in such things as, mending garments, grinding the wheat, making garments and so on. The results are most gratifying. His Legionaries have become most zealous and have advanced fast in the spiritual life.

Next stop was Ichang, where Msgr. Gubbels OFM lives. I had one night there. I was pleased to hear that he had two Praesidia. These came about as a result of a chance meeting I had with him two years ago. He also gave news of Fr. Yang, the first priest in Hankow to adopt the Legion. Msgr. Gubbels asked me to give a talk to his priests and I must say there was great enthusiasm. The following night I was lucky to get a small Steamer to Hankow. We arrived after two and a half days and I went to my Mission where all were surprised to see me. I met Bishop Galvin and the other Fathers, and heard with much delight that they had about eighteen Praesidia and were thrilled with the Legion.

Two and a half days on a further boat brought me to Shanghai, July 23rd, so early that I had trouble getting my house opened. I was tired beyond words and determined to rest for about a week. It was not easy, for the word went around that I was back and I had many visitors. Even during those days, I was present at some Praesidia meetings and even one Chinese-speaking Curia. I am deeply impressed with the work that Fr. Sheng has done - it is no easy task to keep up with things. Apparently since my departure he has given his whole time to this work and is undoubtedly capable. The enthusiasm here is perhaps difficult for you to imagine. I do not know if I ever mentioned in the early days how a young girl, just married and on her honeymoon in another district, landed back by train the next week for her Legion meeting! I am wondering what the husband thought. I wonder if you have anything like that on your records?

The speed with which things have moved here is amazing: The number of Praesidia runs to about forty-three, including ten foreign groups. Fr. Sheng is still in charge of the latter and Msgr. Prevost, a French Canadian who cannot return to his Mission, is very zealous indeed with the Chinese groups. We must now prepare for the formation of a Comitium and eventually a Senatus. The difficulty to date is that the Chinese Curia was almost entirely made up of Senior students and it is not easy for them to give time for outside work.

As to the Handbook, Shanghai alone has printed the Chinese one with some corrections. They have sent books to Hong Kong as requested. We are in an impossible position as to getting books from that city. The Shanghai printers have produced English copies. They printed seven hundred copies by the photographing-method in Shanghai. Production is cheap and it filled a need.

Frank mentions Rosie Yeung again. She truly is a fine Legionary, but when I asked her about Envoy work, she backed out on account of her mother. I heard from Mary Cheng that Rosie has gone to the country on Catechist work.

Frank's remarks about Teresa Su opened my eyes. I had no notion that she had made such a request[41]; she is timid and listens to suggestions. She may have been pressed by the Chinese in Manila to delay her departure. The pity is that she has delayed so long. I have written to tell her to visit Shanghai as soon as she can. She will know more than I do about the Senatus and the various Councils.

We have a wonderful Bishop here who cannot get back to his Diocese.[42] He is so enamoured with the Legion that he has six Praesidia and assiduously studies his Handbook. His Legion talks are all typed out as he goes through his book, which shows a keen spirit. I enclose his Coat of Arms, which has the Vexillum in the middle, without the figure of Our Lady, which it seems, is not supposed to be on a Coat of Arms. Instead, he has a big 'M' where the *Legio Mariae* normally is; underneath is the motto 'Sicut Acies'[43]. That is to be the spirit in his Diocese; he has sent word to his priests. He is from Shantung, Wei Hai Wei. He is so humble and asked me many questions about the Legion and the True Devotion – which is now being translated into Chinese.

All through the country requests are made for the Handbook to be produced in a simpler language and that a synopsis be written. I checked for the latter everywhere. Apparently in Peiking and Hankow, they have made up their

---

[41] To remain on in Manila for a further period of time.

[42] Bishop Gabriel Olbert.

[43] i.e. literally 'as keen' or 'as a sharp edge' or 'as a battle line' – understood in Legion of Mary terms as 'terrible as an army set in battle array' with particular reference to Our Blessed Lady.

own synopsis! They are books of the essential things to know, written in simple language. I was glad to hear Joe Sheng saying he had written to affirm that nothing can replace the Handbook and, even though they had those books to help out, still the Handbook must be studied systematically with the help of a priest or the Praesidium President. I have not seen these synopsis-books yet, but I mean to study them. I shall let you know the verdict later. The Legion rules as such, can be learned after holding a few meetings and are imbibed easily even by the older members. It is the 'spirit' that counts and this will only come by the reading and explaining of the Handbook. If someone started the Legion with the book of regulations alone, we might expect disaster.

You may have heard that the name 'Holy Mother's Army' has been changed again! It was causing suspicion to the authorities and nervousness among Legionaries. The name seems to have been unsuitable from the beginning. Now it is called 'Our Lady of Mercy Prayer Meeting'. The title is only temporary, but such was necessary. Until recently, I heard nothing of these things, as it was impossible for the relevant people to contact me; but the Internuncio was behind the move and also the idea of printing the Handbooks in English and Chinese. Joe Sheng came back from Anthony's place this morning and told me that he presided over the Curia meeting boasting nine Praesidia.

Very sincerely yours in Jesus and Mary,

Aedan

CHAPTER TWENTY THREE

SHANGHAI - JULY TO SEPTEMBER 1950

"EACH CATHOLIC IS A SMOULDERING FIRE"

Whoever is not just is not of God, nor is he just who does not love his brother.
For this is the message that you have heard from the beginning,
that we should love one another. (John 3:10-11)

Shanghai
12th July 1950

Dear Frank,

I recently met with Antonius Riberi and he asked me questions for two hours, commenting in the end: "Tell Frank that I wish he could be here to witness what is going on. I can almost feel with my hands the Faith which has been inspired by the Legionaries." Again he said: "We realise now that each Catholic is a smouldering fire which only needs to be opened to the breeze."

He has not received a letter from Dublin for ever-so-long, nor did he receive the last two editions of *Maria Legionis*.

Hoping you got my last letter and that you will approve our plan to split the Curia. Now that I have been around a bit, I think that there should be plenty of capable people to help us with correspondence. I want to get the Chinese Legionaries writing. Up to the present, it was mostly done by Fr. Sheng, with a few exceptions. Of course our plans for these things may not materialise.

At my request, Fr. Joe Sheng is continuing to run the office officially and more or less taking charge of things. I shall be rallying around all the time.

Aedan

Dublin
10th August, 1950

Dear Aedan,

Your very welcome letters of July 4th and 12th have just come to hand and we are more than delighted to know that you are back safely in Shanghai and

152

as busy as ever. We quite understand the various problems which arise from time to time and I hope that Jim Jantzen has been able to solve his various worries since you last met him.

I have little news from your part of the world although I have written to quite a few of our mutual friends, but without reply

It is good news to know that you found our various friends in Shanghai full of energy. We are deeply grateful to Joe Sheng for the care and attention he has given to all and sundry and we appreciate his zeal and earnestness. Will you kindly convey to him our warmest gratitude and regards? In the present circumstances you should act as you think best in regard to dividing the Groups, since you are on the spot. I would not be inclined to make them too small because the many duties demand a large number of willing and experienced workers. The average number of Groups here in Dublin is about forty.

I note that you are emphasising the importance of reading the Handbook in all places and not relying on a synopsis or substitute. The synopsis would not produce the necessary spirit and high qualities which are so much required.

I shall ask our friend here to send you some Magazines and I hope they reach you safely. During the suspension of post, I presume the Magazines were returned. I understood that such literature would not be welcome at the present time, but I gather from your letter that this is not the case.

You are wise in getting your friends to assist Joe Sheng because it is important that they participate fully in carrying out the various functions. It would be impossible for Joe himself to deal with everything requiring attention.

With every good wish,

John Nagle

197, Yoyang Road,
Shanghai
4th September 1950

Dear John,

I was more than delighted to receive your letter of August 10th. I was wondering if you had received mine. Now I am at rest. I had a letter from Mary Cheng telling of their enclosed Retreats for men and women - both successful. She mentioned that it might be good for you to send your letters direct to her - as with written Chinese characters they are more likely to get there. At present it is not good for us to send records as such - they are too bulky. Letters giving general news can be short enough and will surely get there.

Fr. Sheng is away at present seeing his mother in Hankow. He will be able to help there. That place is doing splendidly. I received a copy of the minutes of the Spiritual Director's monthly meeting which the Archbishop attended. They discussed all questions of the Legion and it was an example for us. We have more difficulties here of course, as the Jesuit's have most of the parishes. However, we are going to do something similar. We have a new Secular Bishop now and he had the Legion in his former district, so we hope that we can get a push. Hankow now has twenty-three Praesidia.

I was extremely busy last week with all the people here. We divided the Curia and you need not fear; all will be well. We have plenty of willing workers.

I also held an enclosed retreat for the Chinese-speaking active Legion members. The Sisters of the Sacred Heart allowed us the use of their Convent facilities. Sixty girls stayed the two days there and the others came each morning, men and women. I was staggered with the turnout! In total, about one hundred and fifty enthusiastic people were present. They kept the silence perfectly. In the middle of each day I conducted a sort of Legion meeting, going over the various points. I knew that there was much off line and it was the only way to do it. They all took notes and got things straight. I gave them plenty on Praetorian membership and the True Devotion. One priest next day scolded me in fun saying: "What did you tell them yesterday: for my boys came back and told me that I was wrong in ten places on the Legion System." I was amused. Work sheets are all in line now and everything else, so I am happy. In the next couple of weeks, I am going to give the English-speaking Legionaries the same dose!

We got Hilda Firtel's article on the *Thirty Nine Steps* translated and it is very popular. We are also getting Frank Duff's *The De Montfort Way*, the *Secret of Mary* and *The True Devotion* translated into Chinese. We got the latter in English here, and there is much demand. We had letters from Wenchow, Chekiang saying that they have a Curia and had heard from you. Now they are writing to us so that we can help them. Fr. McGoldrick told me lately that the Legion has been registered with the police there and all was done politely and without fuss. All goes well this way.

One question: Is it permissible to let Legionaries give a little medicine when they are going around to the very poor and sick people? Ordinarily, this is a common practice in most of the Missions, not including the Legion. It may take the form of an Aspirin, or the bandaging up of a leg and as such opens the door.

I think it is true what Frank says, that if the flame of faith is fanned in the proper way, nothing can stand before it. Communism and all the other 'isms' will ultimately yield to it. Communism is but the product of force and that force is exerted by the tiny few on an inert population. The permanence of the Communistic system depends upon the reins of authority remaining in the hands of those few people and the mass remaining inert. This inertia can usually be counted upon. It proceeds in part from fear and the yielding to force. For after Communism has been enthroned for some little time, it has been able to work by propaganda on the people and to make them willingly inert and even complacent. The only remedy for this position is the setting at work of a counter-force in the community, one which will play on the mass and tend to deprive it of its character of inertness.

Very sincerely yours in Jesus and Mary,

Aedan

Shanghai
11th September 1950

Dear Frank,

Many thanks for your letter of August 27th. The news of your ill-health gave me quite a jolt. You know Frank that my heart is not strong; and in fact Anthony's is just the same. Some of that news would surely kill us! For heaven's sake be careful about your wellbeing.

About letters coming through Hong Kong: We have no proof that they are any quicker or surer in getting here. You can of course send them that way, but don't be under any illusion.

The police have been very nice in asking about the Legion in many places. I shall write again and answer your different questions.

Keep praying for us.

Aedan

Shanghai
28th September 1950

Dear Frank,

Msgr. Antonius Riberi came here and showed me your letter which was sent to him. He was delighted to receive it without delay. Most of the content was wonderful and could be put on a public notice board. Many thanks for the nice things you said. Our Lady is still smiling on our efforts and this is a great consolation. At the moment there must be about fifty Curiae throughout China. That is rather staggering for you, and for us it is a problem to keep up. But in such circumstances we must trust in Our Lady to add extra graces, for it was Mary who inspired it all.

I have rarely seen Msgr. Antonius in such high spirits at all the news of the Legion.

Fr. Sheng continues to work hard for the Legion here. He was up in Hankow lately for a holiday and spent the time addressing groups of priests and others. The Praesidia are splendid there and the priests get together twice a month with the Archbishop for a conference on Legion methods. I may enclose an agenda. Msgr. Prevost. He is the French-Canadian who cannot get back to his Mission. He works hard here in the Bureau book department and is heart and soul in the Legion cause. He resigned as S.D. of the Chinese-speaking Curia, as he did not understand the Shanghai language. Now we have four Curiae and I am temporary S.D. of the foreign Council. One of the Curiae is now the Comitium with Fr. Sheng as S.D. and Msgr. Gabriel S.D. looking after one of the other Bodies.

The June volume of *Maria Legionis* has just arrived. Many thanks; it is splendid. Msgr. Antonius asked me to send you the list of Bishops' names so that you may send copies straight to them. There is no trouble about that. Please, in your next edition leave out the flag beside the report from China. You know that is very much out of date now and would hurt my personal friends very much. Please note: it would be better to put nothing at all in the flag spot.

I wish you would send me extra information about the running of a Comitium. Members consider what is in the Handbook rather short. We now have one here, another in Tientsin, Peking, Tsingtao, Tongshan and Chengtu. We keep a general eye on all places and they have their own responsibilities. Msgr. Antonius wishes that we in Shanghai remain in charge of all Councils. We are now working as a Senatus... The two Curiae in the north are capable of doing their duties.

Teresa Su will help us when she comes, but she has to wait one hundred days after her father's death before travelling here. However, she is doing well in Hong Kong. Reports comment on her great enthusiasm. Last I forget: Msgr. Gabriel, who's Coat of Arms had the Legion standard on it, has no objection to your publishing it.

So many requests have come in for the revision of the Chinese Handbook that we have decided to deal with it. The translation by Fr. Chen was not easy enough and we are preparing another, in simple but good Chinese. You can imagine my difficult position. Mr. Fang, who had a great part of the book done, was not allowed to print it when I was in Hong Kong. Now when we are going to do it again, it seems impossible to ask him for his translation. There is a certain amount of ill-feeling present and I have to keep out. So as to avoid friction, it will be done by another person. Do you approve of the new translation? It is essential, as only about ten per cent of readers understand the old version. I cannot understand it yet. Fr. Sheng suggests that those who want to use the more difficult one can do so. What do you think?

Very sincerely yours in Jesus and Mary,

Aedan

Chapter Twenty Four

On the Giving of Medicine

October to December 1950

Your decrees are worthy of trust indeed;
holiness befits your house, O Lord,
for length of days. (Psalms 92:5)

Dublin
2nd October 1950

Dear Fr. Aedan,

Your letter of September 4th was very welcome. I trust that by now you have received the Journals, which we sent direct to your address. It is good news to know that your various interests continue to meet with success. Yourself and Joe Sheng have been working very hard. I note that Fr. Joe was able to do a spot of work while visiting his mother. Apparently the 'Chief' in his home place, is a most zealous man. Twenty-three people are now helping locally.

Do you remember your old friend Meijs? He called to see us recently and gave us a thrilling account of his adventures. He stayed with his brothers in Phibsboro, so we saw quite a lot of him. Previously he had been to see Antonius who appeared to be delighted with all he had to tell him. He also visited the place where Mary Ingoldsby is working, saw the 'big shots' there and the Boss, who listened with intense interest to his yarns.[44]

I had a letter from our mutual friend Van Coillie.[45] He followed the same course as McGoldrick, who put all his cards on the table, gave the boys[46] a copy of his Handbook to read and told them to come back to him if they

---

[44] Fr. Meijs CM visited the Concilium in August 1950 staying in the Vincentian house in Dublin. He was en route from the Vatican for the purpose of reporting on the state of religion in China. He spent three and a half hours with the Secretary of the Congregation of Propaganda after which he was received by Pope Pius XII and gave him a laudible account of the part played by the Legion.

[45] Fr. Dries van Coillie, a Scheut Missionary, author of *Brainwashed in Peking* (1969), a thoroughgoing account of his maltreatment in Communist captivity.

[46] i.e. The Communist authorities.

required further knowledge. So far things seem to be going well with him. He mentioned that it was he who produced a summary of the Handbook, which ran to one hundred pages. I must say that alarmed me because it is obvious that a summary of that size would hold the field and take the place of the original. I urged him not to allow this to happen and asked him not to make further copies. You realise that if every location produced a summary of its own there would be chaos and before long, little or no similarity with the original would be evident.

I hope Teresa will soon be able to meet you and give you a helping hand.

In regard to your query, I think that your fellow Legionaries should by every means possible and particularly by personal service, assist the poor and sick people in every way, short of material aid. It is difficult to say whether it is advisable for Legionaries to give out these things, since the problem may be, where to draw the line. Also, when the 'giving out' process stops, will the sick have the same welcome for visitors? They should concentrate as much as possible on personal service: nursing the sick, cleaning their rooms, collecting messages, reading to them and so on. This is the best way to prove the sincerity of their service. Perhaps others could be found to dispense medicine, just as now and again the St Vincent De Paul folk are asked to help people who need aid.

Very sincerely yours,

John Nagle

197 Yoyang Road
Shanghai
2nd October 1950

Dear Frank,

We have just returned from the Sacred Heart Convent, where the active Legionaries gathered together for Mass celebrated by the new Bishop of Shanghai. The ceremony was planned by local Legion members, as a welcome. There must have been about six hundred active members present. Nearly all went to Holy Communion and the Legion Hymn *Totus Tuus* was sung, first in Latin and then in Chinese. After Mass each President of the Curia brought up Spiritual Bouquets from their Praesidia. A fine number of priests and Sisters also attended. It was really a wonderful turnout and I think that the Bishop was duly pleased.

Very sincerely yours in Jesus and Mary,

Aedan

Dublin
18th October 1950

Dear Fr. Aedan,

The Comitium ratifies the election of Curia Officers directly related to it. The Officers of the attached Curiae should attend the Comitium meeting at least every second or third month to report on progress and problems. If this is not possible, the Curiae should send a copy of their Minutes to the Comitium and correspondents should be appointed to deal with same. Also, the Comitium should visit the Curiae periodically in order to assist them in every possible way.

The Concilium keeps in touch with the Comitium as the Diocesan Body and has no direct contact with the Curiae. This should also apply where there is a Senatus.

Recently we formally agreed to the conferring of the status and functions of Regional Senatus in regard to Tientsin, Peking and your own place Shanghai, with the proviso that later on it may be necessary to review the situation and make certain adjustments. The two first named places have been acting for some time as Regional Senatus' and I now see that your place has been doing likewise.

The office of Tribune has been abolished, but since no new edition of the Handbook has appeared here, the necessary change has not been made. Hence, no appointment of new Tribunes should be made and when the term of office of the present one is expired, it should not be renewed. It was found that the office in question was an unreal one, and created problems: the Tribune was attending a meeting and doing no work. Further, in practice it was found that there was no demand or need for the Officer in question. For example here in Dublin, there was only one Tribune in the entire city.

I see that your own Legion Handbook is being revised with the idea of having it done in simpler language. It will be a little awkward having two versions of the book, but I presume that the new version will gradually supersede the older one. Hopefully the revision will keep closely to the original and no innovations will be introduced. This is a vitally important point.

John Nagle

197 Yoyang Road, Shanghai
3rd November 1950

Dear John,

Your two kind letters of October 2nd and 18th to hand. The latter one about the Comitium I copied out to send to the places concerned; it will be a great help.

Thanks for your lines on the giving of medicine. This is not a common thing in the Legion. Where the Franciscan Missionaries of Mary go out among the poor, they take Legionaries with them. What they give by way of medicine is negligible and the places they visit are just little mat sheds. These extremely poor and sick people love to see the visitors and I would put the work on a par with the visiting of real houses. The work is done so as to encourage parents to get their babies baptised. The mortality rate is very high among the children. Sisters in religion do this all over China and priests also. If the workers can be multiplied, the Baptisms can be increased also.

Many thanks for the dozen copies of *Maria Legionis*; they came straight to us here. I think that your letters can best come direct too.

Mary Cheung wants to go to Rome and then Ireland. She hopes to visit you all and asked me for Legion addresses in Paris, Rome and London. I could not give them but I told her to ask you. Then she asked me for an address where she could stay in Dublin for a few days. I suggested the Sancta Maria as being central and as the place she would learn most about the Legion. She is a most capable girl, works as Secretary to one of the most wealthy and influential persons in Hong Kong and manages all things suavely. Give her all the welcome you can and all the information too.

Again there is a Mrs. Wilson going to Ireland and she too wishes to see the Legion H.Q. and meet you all. She is the President of the first Slavonic Rite Praesidium in Shanghai and is now President of the parish Praesidium here. When she looks you up, do what you can for her. She was in Dublin lately for a few days and went to Dalgan Park and met my brother.

Today Mother Duff, formerly of the Sacred Heart Convent Leeson Street showed me letters of yours and Frank's written in 1934; some were to Mother Connolly. You will remember them I am sure. At that interchange of letters, the Legion was turned down. Popular as the Legion is here in this place, we are getting plenty of backbiting lately. The local Chinese clergy are going to some lengths, but it is not worrying us. That seems to be the history of the Legion.

Don't forget Cecily Hallack's book. The first edition is finished here in China and we are waiting for the newest edition in bringing it up to date. I must cease!

With all best regards.

Aedan

P.S. From now on, could you please send my letters direct to St. Columbans, number 287 Wu Yuen Road, Shanghai.

Dublin

15th November 1950

Dear Fr. Aedan,

Your very welcome letter of November 3rd has just reached me and I am delighted to know that recent letters arrived safely.

Will it be possible for your Senatus to keep in touch with us? I am hoping that the other two Councils will also be able to send along a copy of their Minutes regularly, so that we may be able to follow the progress and perhaps offer assistance.

I trust that the new arrangement will result in every Centre in China being linked up with one or other of the Senatus. This is very important to ensure that three will be no isolation or unattached Centres. On the question of the Junior Curia: where there is but one such Body, it could be directly related to the Senatus?

We shall be delighted to see Mary Cheung and already I have told her that we shall accommodate her in Sancta Maria.

I am glad that you advised Van Coillie against mixing up the age groups. Apart from cutting across important rules, it could cause endless confusion. I hope that he will act on your advice. It is vitally important that the division between Senior and Junior be retained.

Concerning the trouble emanating from the 'locals', what exactly is the reason for this? I presume that they have a full share in the work and do not regard the Legion as an imported article. It is necessary that this should not be so and I feel sure that there is no real reason why the 'locals' should be antagonistic. However, I suppose it is one of those passing problems, which keep cropping up now and again. I do hope it will not remain a permanent problem.

I suppose you know that Agnes Orlebar is now in Japan and is making good progress there. Of course there are many real difficulties and strange to say, some of these also come from 'the locals'.

With every good wish,

John Nagle

287 Wu Yuen Road,

Shanghai

13th December 1950

My dear John,

Sorry to delay so long in answering your letter of November 15th. I have been very busy and just now have finished giving a Retreat to a school. It is

162

always a good chance to get the Legion across and to give myself a spiritual uplift. Many thanks for all your careful answers to my questions. I was glad indeed to see that Mrs. Wilson had been with you all and wants to visit again. Not long after the arrival of this letter, Mary Cheung also should be with you in Dublin. She sent me a card from Bangkok.

Let me wish you, Frank and all in the Hostels a very happy Christmas. May the Child and His Mother continue to shower blessings on your work. I shall be thinking of you all in that Mass on Christmas morning. I am sure that you will not forget us.

I am sending the headings of the Peking Handbook synopsis; it is the table of contents and I hope that it will give you an idea. As you see, it is formidable. There has been a demand for such a synopsis on account of the difficulty of reading the full Handbook. Seeing that the Legion is mostly amongst the less educated persons in the country, it is hard to expect that the new members understand what is read.

We have now held two Senatus meetings. At the second one, Officers of the other three Curiae attended, though for a couple of members it was rather a torture, not understanding the language. I think we might excuse them the next time. Brother Allen and the new Secretary in Ted's place, Sr. Dolly Gutteres are both able to understand what is going on. For the moment the President is not writing to you. Everything went well at the meeting and the English-speaking Curiae generously handed over all their funds of three years to the new Council: it amounted to about US$150. It was needed for printing. The Senatus was very grateful. A fine report was read by the Praesidium assigned and then each Curia made a short report on its work and financial status. At all the Curiae lately, the discussion subject was on the fourth rule, confidentiality. It was necessary from many points. There had often been untimely remarks made about the Sodality, words which did no good and created bad feeling.

We are still able to contact most of the Senatus Councils. I had reports and letters from Chengtu today and the Legion is doing very well. We have lifted them up to Comitium level so that they can deal with their neighbouring Curiae. Fr. Audren keeps things well in line. I often hear from Fr. O'Meara SJ and he asked lately if he should affiliate with us and send us the reports. We replied that it would be a good idea, for his sake and ours. We often hear from Kaifeng and the Legion is doing well there too. The fact is that there are so many people interested makes it hard to keep up correspondence. Fr. McCabe wrote to me lately after he had begun a Curia, and they have Praesidia in Liuchow near Kweilin.

The Legion Hymn, *Totus Tuus*, which I got from the *Maria Legionis* when in Hong Kong and which we printed, has taken on strikingly in Shanghai. All the Legionaries, both Chinese and English-speaking love it. The Hymn is magnificent at big gatherings; we have the Chinese words there too, to go with the melody.

I had a letter from Van Coillie and all is settled about the school problem. They have followed the right course, forming a Senior Curia and attaching to it the Junior Praesidium.

I have written to Teresa Su telling her to come here as soon as possible. I hope that she gets moving. By the way, when she does come up here, who has the authority to tell her what to do? I know that it is the Concilium of course, but have I any authority to advise her? I would like to have things clear. Please give me a couple of lines on this delicate subject. And how does she stand with the Senatus? Fr. Joe and I had small differences. He is inclined to make decisions on his own and I would like them to go to the Senatus to test them if for nothing else. I hope there will be no difficulties.

Our Reunion and other functions have been carried out well and all enjoyed them. Each Curia held its own so that they might have a chance of knowing their own members.

The Concilium minutes are arriving still through Chungking - please advise that they be sent direct. All came safely.

The *True Devotion* and Frank's *De Montfort Way* too are translated and should be printed soon.

Deepest sympathy on the death of Fr. Creedon; he certainly had a special hand in the pushing of the Legion in those difficult first days. R.I.P.

This letter must go now, if at all; forgive scrappiness.

Happy Christmas,

Aedan

287 Wu Yuen Road,
Shanghai
29th December 1950

Dear John,

...Fr. Sheng is now looking after the Lay Apostolate here and has resigned from the Senatus and other connected work. He intends to help the Legion through his review. It is a funny situation and there was a little "feeling"; but Anthony has decided so. I have been very upset for a couple of weeks, but nothing can be done. I am going to get the Senatus people to do more, as they ought. Fr. Joe was doing a lot, but I always thought they should have been helping.

Msgr. Gabriel Quint is still burning with zeal for Our Lady's work. He loves the *Maria Legionis*; but he suggested to me, to pass on to you, that there should be more about facts, methods and difficulties and less about scenery...

May Our Lady protect you all,

Aedan

CHAPTER TWENTY FIVE

COMMUNICATION GRINDS TO A HALT

SHANGHAI - FEBRUARY TO JUNE 1951

The heavens proclaim His justice,
and all peoples see His glory. (Psalm 96:6)

287 Wu Yuen Road,
Shanghai
14th February 1951

Dear John,
Your letter of January 15th came safely.[47] Many thanks for all the good news, including that of Mary Cheung's arrival. After her return I had a letter from her and she gave me a wonderful description of her visit to the Holy Father and then Dublin where she visited my mother. She was delighted with with the kindness shown to her. Yes, she is a great personage and will become even better with knowledge of the Legion. Many thanks for being so good to her and for putting her up in Sancta Maria. Please convey my special thanks to the indoor Sisters there for their kindness.

I have delayed in answering your letters, as I have not been well for a few days and besides, the many inconveniences continue. Everything here must be registered and you have no idea how troublesome it all is. The Sodality also has to be listed and the procedure is a bit of a nuisance. Don't expect much by way of letters as we are all busy and tired from the extra work load.

Teresa Su came along at the end of the month and is well. She is resting up after the shock of her father's death. We are all delighted to see her and are favourably impressed. She has strong faith. She is not in the least upset by the terrible weather we are enduring.

The S.D. of the Senatus is Msgr. Prevost. I am already the S.D. of the English-speaking Body and also the Chinese-speaking Junior Curia. We have not got under way yet. The situation is more difficult than you might realise.

---

[47] Not on file.

The Concilium Minutes arrived safely and I see that you are again Secretary. Congratulations, though I don't envy you the work. We sent up the new translation of the Handbook to Peking and asked their opinion, but no reply has come as yet.

Aedan

Dublin
1st March 1951

Dear Fr. Aedan,

I am sorry to learn that you have not been well recently and also had a number of worries. I am not surprised at this, but I do hope that the inconveniences will not tend to increase and that before long you will be feeling your old self again. I have not heard at all recently from any of our mutual friends, but I understand that the bad weather and severe illness of so many people are not conducive to letter writing.

You will be sorry to know that Frank has experienced another death in his family, the fourth in a short time. I refer to the recent death of his sister Ailis, who was residing at Navan with his married sister, Dr. Monahan. Now this latter is the only member of the family left. I know that you will remember the deceased in your prayers.

Some time ago I wrote to Anthony's boss to let him know how we are getting along. I have just received a fine reply: The letter is signed by the boss and his secretary. The boss says that he and his crowd are delighted with the progress made. He has noted the solid training that the staff received, enabling them to work hard and secure such notable results in spite of the problems and worries. Tell Anthony that I put in a good word for him with the boss! Also tell him that Peter and Celso were asking for him.

You are always remembered by the family, all of whom join with me in warmest greetings and regards.

John Nagle.

Shanghai
13th March 1951

Dear Frank,

I was so glad to receive John's letter and many thanks for his replies, always so prompt and to the point...

167

I was so glad to hear the Holy Father was pleased with the progress made here and had such an interest. Yes, Van Coillie will be happy to receive word from him. We had a letter from Van lately and he mentioned that at the last Senatus meeting one hundred and fourteen were present, representing ten Dioceses, some having travelled for six days, others two days and nights to attend. It is much easier in his place than here, which is a good sign. Our little Sister[48] is helping to a great degree and is very happy. All find her gentle and tactful.

The February Concilium report came to me; thanks, also my *Maria Legionis* arrived. So pleased to receive them and looking forward to Msgr. Suenens' book on Edel Quinn.

Van Coillie wrote the other day saying that they had studied the manuscript of the new Handbook translation and were pleased with it. We can go ahead and print it soon. He was so pleased, that he decided to drop the Synopsis for the present. If he has to print that book again, he will make it more of a help for Officers.

Aedan

Dublin
18th June 1951

Dear John,

I had a letter from home; my mother though so old is still in fine health *Deo Gratias*. Ronan is busy and glad to be so. I am wondering how my nephew and niece in Dublin did in their examinations?

...I know how very busy you are and I do not expect you to write to me. I just want you to know that I am well; *Deo Gratias*.

Aedan

Dublin
26th June 1951

Dear Fr. Aedan,

Just a short note to say how relieved we are to know that you are well. We have been thinking of you and praying for your safety very much in recent times, and wondering how you are faring. I don't know whether you received my recent letters, but I was always in a dilemma as to whether to write to you and as to what to say. I think in a letter to Frank, you thought I was ultra-cautious, but

---

[48] Teresa Su.

I believe that I followed the wisest policy. I found it hard to understand the situation, because on the one hand we were warned of the danger of writing and of mentioning the Legion, and on the other hand you said it was alright to forward the Legion journals and Concilium report. However, it is great news to know that you survived the very trying and dangerous experiences of recent months. Warmest congratulations on your courageous and zealous work for the Legion through all the difficult and testing time in China. The Legion has a grateful heart and will not easily forget your wonderful services as a builder of the Legion throughout the vast country. I do hope that this wonderful work will continue, as also your Providential Mission of extending the Legion.

I trust that you are none the worse for your very trying experiences. Teresa Su has written to me at great length about conditions in China and the cruel and ruthless persecution with which the Legion is faced. It all makes very sad and sorrowful reading, but of course there is a Divine Plan behind it all. Our thoughts and our prayers are very much with the heroic Spiritual Directors and Legionaries whose record of sterling service will guarantee the final triumph of the Legion. And all this is in no small measure due to your own self-sacrificing and courageous building-up of Legion spirit and outlook throughout the years. Our consolation now is Our Lady's maternal protection and inspiration: we can trust Her to fortify the Church and the Legion in China in these dark and depressing days...

Fr. Ivar wrote to me from Formosa (Taiwan). At the request of the Bishop he has established three Praesidia and a Curia with the help of a former Chinese Legionary.[49] I replied to him at great length and more recently I have written to the Chinese Legionary, but so far, no reply. Fr. Ivar was anxious to have the Curia affiliated here in Dublin because of the difficult situation in Formosa. I wonder would it not be more practical to have the Curia affiliated to Hong Kong for the time being? ...

We eagerly look forward to hearing from you when you have time to write. I suppose that the poor Internuncio (Riberi) will be "expelled" shortly. Certainly the Legion owes His Excellency a very great debt of gratitude. Did you ever receive the copy of Bishop Suenens' book, which I sent to you in Shanghai quite some time ago? Or has some "Red" censor grabbed it for spiritual reading?

John Nagle

---

[49] The Legionary referred to is Christa Shih who was instrumental in setting up 40 Praesidia in Formosa with Fr. Ivar.

170

PART FIVE

THE NOOSE TIGHTENS

1951 - 1954

Sept 9th 1951 - Chinese Communist troops occupy Lhasa.

Oct 25th 1952 - New York: China application of entry to
the U.N. refused for the third consecutive year.

Feb 23rd 1953 - Taipei: Chiang Kai-shek repudiates 1945 alliance
between Nationalist China and the U.S.S.R.

Mar 15th 1953 - Tito's visit to Great Britain - the first by a
Communist Head of State.

Feb 1st 1954 - Washington DC: Senator Joe McCarthy's
anti-Communist Committee begins investigation of U.S. army
personnel.

CHAPTER TWENTY SIX

LATEST REPORTS FROM
THE CHINA MISSIONARY NEWSLETTER

Brethren, do not speak against one another. He who speaks against a brother,
or judges his brother, speaks against the law and judges the law. (James 4:11)

Correspondence from Ireland ceased. While Fr. McGrath, under increasing duress, continued his efforts to consolidate the Legion from Shanghai, the following startling extracts appeared in the China Missionary Newsletter, No. 28, June 30ᵗʰ 1951. This Catholic periodical was published by the China Missionary Bulletin Editorial Board in Hong Kong and sought to highlight the false Communist Propaganda against the Catholic Church and specifically against the Legion of Mary.

(A) LEGION DIRECTOR IN TIENTSIN JAILED

Rev. Fr. Henri Hermans, Dutch Missionary of the Congregation of Missions, a Vincentian priest, has been arrested in Tientsin for participation in the Legion of Mary. This was announced by the Communist New China News Agency on June 24ᵗʰ, 1951. According to the Communist Press, Fr. Hermans and three Chinese lay Catholics wrote "threatening letters" to the leaders of the Government's movement for "self-Government, self-support and propaganda".

The report stated that they had threatened the life of Wu Ko-chai, who immediately denounced them to the police. Wu Ko-chai is one of three former Catholics who strongly favoured and promoted the "reform" movement in Tientsin.

Although Communist newspapers had falsely announced the signing of a "manifesto for an independent Church" by more than ten thousand Catholics of Tientsin, opposition among the faithful remains resolute.

The Communist *The People's Daily* editorial of the same day said Fr. Hermans and the three laymen would be punished according to the "Regulations for punishing counter-revolutionaries," under which the guilty are liable to execution. It also offered amnesty to all Catholics who resigned from the Legion of Mary, and who accuse and disclose the names of the "imperialists and counter-revolutionaries who hide behind the Legion". The Communist editorial went on:

"The Tientsin Legion of Mary is a reactionary organisation under the direction of Bishop de Vienne, who has already been expelled. The Tientsin People's Security Police Bureau has arrested the organisation's anti-revolutionary elements, and will punish them according to the 'Regulations'. As for the reactionary group in the organisation, they must immediately register with the Government, render up their reactionary movement and paraphernalia, confess all the organisations reactionary activities and thus the People's Government may judge them leniently; if they obstinately adhere to their errors and continue their reactionary activities, then they must inevitably be destroyed by themselves…After they have announced their resignation from this reactionary organisation, the People's Government will regard them in the same manner as other Catholics and protect the freedom of religion from aggression. We trust that these Catholics who have joined the Legion of Mary will hurriedly acknowledge their error and decide to cease all their evil deeds, break off all relations with the imperialists and on the ground of patriotism, fight for the practical realisation of the Catholic reform for independence. All patriotic Catholics, arise in unity to disclose the new plot of the imperialists, raise the standard of political consciousness, determine to oppose the imperialists Riberi, de Vienne, Hermans and the like etc. …"

Typical Communist Propaganda cartoons
The Bishop is depicted as concealing United States espionage behind a Legion façade

(B) CHANGE OF TACTICS SEEN IN THE NEW COMMUNIST CHARGES AGAINST INTERNUNCIO IN CHINA

Accusations in Communist newspapers against Archbishop Antony Riberi, indicate a new line of attack against the Prelate. The latest and by far the most absurd allegations indicate the frustrations of Communist propagandists to excite the Chinese people against the Papal Legate.

The Liberation Daily, Communist Party paper of Shanghai had headlined on June 20th, its latest propaganda: "Blessed Mother Orphanage in Wuhu under the direction of Riberi, has killed a large number of Chinese infants," and concludes by saying that various groups in Wuhu, "unanimously petitioned the People's Government to deal sternly with Riberi."

The Communist technique in accusing Catholic orphanages of "killing babies" and imprisoning the personnel of these institutions is now months old. Two Nanking Franciscan Missionaries of Mary were sentenced to ten years imprisonment on these charges, while many other priests and Sisters, including Bishop Rombert Kowalski of Wuchang and the five Canadian Immaculate Conception Sisters of Canton, are still in jail awaiting formal "judgement".

Previous accusations against Archbishop Riberi were made on the grounds either that he was a diplomatic representative to a now defunct Government (the Kuomintang), or that his warnings of the schismatic nature of the Government programme for an "independent Church" constituted "meddling in the internal affairs of China." On the basis of these contentions, the newspapers reported, the people are "petitioning the Government for Riberi's expulsion." *The Liberation Daily* might be interpreted as asking for the punishment of the Papal representative instead of mere expulsion.

Attempting to place the affairs of the Wuhu Orphanage on the Apostolic Internuncio reveals the complete absurdity of Communist propaganda. The vicious campaign to vilify Catholic priests and Sisters through this propaganda has proven effective in the Communists war against religion.

The Orphanage of the Blessed Mother in Wuhu was established in 1940 by the Mercederian Sisters from Spain. Two Nuns, who according to the Communist propaganda share the responsibility, are identified as Sr. Mercedes Isasi and Sr. Teresa Elorduy. There are fifteen Sisters of the same Order in Wuhu, who also conduct a large Middle Secondary school for girls besides the Orphanage. The latter institution was originally very small prior to last year.

When the Protestant Missionaries evacuated the area during the war, they requested the Nuns to look after their orphans also. Substantial material aid was also turned over to the Nuns at the same time. About fifty orphans are cared for in Wuhu Orphanage.

More than ten Orphanages so far have been targets of such Communist attacks. The facts in each case are identical, namely that these Reception Centres for unwanted infants received the babies in such weakened condition due to neglect, disease, or exposure, that it was impossible in many cases to sustain life in their tiny frames.

Fr. Robert Kennelly, fifty-one year old 'Maryknoller' priest from Connecticut was arrested on March 17th and accused of killing thousands of babies since the Loting Orphanage began in 1919. A month later, Sr. Colombiere Bradley from Brooklyn, New York was imprisoned. During the following week the remaining foreign personnel of the orphanage, Fr. John Graser of Syracuse New York, Sr. Monica Mario Boyel of Minersville Pennsylvania and Sr. Candida Marie Basto (Portuguese) of Hong Kong, were also detained.

While in prison, the priests and Sisters were subjected to many interrogations and were obliged to undergo the course of indoctrination given to all prisoners. They were not physically maltreated, although they were obliged to live on prison fare. The food ration was gradually reduced, probably reflecting the general shortage in the area, until at the end of their imprisonment they received a mere eight ounces of rice twice per day, prepared in a gruel. A few green vegetables were divided amongst the prisoners. Meat was never served.

It appeared that the authorities were unable to make out a case against the priests and Sisters solely on the charges of baby-killings. The good reputation of the orphanages was locally well known during the years and the people were not influenced by the Communist propaganda. When the Communists took over South China, the priests had reported the conditions in which the abandoned babies were received and the impossibility of sustaining life in some of those unwanted day-old tots. The authorities told the orphanage to continue its regular operations. Other charges were brought against the religious, and their expulsion from China, they were told, was for using religion to cover their reactionary teachings, killing orphaned babies and concealing weapons and foreign currency.

The priests and Sisters left Loting handcuffed, but their manacles were removed after a day's journey. The remainder of their journey under guard to the border was uneventful. They were not molested and experienced no especially harsh treatment. All had lost a considerable amount of weight due to their frugal diet, but were otherwise in good health.

176

Observers are apprehensive of the eventual effect of Communist propaganda against religion and the Catholic Church on the simple but good country Christians, especially where recent converts are in the majority. The people are being subjected to unremitting pressure on patriotic grounds to break all relations with the "imperialists"(foreign missionaries) in the Church. Add to the pressure, a campaign of lies, malice and deceit in the promotion of the "independent Church" and the apprehension of missionaries becomes alarmingly realistic.

A vivid story of Communist terror exercised over native Christians in China was revealed by Fr. Justin Garvey, a New-Jersey-born American missionary in China. The campaign to turn Catholics against their priests, both foreign and native, is carried on mainly through the Red-devised "Reform Church" movement, which is being imposed upon all Catholic communities under penalty of denunciation as reactionaries, a "crime" punishable by death under the Red Regime.

The faithful are forced to attend compulsory indoctrination courses that are being conducted specifically for Christians. Under the direction of Communist agents, the Catholics are being manoeuvred at these meetings into such a position as to make it appear that they themselves are "demanding" the destruction of the Church.

In a story that is typical throughout China today, Fr. Garvey explained the methods, which the Communists employ to terrorise the Christians. "Some weeks ago all the Christians here were forced to take indoctrination courses; one was held at the Mission, two others at different places in town. Each meeting had its comrade-in-arms, appointed by the authorities. His job was to whip the people to a frenzy, to show our Christians the 'error' of their ways and lead them along the path of 'enlightenment'. "The early meetings followed the usual Communist programme of learning songs, listening to prepared speeches," the priest said. "At first, the course stressed the single theme of patriotism. Imperceptibly almost, the question of religion was introduced. Emphasis slowly turned to the 'independent Church' and attacks were made against the 'imperialistic Church', used by China's confirmed and age-long enemies, it was claimed, to carry on aggression against their Fatherland. Before the people realised it, they were face to face with the question of schism. It had already been made lucidly clear that any deviation from the path marked out by the Government's wishes would stigmatise one as a reactionary, a traitor to the country, a candidate for the black list.

The indoctrination meetings go on every night. Forced to sit in nearby rooms awaiting our turn, we hear the racket. Though we cannot make out what is being said, yet from the animated shouts and cheers we know that the class is kept at high pitch. In each session a certain number of Christians are picked to stand up and say something against the foreign priests. No one may refuse; each must offer his own personal morsel; to fail in this is to be cursed and branded a reactionary. While all this is going on, the Comrade periodically calls out pre-arranged slogans and the foreigners are roundly cursed. One phase of the course has just ended. Each Christian was obliged to put in writing his opinion of the course, what he learned and what his views of the missionary priests were. A committee was appointed to receive these essays, to ascertain if everyone's mind had been properly 'washed'. For those who could not write, secretaries were assigned to take their dictation. When it was all finished, a summary of 'the people's will' appeared in the local Newspaper."

Commenting on how these methods were applied in his Mission Hospital, the priest said: "The authorities appointed three agents to conduct the indoctrination for all employed at the Hospital, doctors, nurses, workers and even patients. The Leader was in effect the Superintendent at the Hospital. After several public talks he made it known that he wanted to see the fifty-odd personnel individually, that they were not obliged to seek him out, but failing to do so would 'not be so nice'. Thus all, from the head doctor to the lowest employee, 'freely' went to his private interview. The next Sunday many failed to appear for Mass. When I sought out the leader and asked him why they were not permitted to come to Church, since the Government guaranteed freedom of religion, I received only a bland smile and the answer: "The people are all free to practice their religion if they want to, but there is no one in the Hospital who cares to practice." I couldn't swallow that as I knew the Christians too well. What I couldn't tell him was that I was aware he had threatened those who came to Church, because such an action on my part would be taken as a denial of the revolutionary principles he had taught them."

Speaking of the constant searches and examinations the foreign missionaries are subjected to, Fr. Garvey said: "Last week, forty soldiers armed with picks, shovels and axes entered the Mission. They did a day's work digging all over the place to find radios, guns and gold. They tore down sections of the house and must have been frantic when they found nothing. Just as the search was ending, one of them happened on an old brick stove in a building used as a Catechumenate. He and his buddies tore down this stove and the brick chimney attached. It was then one of the Sisters remembered that some Aspirin and

Bicarbonate of Soda had been hidden there during a bandit raid two years ago; when the searchers found these, there was instant jubilation: at last the foreigners had been caught red-handed at their bare-faced tricks! Word was sent to headquarters and a photographer was rushed to the Mission. The medicines and the Sister were photographed. The medicines were confiscated and the priests and Sisters roundly berated for their crimes. Then the search party left."

"Under such circumstances," the missionary said, "the position of the Chinese priests is extremely difficult. One of them was taken from the Mission six months ago and nothing has been heard of him since. Fr. Raphael and Fr. Bede are continually risking their necks to instruct the Catholics. Fr. Raphael, the older of the two, has not yet been granted permission to live here. He can make only occasional visits. Thus the burden fell on Fr. Bede, a job that is sometimes beyond his years and experience, as he was ordained only seven months ago. He is doing nobly, absorbing much bitterness on behalf of the Church; but his experienced, crafty opponents often get the upper hand by sheer trickery. Responsibility for the whole Diocese has in fact fallen on his shoulders.

"The Communist propaganda machine is a marvel of efficiency: when the Reds decide to do a job on someone, it's thoroughly done", Fr. Garvey concluded.

Further pictorial Communist propaganda.

The Legion of Mary emblazoned flag flies over the Prelate who is depicted as broadcasting his 'reactionary literature', 'secret reports' and 'anonymous letters'

(C) FATHER BONIFACE WRITES

On July 25th the Legion of Mary was outlawed in Tientsin, and the Shanghai Municipal Security Police issued a like order on October 11th. Similar actions were carried out, the Communist Press announced, in Nanking and Shih Chia Chuang.

The "outlawing" of the Legion in Shanghai was accompanied by an enormous amount of newspaper publicity. The October 6th issue of the Liberation Daily, a four-page Shanghai, Communist Party Publication, printed 260 inches on the Legion and the October 9th edition had 307 inches, or fully one-fourth, of the entire paper. Exclusive of pictures, the Liberation Daily devoted 1,645 inches to the Legion of Mary, during the month of October.

CHAPTER TWENTY SEVEN

'PUBLIC ENEMY NUMBER ONE'

JULY/AUGUST 1951

Now we know that for those who love God all things work together unto good,
for those who, according to His purpose, are saints through His call. (Romans 8:28)

Newspaper extract from a July edition of *The Catholic Herald*

CHINA REDS CLOSE DOWN LEGION

All meetings of the Legion of Mary have been forbidden by the Security Police in Tientsin, China. The order was issued because, it was alleged, the resistance of Catholics to the Government's "Independent Church Movement" sprung from the influence this group exercised over the Catholic population.

Following a vain attempt to prove allegations of spying against the Legion, the authorities finally proscribed its activities on the grounds that it was the source of Catholic resistance to the "Chinese Patriotic Independent Church Movement."

The Legion was charged with being "reactionary" at several "accusation meetings" convened by the city authorities. The accusations were sustained, but the "reasoning" at these mass meetings followed the line that "foreign priests were influential in organising the various groups of Legionaries, and since foreigners were imperialists, the Legion was therefore a tool of imperialism."

In Tientsin alone there are fifty-eight Praesidia. In North China there are at least five hundred Praesidia. The main efforts of the Legion of Mary have been directed to convert-making and to bringing lapsed Catholics back to the practice of the faith. After its establishment, the annual number of converts in some areas more than trebled over previous efforts. The Legion has been established in ninety Dioceses.

Dear Mr. Nagle,

I presume that the enclosed letter from my brother Aedan is for you. As you can see, the matter in the beginning of the letter is just padding for the sake of security. My letter was dated June 21st, so it seems he is still in Shanghai in spite of the news of his expulsion. In a letter to me, he says: 'You may have heard that our business had to close and that I may be in a predicament. When you are going around the beads, keep us in mind.'

The reference to you is: 'I enclose a letter for cousin John of Brunswick Street. I owe him a letter for a long time.'

If the Communists decide to make a case against Msgr. Riberi, it is very likely that Aedan will be involved. In that instance, he may need all our prayers.

Every good wish,

Fr. Ronan McGrath

Navan
20th August 1951

Dear Mr.Nagle,

Fr. Carty who used to work in our Shanghai house wrote to me from Hong Kong on August 10th. You may have got his news direct, but to be on the safe side I am quoting from his letter:

"You have probably heard that the Legion has stopped functioning in Shanghai and in nearly all other places. In Peking it was formally condemned and also in Tientsin, but in Shanghai it didn't happen that way. All along, things happened in Peking and Tientsin before they happened in Shanghai and we more or less took our cue from them in these matters. In Shanghai the condemnation appeared in an article written in the daily newspapers. It condemned the Legion as a spy ring of Riberi, and in turn it condemned Riberi as an imperialist working for the Americans. It said that the 'Legion of St. Mary', as they called it, must stop its work immediately and that those responsible must be duly punished. It gave what they considered the origin of the Legion in which Frank Duff and Aedan got honourable mention. Aedan's history was given, all upside down, of course. He was accused of working for the Japanese when they were in occupation. When the Japanese were defeated, he had to leave China because he could find no one to take his part. Then he went home to Ireland and was sent back by the imperialist agent, Frank Duff to organise this spy ring in China. He travelled through America to get more instructions from the American imperialists. They gave his travels through China, all wrong again, and they ended by calling him "the Cat's Paw of arch-imperialist Riberi."

Aedan and those in charge of the Legion got worried over this propaganda, because they were afraid for the safety of Chinese Legionaries. In the schools, the Chinese girls and boys suffered because of their activities as Legionaries. A few of them were arrested and the parents of those children were forbidding them to attend the Legion meetings. Many of their parents hold no set beliefs. After a lot of discussion it was decided to stop the meetings, but where possible to continue working as circumstances allowed. Quite an amount of work is still being done. The Communists never made any comment on the fact that the Legion had ceased, but continue day after day to tear it to pieces in the newspapers. Many of the articles are written by the head of the Aurora College for men, a Catholic, who publicly apostatised. He was excommunicated by the Bishop but, strange to say, he continues to go to Mass and has even tried to receive Holy Communion. It seems that he has got more from the Communists than he bargained for, and they are just using him and forcing him to write these articles. I think that one of the articles was sent out and you may have seen the translation.

Msgr. Riberi was singled out in their newspaper articles. All kinds of accusations were made against him and he even appeared in cartoons as a gramophone which was being wound by America; and his song was 'Our Church is above politics.' The Communists quoted from a letter he had written to the Chinese Bishops, or rather I should say, they misquoted. An example of their method is this: they said that Riberi wrote a letter to the Hierarchy of China and they added as an explanation of Hierarchy: "In other words, the imperialists in China". In the same way, they took up the Legion Handbook and misquoted it. A typical example of their method is: they took the three characters which mean 'against the devil' out of context and explained: "By this they mean that the Chinese people are Devils." Almost every day there is an article in the paper demanding the expulsion and punishment of Riberi and of those who are working for him.

Some six weeks ago the Catholic Bureau was closed. The Communists came and took away all the files, sealed some of the offices and ordered all activities to cease. They rounded up all the priests there into one room and told them that they were to go to their respective homes and stay there until they were told what to do. Since then nothing has happened, except that segments of the matter they found in the files have appeared in the newspapers and needless to say, have been twisted to suit their propaganda.

Aedan is still in Rue Maresca and free to move about as he pleases, but we know that he is being watched all the time. In this regard, operators of the pedicabs at the gate and also the watchmen are in the pay of the Reds.

An interesting but tragic story is that the Legion numbered in its ranks an Austrian who was paid by the Communists. He once worked in the Austrian Embassy in Nanking. This man, who had spent one year in a Buddhist monastery in the Interior of China, spoke thirteen languages, including Latin and was perhaps the most learned Chinese scholar in the country. Baptised by a Jesuit in Shanghai, he was recommended by Msgr. Riberi, whom he got to know in Nanking. Riberi insisted that he should be accepted as a member of the Legion and he became a member of Luke Lynch's Praesidium in Rue Maresca. The Austrian then joined every Confraternity and Sodality, and came to Mass almost daily. As a Legionary, he brought forward lots of people for baptism and wanted them baptised after a short course of instruction, giving as excuse that they were going away or something similar. His wife told someone that he was a Communist spy and that he had obtained Riberi's letters with a view to translating them into Chinese. Further details of his personal life became known some time after he was admitted into the Legion. Rumours began to go around and everyone got suspicious of him. It later emerged that the Austrian had been married four times. His last wife, a Chinese Catholic girl, eventually escaped from him to Hong Kong. Aedan and Luke were concerned, but after talking it over decided that if the Communists wanted to know anything about the Legion, they could do so without the Austrian's help; and in any case there was nothing to hide.

The week before I left, eight foreign priests were arrested in Peking. Among them were Frs. Rigney of the Fujen University, Cavanagh the Irish Vincentian and Van Coillie, the Belgian who was running the Legion there. We did not get any other names. There were about six Chinese priests arrested. We do not know on what charges they were arrested, but it is thought that the arrests were on account of their Legion work.

The big news was the story of the Chinese priest from Shanghai who was sent to Chungking by Riberi. In Chungking it seems that the Chinese priests led by their Vicar General had given in to all the demands of the Communists, including the signing of a document demanding the expulsion of Riberi. This visiting priest, Fr. Yung came to Chungking just at the time of a meeting and demonstration in which all Chinese priests and people were to take part. During the meeting he made a speech in which he told the Communists that they could have his body if they wanted it, but he had something to say to them first. He began to tell them that just as they had certain principles to follow, so had he, and that just as they had no use for people who were prepared to take whatever side suited them best, so he too...and so on. The Catholics cheered so loudly that the meeting had to be called off. On the following Sunday the Vicar General and the other priests publicly apologised to the people for the example they had given, and declared that now they were determined to hold out no matter what happened. Fr. Yung was arrested and the latest news is that he was beaten to death, but this is not certain. His speech has been printed and most Catholics have a copy of it. I will try to get a copy myself."

Fr. Carty says that Aedan has not been well: the heat, I think. He presumes that Aedan will be imprisoned before he is expelled. In a recent guarded letter, Aedan said that the last two 'Blesseds' in the 5th Chapter of St. Matthew were a great consolation to him.

Yours very sincerely,

Ronan McGrath

Dublin

21st August 1951

Rev. and dear Fr. Ronan,

Recently we received via Hong Kong extracts from the Shanghai Communist newspapers, which contain a good deal of the vilification of the Legion and those connected with it in China. The Communists have made the Legion 'Public Enemy Number One' and I have just learned that the Legion in Peking has endured a very bad time.[50]

I am delighted to know that Fr. Aedan is apparently not in prison. I was under the impression that he had been locked up and we were greatly worried as to his fate. I do hope that he will be expelled in the near future. I wonder what is the idea of permitting him and the other Missionaries to remain in the country? I thought that perhaps the Reds had in mind one of these infamous trials of the Inter-Nuncio, and that they might be holding Fr. Aedan as one of the witnesses. This is unlikely because of the diplomatic status of Archbishop Riberi.

It is disturbing to find that there are so many spies planted everywhere, and I imagine that one of those mentioned in your letter was the gentleman who kept trailing Miss Teresa Su in Shanghai when she was endeavouring to do some Legion work under the supervision of Aedan. I think I told you that she had to clear out and go to Hong Kong on the explicit instructions of Archbishop Riberi and Aedan. However, this appears to have been Providential since she is now free to go to Indonesia to organise the Legion there at the request of the Internuncio.

Have you heard recently from Fr. Ivar in Formosa? You will remember his writing to me about the Legion some time ago and asking me to have the Legion there affiliated to the Concilium. I replied at once to him, and later I wrote to both him and the Chinese Legionary whom he had put in charge of the Legion, and who had valuable experience of the working of the system in China. However, I received no reply of any sort and I am wondering whether there is a difficulty in corresponding with us from Formosa? I presume it is best for me not to write again. I trust that soon you will have good news from Fr. Aedan.

I am very sincerely yours,   John Nagle

---

[50] "A Bishop driven out of China has told us that this invocation to Saint Michael which we repeat in the prayers after Mass, is expressly prohibited in Communist China. Similarly, the acts of naming the devil, or the Legion of Mary expose one to drastic penalties. *Fas est ab hoste doceri* - It is permissible to learn from our enemy - the devil could not more clearly reveal his presence and his hatred than by inspiring such sentences of outlawry. So we have the right to conclude that the Legion of Mary and Saint Michael are objects of fear to him." *Maria Legionis*, 1953, No.3, p.3.

186

Chapter Twenty Eight

The Hammer Falls

Shanghai - 7th September 1951

But we know that the Law is good, if a man uses it rightly, knowing that the Law
is not made for the just, but for the unjust and rebellious ... (Timothy 1:8)

E. S. K. Ho-Tung,
59, Pearl Street,
New York
12th September 1951

Dear Br. Nagle,

I read in the *New York Times* this morning that Fr. McGrath has been imprisoned since September 6th. The Hong Kong newsagents are usually reliable if they can give the full names of the victims, and the names of the organisations they are associated with. I enclose the news clipping for your interest, as I know you must be very anxious over news of Fr. McGrath.

I have contacted Miss Berryman here, and met some Legionaries at a Maryknoll Motherhouse, outdoor function in Ossining, New York; but I had no opportunity to attend any Legion meetings yet.

Greetings and good wishes to all at Concilium,

Yours sincerely,

Mary Cheung

FOUR PRIESTS SEIZED IN CHINA

Belgian and Irish Clerics Have Been Held in Shanghai.

The New York Times, 12th September 1951

Hong Kong: Two foreign and two Chinese priests attached to the Catholic Central Bureau in Shanghai, which formerly served as a coordinating agency for Roman Catholic missionary activities in China, were authoritatively reported today to have been jailed on September 6th in Shanghai.

The two foreign priests were Belgian, Fr. Francis Legrand, director of the Bureau's cultural department and Irish priest, Fr. Aedan McGrath, director of the Legion of Mary, an organisation for Catholic laity. One of the arrested Chinese priests was identified as an associate of former Archbishop Anthony Riberi, Papal Internuncio, who recently arrived here following his expulsion from Red China.

The Evening Herald, Dublin, 14th September 1951

Fr. McGrath, a Dublin man is a son of the late Mr. William McGrath K.C. and Mrs. McGrath. Fr. McGrath was educated at Belvedere College. He joined the Maynooth Mission to China in 1924 and was ordained in 1929 at Dalgan Park. He ministered in the Hanyang Diocese all through the Japanese war and when hostilities ceased returned to Ireland for a holiday in 1947. On his return to China he was commissioned by Archbishop Riberi to undertake Legion of Mary work, starting in the Diocese of Hanyang. Fr. Ronan McGrath, Director of Probationers, St. Columban's College Navan, is a brother of Fr. Aedan. Another brother is at present attached to the Hanyang Diocese.

Fr. Ronan McGrath told an "Evening Herald" representative today that Dr. Joseph Sheng, a Chinese priest and one of those detained, visited Ireland two years ago after his ordination in Rome. He spent two months in Dublin before leaving for China, where he joined the Catholic Central Bureau organised there by Archbishop Riberi.

Dublin
17th September 1951

Dear Sister Cheung,

Many thanks for your letter of September 13th. We had already heard the distressing news of the arrest of Fr. McGrath, but we are hoping that it is the preliminary move to his expulsion from China. Latterly, this appears to be the procedure followed in regard to non-Chinese priests: arrest and then formal expulsion from the country. I understand that Rev. Fr. Sheng has also been arrested. He had been a prominent Legionary Spiritual Director in Shanghai and closely connected with the Internuncio. I am afraid that arrest in his case is really serious since he is a Chinese priest and quite a number of them have been executed. We have asked the Legion everywhere to pray earnestly for the Chinese Spiritual Directors and Legionaries and for the welfare of the Church in China.

By now you are aware no doubt of the expulsion of the Internuncio. His Excellency declared in Hong Kong that the Legion would eventually save the faith in China if all the priests were expelled or immobilised. This is a wonderful tribute coming from the Internuncio.

I am delighted to know that you have made contact with the Legion in New York and I trust that you will have a further opportunity of attending some Legion meetings.

You will be interested to know that Teresa Su has now secured her Passport, and as soon as she gets the necessary Visa she will be setting out for Indonesia.[51] I do hope that Fr. McGrath will reach Hong Kong before she leaves for her destination.

It is now necessary to try to print the Chinese Handbook in Hong Kong because supplies in Shanghai are frozen. Unfortunately, nobody in Hong Kong has a copy of the revised edition printed recently in Shanghai by Fr. McGrath. This is a great drawback because it is unsatisfactory to have to print from the old edition. There does not seem to be any possibility now of getting a copy of the revised edition.

I am sincerely yours,

John Nagle

---

[51] Teresa Su transferred her Envoyship of the Legion of Mary to Indonesia. Over a period of years, she set up the Legion in many vicariates there. Fr. Aedan says elsewhere that, "the priests whom I have met, all agree 'that she is a wonderful little girl but that she is working herself to death. She is going day and night without ever a thought for herself.' Incidentally she is familiarly known as the Edel Quinn of China."

Fr. Aedan McGrath's Prison notes

In a Prison Cell - Shanghai

On the night of September 6th 1951 at 11.30pm, my fellow-Columbans and I were rudely awakened by a loud knocking on our door. Fr. MacElroy went down, opened the door and called up to me: "Aedan, the police are here!" Strange to say, I breathed a sigh of relief. The suspense and strain of waiting were over; the long-expected hour had come and the future was safe in God's hands.

The police rushed in, revolvers drawn. Producing a warrant for my arrest they requested Fr. MacElroy, my superior to sign it. On enquiring the purpose of my arrest, he was told: "It's just another case". Five or six detectives then entered my room; others were guarding Fr. Murphy, who had emerged from his bedroom; others still were rushing in and out of the various rooms. Outside, the road was awash with police guarding the approaches to the Columban Procuration, while many others surrounded the house and garden.

After some time they ordered us to sit down while they searched my room. Within a few minutes an Officer had discovered some letters for which I myself had been looking in vain for months. I was fortunate in being able to get a peep at some of the contents, for later during my frequent interrogations I could admit to having written them. Though containing nothing "treasonable", it was well to know the content. Next, they found many photographs of my own family, but no snaps of individual Legionaries; these I had already destroyed, lest the members of the Legion be implicated.

One of the detectives picked up my little long-wave radio, which was capable of receiving Shanghai broadcasts only. He placed it on the floor and was beginning to wrap it up, when prevented by another Officer, who shouted: "Leave that gadget alone. We will take a photograph of it in order to 'prove' that he used it to tap messages to America."

When finished their ransacking, they ordered Fr. MacElroy to get out. A policeman was detailed to guard him in another room with a revolver, not allowing him to budge. As I sat in my room, a man and young woman walked in holding some objects in their hands. After looking around, they stood directly behind me. Then I was led away from a table that stood in the middle of the room, so that I could not see everything that was going on. A short time later, I realised that the objects carried by the man and woman had been placed on the table, while other items such as photographs and paintings were pinned to the walls around me. After I was taken back to the table and made to stand in front of it, the young Communist woman took several photographs with a Leica camera from various angles. I was subsequently to discover that weeks later, pictures of my room were not only published in the newspapers, but displayed on buses, trams, walls, schools and church buildings. These photographs showed my table strewn with pornographic literature, knives and guns, while the walls were covered with photographs and paintings of nude females.

After the photographs were taken and the room tidied, Fr. MacElroy was told to come back in. I was then ordered to get ready for departure. I gathered up a few toiletries; then an Officer took possession of my toothbrush, paste and a little towel. Fr. MacElroy interrupted saying: "Father has been very ill recently; unless he takes a rug he will die of cold".

They accordingly gave permission for me to take extra belongings and Fr. MacElroy quickly wrapped up two rugs, a small one, a military rug and a few cardigans; these, he bundled into my arms. I knelt down and asked him for absolution. The Officers tried to interfere but Father ignored them. When finished he commented: "Well, keep your chin up; goodbye".

Two of the men then escorted me downstairs. Fr. MacElroy came with us. They ordered him back but he continued, saying: "In China it's the custom to see visitors to the door". One of the officers replied: "In this case, it's not necessary". Father accompanied us to the foot of the stairs and asked: "Where shall I enquire for Father Aedan?" The officer in charge responded: "In Zikawei Police Station". I was then pushed out the door and thrown into one of two cars parked outside.

We set off for Zikawei, but soon veered off in another direction. I ended up in Lokawei Police Station, which also doubled as a small prison. The time was now two o'clock in the morning of September 7th, two hours into the date of the thirtieth anniversary of the foundation of the Legion of Mary.

At the station I was ushered into a room with a concrete floor, pushed into a corner and left standing. A guard holding a Tommy-gun stood opposite me while two policemen took away my spectacles, Rosary Beads and medal-chain from my neck. But, in spite of their determination to deprive me of my sacramentals, they failed to see my scapular, which remained with me for the next three months, though I was subjected to a weekly strip search.

While standing in the corner I heard a policeman remark about my medals: "Ha, they all have these things", from which remark I surmised that other priests had been recently arrested. My guess was to prove correct.

Prior to my arrest I had been reading St. John Eudes' book *"The Hearts of Jesus and Mary"*. It was a good spiritual preparation for this ordeal and I felt

191

very close to the Saviour and His Mother. As I've stated before, I was convinced that the blue mantle of Mary was close around me. Had I not already given myself completely into her hands and what had I now to fear? After an hour of standing still in the corner of that room, a policeman came in, escorted me to a cell and threw me onto a mat on the floor. After I got up, he then ordered me to lie down. I did so, and with the foregoing spiritual thoughts of The Hearts of Jesus and Mary in my mind, fell peacefully asleep within five minutes.

At five in the morning I got a rude awakening in the form of a kick in the ribs from a guard. I was ordered to get up, roll up my blankets and sit on the straw-strewn floor, though it was not yet dawn. Apart from being allowed to use the toilet, there I sat for the next two days and nights, without exercise, or good food, listening for every sound and inhaling prison smells while staring at blank damp walls. This was merely a foretaste of things to come.

Constantly watched by an armed guard, I was not allowed to stand or lie down. Instead, I had to sit with my back against one of the walls. Having been deprived of sleep, I frequently nodded off during the day; but a shout or a kick from the guard, would sharply remind me that such comforts were prohibited in this place of detention.

In my sitting position, I found it difficult to eat the meagre portions of rice which I was proferred. When once I changed to a kneeling position the guard objected. I explained that I was uncomfortable while sitting, to which he replied: "This is not meant to be a comfortable place."

Towards the end of a trying and tedious third day, at nine o'clock, I was told to lie down and immediately fell asleep. Within a short time, I was awakened by a kick from one of the guards and ordered to dress. Escorted upstairs by two armed guards, I was ushered into a brightly lit room. Several judges sat around a table over which hung an illuminated picture of Mao Tse-tung. Though physically exhausted, I felt spiritually at ease in this situation. My trial under the Communist Regime had begun.

I was told to sit down, asked for my name and the reason for my arrest. "I presume," I said, "I have been arrested for spreading the Legion of Mary in China". One of the judges then asked: "What is the Legion of Mary?"

In reply, I was allowed to speak freely for the best part of an hour on my work of spreading the Legion of Mary. All this they knew already, so I was not telling them anything new. When I had finished, another of the judges accused me of having spoken nothing but false and empty words. "You are now being tried," he said, "and if you confess the crimes of the Legion of Mary, you will receive leniency. Otherwise, you will be punished." He spoke in this strain at great length and after a few hours in that interrogation room, I was brought downstairs to my cell.

As my tongue was parched, I asked for and was given a drink of water, after which I was allowed to sleep for a few hours. I was awakened at about five o'clock next morning and for sixteen hours I sat on the mat in my tiny cell. During the day, guards were changed every two hours. Many people, including some of my interrogators from the previous night, approached my cell, looking in the small window and jeering at me.

Next day at about noon, I was removed to cell number 12. Two native Chinese prisoners were already housed in this cubicle. One was to remain for only a short time. Removing my shoes, I sat beside them against the wall, facing the door where the guard watched through a pigeon-hole. Forbidden to cough, to speak, to laugh, to shut our eyes or even sneeze, all three of us sat in silence through the long day, without reading material, Rosary Beads or prayer books.

Each morning, all three of us were twice escorted by guards to a water tap in the yard: first to wash our faces and brush our teeth and then to wash our cups and chopsticks. It was good to get out into the fresh air, but the spells of relative freedom were short.

The prison had cells of different sizes. Number 12 cell was quite small, with two or three tiny windows high on the walls. The bars of the door were covered by boards. Thus, I could not recognise priests and other prisoners whom I could hear were constantly being led in for interrogation.

A total of about eighty prisoners used a single common toilet. Inmates were allowed four or five visits to this toilet during daylight hours. No such toilet facilities existed at night. Though we were permitted a drink of boiling water after each meal, we restricted our drinking as the inconvenience of getting permission for extra toilet visits was too great. On this account, prisoners suffered from dehydration. Requests for a toilet bucket to be placed in each cell were refused. Through insufficient intake of liquids, our tongues became swollen and we found it difficult to swallow food. This was one of many aspects of prison life that I had not bargained for. I began to trust more and more in the power of prayer, to give me strength in my captivity.

One night when I was in great pain, I begged the guard to allow me to go to the toilet, but he refused and it was only after half-an-hour's urging by the other two prisoners that he eventually consented. Suffering this inhuman treatment, many prisoners became sick. One young Jesuit priest died from this abuse.

A short time later, by way of a concession, the prison authorities eased up on the toilet-rules. A wooden toilet bucket was introduced into each cell, which prisoners were allowed to use on special request.

This was my first taste of prison life. It was horrendous, but somehow, I was coping. By the grace of God, the first round was won. I was fortified by the thought that millions of pious laity and our Brothers and Sisters of the Legion of Mary worldwide were storming heaven for prisoners such as myself.

After a short period in this new cell, the ordeal of constant interrogation began - Communist style and continued by day and night for several weeks. Looking back, I am not clear as to the exact number of interviews. In this new phase of questioning, the first interrogation took place at night. Violently awakened from sleep, I was escorted by armed guards into a room where I was confronted by a judge and two secretaries. Having asked my name and country of origin, the judge began to question me critically on the Legion of Mary, its activities and motives. I had already decided in advance to play the Communists at their own game. In this instance, I did not answer questions directly, repeating and emphasising as often as possible that the Legion was purely a religious organisation and was neither reactionary nor secret.

One particular judge had a harsh and accusing voice: for this reason, I mentally branded him, 'the Barking Judge'. During a subsequent interrogation, when this man asked me to name the spiritual directors in the district, I gave the names without hesitation; I knew full well that these names were available in all police stations, having been supplied when the Legion was asked to register in each of the churches some months previously. When, however, I was asked for the names of the officers of the Senatus, I decided to refuse despite the fact that these names also were known to all police stations in Shanghai. I merely wished to test the reactions of the judge. Showing no annoyance, he reverted to general questions, allowing me a short interval before again asking: "What about these names?" I again refused to give the names and after a third refusal I was ordered to stand up and was lectured on my position as a prisoner, liable to severe punishment should I persist in my refusal to answer questions. Asked a forth time for the names, I replied, jokingly "You are back again to the same question, aren't you?" This caused an outburst of giggling from one of the secretaries, which so enraged the judge that he cut short the session. Ordering me back to my cell, he threatened to resume his questioning at a later stage, when I would be expected to confess my crimes against the people of China. 'What crimes did I commit against the people of China?' I asked myself.

The next interrogation was conducted in daytime by a judge who had given up the practice of his religion and joined the Communist Party. A former Christian, this man had been responsible for organising several hundred agents in an attempt to secure detailed information concerning the Legion's activities in Shanghai. His questions related to general organisation and administration of the Legion, avoiding any demand for names. I answered his questions in a forthright way, but my replies did not match what he expected. The constant torture of repeated questioning and accusations succeeded in mentally wearing us down.

The Barking Judge, on resuming his interrogations the following night, produced a photograph of my father, and asked: "What would your Irish Government do if I went to Ireland and stirred up the people as you have done here?" I told him that it was never my intention to stir up trouble. Then, with a sneer, he continued: "We will be in Ireland to liberate you some day".

"Thanks", I replied, "but we are already liberated!"

His dream of liberating the world contrasted sharply with the apparent inaction of his Chinese countrymen in recent times, when they had failed to guard their own coast against English and American commercial enterprise. He had now become an apostle of Communism and was determined to make a name for himself. While listening to his questions and noting his zeal, I couldn't help thinking that by contrast, we as Catholics who are obliged to be apostles, often fail in our duty.

Handcuffs and chains were produced before the end of that particular interrogation. The guards did not apply the chains to my legs, as was the case with some other prisoners.

From then on, I was often dragged out of bed while half asleep and brought before a judge with my hands manacled behind my back. The screws in those shackles were so tight that circulation was impeded and my hands became swollen. After repeatedly asking the same questions, the Barking Judge would shriek and jump around the room in his endeavour to force me into divulging the names of Legionaries, while a revolver pointed by a guard, threatened me. But I still refused to give the names. At the end of each interrogation, renewed threats were made of further punishment and long imprisonment. The handcuffs were removed outside my cell door and I was thrown back inside to once more ponder my, "crimes against the people of China."

After weeks of this ordeal, I was brought out as usual one night, a short time after falling asleep. The handcuffs were again screwed tightly into position, with my hands in a behind-the-back position. After being escorted to what seemed like a courtroom, I was confronted by seven or eight judges, who sat around a large table. Guards holding two Tommy-guns stood close beside me. The Barking Judge, looking more wicked than ever, fumed and shrieked while demanding the names of key people involved in the lay apostolate. I stated once more that the Communist authorities already knew these names; their spies had gleaned data on everyone in key positions. Knowing that my answers could make no difference, I gave the Christian names of three members of the Senatus. Though pressed continually on this point, I eventually convinced the interrogators that I was ignorant of their full Chinese names. After some time on the subject of names, a decision was made that my handcuffs should be removed. Suddenly, the judges pretended to become more friendly towards me. However, I was not fooled by this change of attitude. It was inconceivable that the interrogators could genuinely alter their stance in an instant. Perhaps they regarded receiving the first names of three Senatus members as a victory.

The Barking Judge then euphemistically describing the incessant interrogations as 'invitations', informed me in a sarcastic tone of voice that I had been 'invited' to the police station to tell them 'all about the Legion of Mary'. "An invitation received in the middle of the night," I replied, "preceded by a grilling and followed by handcuffing; this appears to me a new form of invitation!"

From then on, in order to create uncertainty in my mind, the judges gave the impression that prisoners whose whereabouts I was anxious to discover, were actually in Lokawei Prison. When one of these judges asked me, with a sneer, "Where is Father MacElroy now?" I felt sure that he too was in prison. A short time later, when this same judge referred to the full name of the Vice-President of the Senatus, I was not at all surprised.

One of the judges asked me questions, which suggested that the Communist spy network had, by some means, gained access to my letters and minutes of Legion meetings. As I had burned all these letters, minutes and lists of names, I concluded that they must have discovered the carbon blue papers, which I had forgotten to destroy. However they came by it, they had apparently obtained sufficient information to enable their representatives to ask intelligent questions on subjects touched in my correspondence. The tone of the questions asked by this particular judge convinced me of the futility of making false statements and of the importance of telling only the truth. However, I refused to give any names not already known to them. "It would be against my conscience", I stated, "to give names". This word "conscience" appeared so important to the judge that one of them asked me to write it down. I afterwards received a lecture on the subject of conscience by an interrogator. He vehemently denied the

196

existence of such a concept and forbade me to use the word 'conscience' again, a prohibition I ignored.

My memory was always bad, but it got worse as a result of my prison treatment. I even forgot the number of my own house in Shanghai. I think I was able to convince the judges of this failure of my memory by asking them to consult the schoolchildren of schools I had visited. When asked to name the different Praesidia of the Legion I was unable to give the name of even my own Praesidium, only to learn that the name was already known to the Communist authorities.

Life in Chinese Jails

In this first prison, I spent seven months under penal conditions. My cell measured seven feet square. The Communists saw from the beginning that I needed much sleep. The interrogations, sleepless nights and whole days in a sitting position were but part of the torture routine. For someone used to freedom of speech, the rule of silence was, to say the least, frustrating. Not to be allowed to laugh, cough, sing or even sneeze was absurd.

Now, I always had a problem with sneezing: I sometimes sneeze twenty times in succession and can find it difficult to stop. When this happened for the first time in my cell, the guard was very angry. He ran to my cell door and shouted: "Do you know you can send messages to the next cell by sneezing?" This had never occurred to me. After that first incident, every time I sneezed a guard reprimanded me.

Prisoners were not allowed to blink their eyes! Can you imagine how hard it is to control blinking? The rule was part of the torture programme. Such rules kept everyone on edge twenty-four hours of the day.

For my part, I tried my best to be cheerful. On the way to each interrogation session, I would brace myself for some new angle of questioning and pray that I might give the right answers. In the 'courtroom' I was often forced to stand for prolonged periods. On returning to my cell any attempts to fall asleep would be thwarted. The word 'weariness' took on new meaning. This form of persecution went on endlessly.

Strangely enough, the guards did not strike or beat us, but relied mainly on more subtle methods of torment. However, the tight screwing of manacles on wrists was part of the physical punishment. This practice caused excruciating suffering, leaving victims in a sorry state. It was all part of the ill-treatment aimed at breaking the will and heart of each individual prisoner.

It was bad enough to have swollen hands, but as mentioned already, the swelling of prisoners' tongues through a low intake of liquids, became a bigger problem. I heard the condition referred to as *beri beri* or Vitamin B deficiency. Sadly, nearly everybody in the prison contracted the ailment. Thank God, in my case it was not too insufferable.

After two or three months in that cell, I began to eat with reasonable regularity and at least had a certain interior peace.

After being interrogated, I made a point of not thinking over the questions they asked me to consider. I haven't the sort of mind to respond to that type of command. I simply continued my prayers, paying absolutely no heed to the judge's threats. I trusted in the Holy Spirit and in Our Lady to give me wisdom when I returned for more questioning. Many times I recalled the words of Scripture: "For words will be given you when the time comes; it is not you who speak but the Spirit of your Father, Who, is in you". (cf. Lk.21:10-19)

One of the Chinese men who shared my cell in the early days, was moved out after a short spell for breach of rules: He had passed on a boiled egg to me, which had been given to him for medical reasons. My second fellow-prisoner had travelled up and down to Hong Kong frequently before being arrested. He was married with four children. His English was fluent. This prisoner turned to me one night and said: "Father, it's lucky for you". I asked why he considered me so lucky and he replied: "You've got religion, I have none". Straight away, he started to learn the tenets of the faith. Over a period of time in the confines of our prison cell, I whispered many things to him concerning the Gospels and various teachings of the Catholic Church. He was a willing listener. Though professing never to have believed in religion, he soon began lapping up doctrine. That is the place to enlighten others about the Gospel. When people in China find themselves in captivity, they fear it may be for a long period and begin to look for spiritual comfort. They start thinking in terms of life beyond the grave.

Day after day and night after night, the guards would walk up and down keeping the prisoners under strict observation. Sufficient light penetrated the boarded cell door that we could see the warden's shadow coming. We watched that shadow all the time while whispering to one another. I volunteered to take on the role of look-out for long periods of time; it filled up the time and I was very glad to do something for the sake of my fellow prisoners. Apart from daylight we never knew for certain the time of day.

In these terrible conditions, my English-speaking companion marvelled at my good disposition and kept asking questions such as: "How could you be happy in such a dreadful place?" I explained that being a priest, I realised that the greater our suffering and persecution in this life, the greater would be our reward in the next. I took every opportunity to speak to him about God and so attentively did he listen that in a few days I had taught him the Our Father and Hail Mary and we even managed to say the Rosary together. Within a month he could repeat the Litany of the Blessed Virgin and all the Legion of Mary prayers.

During weeks of instruction, we said nine Rosaries in English every day and three in Chinese. On the Feast of All Saints, I baptised him by pouring drinking water out of an empty toothpaste tube on his brow. He was simply delighted to be received into the Church.

While at the Catholic Central Bureau I had learned a method of saying the Rosary without beads or fingers for counting: A series of pictures from the Gospel stories are brought before the mind, a different picture for each Hail Mary, so that when the tenth picture is reached, the 'Glory be' follows. A leaflet explaining this method had been distributed widely in China and was popular with the people. I had taught my new convert this method and he quickly got the hang of forming his own pictures for the mysteries. I always had difficulty in remaining awake as we prayed together, and on one occasion when I had apparently nodded off, I was nudged in the side by my friend. "Father", he said, "it was hard enough to find ten pictures for each decade, but how did you manage to find seventeen pictures for that last decade?"

From saying the Rosary in this manner, he progressed to making Spiritual Communions and to meditating. He spoke hopefully of his plans for the future and of his intention, if given his freedom, to make amends for the time lost in God's service. Of all the prayers I taught him, the one he loved best was the concluding prayer on the Legion of Mary leaflet, because it was so indicative of the battle against an evil force, a fight which he knew he would be compelled to undertake if ever released from prison.

CHAPTER TWENTY NINE

"GENERALISSIMO OF THE LEGION OF MARY"

In your hands is my destiny; rescue me from the
clutches of my enemies and my persecutors. (Psalms 30:16)

FEARS FOR DUBLIN PRIEST

The Irish Catholic, September 1951

An announcement by the military authorities in Shanghai that the leaders of the Legion of Mary movement in China were to be "tried" as "counter revolutionaries" has caused concern for the safety of Fr. Aedan McGrath of Dublin, who was arrested by the Chinese Reds in Shanghai recently. The Government Information Bureau said everything possible was being done to extend diplomatic protection to Fr. McGrath.

Fr. McGrath, who was the Legion of Mary director in China, was mentioned by name two months ago in an attack on the Church by the Shanghai authorities. The Reds said: "His political background would be investigated." Peking Radio said Legion members and officials would be tried, but those who registered with the police, made "frank confessions", produced all documents and pledged future co-operation with the Communists would be "treated magnanimously" by the Shanghai Military Control Council. The Communists suspended the Catholic Central Bureau, of which the Legion is a part, on June 6th. At that time, they said all Bureau officials, including the American Bishop, Most Rev. Dr. Walsh were being detained for investigation as "imperialist elements".

In a Prison Cell continued...

A Film Star's Studio

After several months in Lokawei Prison I was suddenly removed to another Detention Centre, I know not where, and brought into a room where several police were menacingly gathered, one of them sneering: "So this is the Generalissimo of the Legion of Mary". After an interrogation, I was placed in a large cell containing about twenty other prisoners, including three Catholics. On learning from me that I was a priest and where I had come from, one of the Catholic internees informed me that two priests known to me, Fr. Martin, the Salesian and Fr. Suppo, had been arrested and were now in prison.

After a short time in this cell, I was escorted to a large room with powerful lights. To my surprise, a number of children were present. Seeing a camera, I realised that I was about to take on the role of film-actor. The camera was placed before me, the powerful lights trained on my face and a short film was apparently made, though I was not aware of any dialogue. For the duration of the movie, two guards with revolvers kept an eye on things. After all the mistreatment, my physical appearance must have been comical, and, as if to add to this farce, my belt-less trousers fell down around my ankles a number of times during the filming.

At the end of the session, I was handcuffed and brought back to the big cell. The three Catholics, on seeing my handcuffs, began to cry. One of them threw himself on the floor, pleading: "Father, bless me", while another made the Sign of the Cross. I had scarcely given them each a blessing when I was again escorted under guard to the film-set room. On entering this chamber, my handcuffs were removed and at a signal, the film-making resumed under the same strong lights. Five judges and several secretaries, all in full uniform and armed with note pads and pens, stood behind a table. A plethora of questions were addressed to me, varying in tone and content. I had heard them all before and gave more or less the same answers. Finally, one of the judges asked me who was responsible for ordering me to come to China. I replied: "Nobody ordered me to visit China. I came of my own free will".

As this was a movie and not a talkie[52], the questions and answers mattered little. I instinctively felt that the script for this film would later be put together later to suit the Communist propaganda machine. On the conclusion of the filming, I was once more handcuffed, put into a car between two soldiers, and driven back to Lokawei. I heard nothing more about the process and never found out for certain what became of it all.

My cell-companions were surprised when I reappeared in Lokawei Prison. They thought that I had been transferred permanently to some other Penitentiary.

The monotony and torture of prison life resumed. Once per month prisoners were allowed about fifteen minutes for washing their clothes. This

---

[52] i.e. with sound.

201

chore took place with the aid of cold-water taps in the exercise yard. Looking down into basins of water at our reflections was our only opportunity of observing ourselves in daylight. The prisoners, including myself, looked frightfully yellow. The hair on the backs of our hands, which under normal conditions would be bleached by the sun, was black in colour. Our fingernails were long and so brittle owing to lack of vitamins that they broke while we washed our clothes. Occasionally, during this laundry operation, we were allowed to wash our feet. This privilege, however, as well as the monthly clothes-washing, was suddenly withdrawn when a great anti-waste campaign was inaugurated in China. For several weeks we were not allowed to wash our clothes. Water was saved, while the bugs and vermin in our cell multiplied.

Most of the Lokawei prison guards were simple, uneducated men from Northern China. When it was considered necessary for one of them to deliver a lecture to the prisoners, the better speakers were chosen. One of these guards we called "The Black Fish" because he was very small and dark. On the slightest provocation he entered our cell and, with a sneer on his face, went on to lecture us, calling us "Imperialists" and telling us that we were such reprobates that any punishment we received, even death, would be of no consequence.

Though we rarely saw the prisoners in other cells, we could hear a prisoner in the opposite unit vomiting day and night for about two months. His condition must have been pitiable. Eventually an ambulance arrived and he was removed. After my release from prison I learned that the prisoner's name was Fr. Bede Chang, the Jesuit Rector of St. Ignatius College in Shanghai. He had died in prison despite the efforts of a doctor to save him.

The Rosary and The Gospel.

The interrogations continued relentlessly. The unfailing reminders by my questioners at the end of each session "to go down and think these things out and come back with an answer" were no doubt geared at breaking my spirit. Apart from the undoubted spiritual helps I was blessed with, my lack of clear thinking and resolution not to worry about the immediate past or the immediate future enabled me to retain my calmness and sanity. Christ's words: "Be not solicitous for tomorrow!" and the words of the song "Just for today" were often in my mind. (cf. Matt. 6:25-34)

Once out of the 'jury room', I banished from my mind the details of interrogations and concentrated on prayer for fellow prisoners, some of whom succumbed to the torture and would bang their heads against the bars of their cell.

As a prelude to what little recollection I was albe to manage, I imagined the towels which hung on nails in the corner of the cell as taking the form of Our Blessed Lady. This brought with it a sense of security, that all was well.

My study of *The Treatise on the True Devotion to the Blessed Virgin* by St. Louis Marie Grignon De Montfort over the years, contributed strongly towards this feeling of interior peace. It was as if the eyes of Mary watched over me; her mantle was ever closely bound around me and no harm could come to me, even though I was at the mercy of my captors.

During the period of my daytime interrogations, I often missed a meal. These 'meals', consisting of cold rice and a little cold vegetable, were most unappetising and in my weary and sleepy condition I could force down only a few mouthfuls. As a consequence I grew gradually weaker and thinner. My belt and shoelaces having been taken from me in case of an attempt at suicide, I felt ill at ease in my clothes.

Towards the end of my stay in Lokawei, a White Russian prisoner with chains on his legs was escorted into my cell. I was soon to learn that he was locked up for being in possession of arms. His offence was having thirty-five guns but declaring only two of them, thinking he could get away with the others. Unfortunately somebody informed on him and he fell foul of the authorities.

On learning that I was a priest, the Russian said: "Father, it is all right for you to pray. You have been trained. But I can't. I can only worry." Later he related to me in whispers, how his detention came about: Fond of wild-duck shooting, he had kept sports guns without a licence. Unable to pray, he worried about his food and the odds against his release from prison. He also dwelled on the identity of the informer responsible for his arrest.

As the days passed and his mentality did not improve, it was a constant struggle to prevent this man from losing his sanity. A strong athletic individual, about six feet tall, he had been a boxer and it was for this reason that chains were kept on him. In addition to the chains, handcuffs were put on behind his back during his interrogations. On some occasions two straight arm-cuffs were placed across his arms. After one such grilling the veins on his head stood out prominently and he was the colour of death. The physical and mental torture had such an effect on him that he soon was prepared to confess anything to the prison authorities. One day he confided in me what he said to the judge during his cross-examination: "Everything you have on your book there against me, I admit." "What do you admit?" asked the judge. "Oh", he said, "I don't know. Everything you've got down there. I can't stand this any more."

The Russian could not bring himself to pray for a solution, and lack of prayerfulness added greatly to his sufferings. I spoke to him at every opportunity about spiritual matters and gradually he showed an interest in the faith. Though this man never joined in the Rosary, the recital of prayers within the confines of the cell and also my instruction apparently had a good effect on him.

The number of prisoners in my cell increased to four with the arrival of a young Chinese man named Paul, who turned out to be a Communist of the Youth Corps. Professing to be a loyal member and a firm believer in the Communist doctrine, he could not account for his arrest until, on his first interrogation, he was accused of being a spy and asked to confess. Dejected and miserable, he was handcuffed with hands behind his back for three months, day and night. In order to help him sleep in this position, I tucked a coat under his arms each night. Like my other companions, he soon began to take an interest in the Catholic doctrine. Within a few days, he joined in the Rosary. Paul listened with evident delight to the Gospel stories and when he asked me to baptise him, I explained that this was not a good idea as he was not yet ready. I advised him to see a priest when released from prison and to ask for Baptism, adding that, should he die without having been baptised, a desire for Baptism would be sufficient to save his soul…

COMMUNISTS IN CHINA ASSAIL LEGION OF MARY

As Fr. McGrath is languishing in his cell, the Communist propaganda machine is busy. The following article courtesy of *The Irish Catholic*, October 18th 1951, gives examples of items published in Chinese Newspapers such as the Peking *Jen Min Daily*, Shanghai *Liberation Daily* and Canton *Nang Fang Daily*. These articles were syndicated and appeared regularly in an effort to undermine and vilify the good work done by the Legion of Mary.

'WHAT THEN IS THIS LEGION OF MARY?'
The Legion of Mary (under various Chinese names) is an organisation under the direction of the Catholic Central Bureau to promote reactionary activities.
The Legion of Mary was established first in Dublin and its founder was Frank Duff, a reactionary guardian of the interests of the ruling class. What sort of an organisation is the Legion of Mary? Is it what the imperialist Duff asserts, merely an organisation devoted to purely religious activities? …In a word, the Legion of Mary is truly an earthly army, hiding

under the cloak of religion, which swears loyalty to serve the reactionary cause of the imperialists. In our country the Legion of Mary became active after the people of our land had defeated the aggression of the Japanese Imperialists, and the great struggle to liberate the masses had begun.

FR. AEDAN McGRATH

When the Catholic Central Bureau had been organised at the end of December 1947, the Imperialist, Riberi, in order to continue his widespread aggressive activities against the people of China set up a central section of the Legion of Mary in the Catholic Central Bureau, and appointed his confidential agents, the imperialist W. Aedan McGrath, and Shen Shih-Chien as the responsible heads of the central department. It must be pointed out that although McGrath and Shen Shih-Chien are the direct leaders of the Legion of Mary, yet in reality the true organiser and director in China is the imperialist Riberi.

'INSTRUMENTS FOR IMPERIALISTS'

Before Riberi came to China he personally directed the activities of the Legion of Mary in Africa and Ireland, and at that time, beside himself with delight, he praised the Legion of Mary, which he led as 'the best instrument' in the service of the Catholic Church. (In truth it is the best instrument for the imperialist and reactionary groups). As soon as Riberi came to China he resolutely regarded the great revolution movement of the Chinese People with enmity and, having decided to oppose the Chinese to the end, make use of what he had already praised as 'the best instrument', the Legion of Mary. He intended cunningly to employ under his instructions in our country that which he had used in Africa and Ireland and also he summoned his loyal and sincere agent McGrath from Ireland to come to China so that in unison they could oppose the affairs of the Chinese People.

ACTIVITIES OF FR. McGRATH

McGrath is a subject of Ireland who first came to China in 1930. After his arrival In China, he was immediately active in the diocese Hanyang in Hupeh. In 1945 after the people of our country had defeated Japanese Imperialism and attained a glorious victory, McGrath was frightened at the increased and widening influence of the Chinese people's power, and - subsequently in that year quietly left China. In 1948 McGrath, in obedience to Riberi's cabled command, returned to China and directed the activities of the Legion of Mary.

Before McGrath came to China a second time he went to Ireland and America to be trained in organising the Legion of Mary. In the year 1948, precisely when the Chinese People's fight for liberation, like a deafening tidal wave, swept forward.

[Riberi] in order to direct and collaborate with Chiang Kai-shek's reactionary administration and to continue the slaughter of Chinese People, in August 1948 sent his agent McGrath to visit Peking and Tientsin stealthily and organise secretly the Legion of Mary. On the eve of the liberation of Peking and Tientsin, McGrath fled away from north China and went South, when in Canton, Kweilin and other areas he continued his activities. When the Chinese People's liberation army was about to cross the Yangtse, McGrath again left South China and quietly went into the interior, and in the Szechwan region continued to organise and expand the illegal activities of the Legion of Mary...They sent reactionaries into schools to disseminate reactionary propaganda, creating and spreading rumours, striking at and attacking members of the Youth Corps, sabotaging the People's patriotic movement. The Catholic Central Bureau published and circulated a large number of 'Legion Handbooks' and 'Catholic stories about the Virgin', poisonous, reactionary publications. ...They temporarily circulated, inside and outside the schools, the Catholic Church's 'Declaration of Principles', 'One Holy Catholic Church', 'Propagation of the Faith' and other reactionary publications to sabotage the patriotic Catholics Three Autonomies reform movement and also to collect secret reports for the imperialists.

...In order to protect the fruits of victory of the people of our country to guard the interests of the people, not to permit the slightest imperialist aggression and to clear the path for the Catholic's patriotic three autonomies reform movement, we must not only advance a step in disclosing the crimes of aggression of the imperialists Riberi, McGrath and others, but we must petition the government to expel immediately the imperialists Riberi and McGrath, and to suppress forthwith all activities of the Legion of Mary and other such unlawful organisations.

(End of Communist propaganda articles)

HOLY FATHER PRAYS FOR CHINA

Not all was Communist propaganda, however. The Apostolic Letter *Cupimus Imprimis*, issued on January 18th, 1952, feast of Saint Peter's Chair in Rome, was addressed by His Holiness Pope Pius XII to the Hierarchy, Clergy, and People of China to console and exhort them paternally in their hardships, anxieties and adversities. The Holy Father begins by manifesting his "warm benevolence towards the entire Chinese people, which added even greater riches to the splendour of its millenary civilization, once it had been illumined by the light of the Gospel." He then declares himself "greatly grieved" because among those, his children, "the Catholic Church is being represented and attacked as an enemy," and because "its Bishops, Clergy, Religious and Nuns are frequently driven from their centres of activity, or impeded in the free exercise of their office, as if the Church were engaged, not in the service of supernatural things…but rather in pursuing human interests and in seeking temporal domination."

The Pope also exhorts his Chinese children to be strong with that strength of soul which is founded, not on human force, but on divine grace; and to offer their sufferings to God so that He may finally grant peace and liberty to the Church in China.[53]

SUPPORT FROM THE CONCILIUM

Neither were the persecuted Legionaries forgotten by the Concilium, which, echoing the voice of the Holy Father, earnestly recommended that "*each Praesidium throughout the World* should participate in a special Novena of prayer to Our Blessed Lady, Queen of the Legion, for our persecuted and suffering Spiritual Directors and Legionaries of China. It is suggested that the Novena should take place prior to the Acies ceremony and that it should terminate with the offering of the usual devotions of the Acies for the same intention. The Adjutorian and Auxiliary members are to be approached and requested to join in this Novena. If possible, daily Mass and Holy Communion and the recital of the Rosary would be a most acceptable offering to place in the hands of Our Blessed Lady. Also, where it is customary for Praesidia to offer a Spiritual Bouquet in connection with the Acies, these should be offered for the intentions of the Novena. The Concilium feels confident that the Legion all over the World will generously respond to this suggestion, upon which much may depend and which will enable our suffering brethren in China to re-echo St. Paul's words, 'We suffer persecution, but are not forsaken.'"[54]

---

[53] Cf. *Maria Legionis*, 1952, No.1, p.6
[54] Ibid., p.12

CHAPTER THIRTY

FROM LOKAWEI TO WARD ROAD JAIL - 1952

Pray for us. For we are confident that we have a good conscience,
desiring to live uprightly in all things. (Hebrews 13:18)

Old photo taken outside the original Ward Road Jail

In a Prison Cell continued... In March 1952, with my new converts, I made the novena to St. Joseph and on the 20th, the day after the end of the novena, Leo the White Russian and the Chinese named Paul who had asked for Baptism, were both taken from the cell. Though unaware of their destination they were delighted to leave this horrible cubicle. Before saying goodbye, they both knelt and asked me for an Absolution, which I duly gave.

Next day, the second Chinese prisoner was taken away without explanation, leaving me alone in that dreary cell. When I went out to wash my cup I estimated, by counting the chopsticks that only about nine prisoners were left in the prison. Among them was Fr. Legrand of the Catholic Central Bureau. After ten more days, my solitude suddenly ended. A batch of new prisoners arrived and I was soon to discover the reason for the influx. Around this time, a determined drive against bribery and corruption in Government circles had commenced. Thus the prison began to fill up once more and I found myself with four new companions in my cell.

208

All four of these men denied having any religious beliefs. Unfortunately, before I had time to speak to them in depth on the subject of religion, I was whisked out of Lokawei Prison.

This happened on the 9th April and so sudden was the order I received that I left my drinking-mug behind in the cell. Without explanation, I was brought to the entrance area, where I was handed back all the articles, which had been taken from me after my arrest. These included a watch, Rosary Beads, Miraculous Medals and my Scapular. I was provided with clothes, which had been sent to me in prison, but which I had never been given.

A short time later, in the custody of a policeman, I was driven at speed through the streets of Shanghai and arrived at Ward Road Jail. Compared to Lokawei Prison, this huge Penal Institution looked like a fortress. The jail, surrounded by sturdy walls, was said to be the second largest detention centre in the world. Built by the British, mainly for Chinese prisoners, one section was reserved for foreigners, this subdivision being provided with bigger and more comfortable cells, each containing such articles of furniture as a table and a chair.

As I was driven through the gates of Ward Road Jail, the accompanying policeman told me that the more comfortable wing in what was to be my new home, was occupied by women!

My fingerprints were taken and I was carefully searched. Buttons were cut off my clothes and, as usual, any articles which could be used to commit suicide, removed. I was assigned to number five block, the Chinese section. On my way to the cell I was assisted by another prisoner who carried my bundle. I was so weak and undernourished that I was scarcely able to move. As we walked along he whispered to me in French: "Father, I am a Christian too. Don't worry".

My cell measured seven feet in length, five feet in width and eight feet in height. A guard soon came along and asked me if I had received anything to eat. A few minutes later, a prisoner arrived carrying a tin. I thought it odd that a prisoner should do this work, but at this stage was more concerned with eating than finding answers. It was the first time that I had seen one of these containers, a shapeless piece of aluminium that looked as if it had not been polished for years. The tin was dirty. It contained a portion of off-white rice, with a meagre morsel of vegetable on top. The appearance of this so-called dish was simply awful. To make matters worse, the food was not only cold, but accompanied by a pair of soiled chopsticks.

Later in the day, a guard asked me what foreign languages I spoke besides English. I told him that I spoke French. Next day, the prisoner who had escorted me to my cell was ordered to instruct me on the prison rules. The guard was apparently unaware that I also spoke Chinese. Well, he never asked me that question! Taking advantage of the guard's ignorance of French, the prisoner contrived to ask for prayers for himself while instructing me on the prison rules. After repeating each rule he would say things like "Pray for me, Father". He asked me for Absolution, which I immediately gave him. He then informed me that Fr. Sheng, Dr. Chang and Mr. Seng of the Shanghai Senatus were here also.

This assistant looked after me well: he even brought a scissors to my cell to cut my finger and toe nails, ordinary prisoners not being allowed to use such tools. After performing this task for the first time, he stood up and looked out the cell window to see if a jailer was in sight. He then knelt down and kissed my feet, dirty and smelly as they were and said before leaving: "God bless you, Father!"

My new home consisted of twelve blocks, in the Chinese section alone. In each block there were four to five hundred cells. Most cubicles housed three or four Chinese prisoners; but I was on my own.

I did not know my adjoining prisoners, either on the right, or the left of me. At first I did not realise how the day was divided, what time prisoners went to bed or got up in the mornings. I found it difficult to get into a routine in this new environment and a struggle to pray. Each night we were told when we could lie down. When a whistle blew in the morning, we were ordered to get up. Water for washing was provided to each cell in a small container. It was never sufficient. I longed to relieve myself of my dirty condition.

About half an hour later, a whistle blew once more. A guard opened all the gates and the prisoners lined up for exercise. I was soon to learn that exercise was curtailed depending on status and conformity to prison protocol. On joining the line-up of prisoners one morning, I found myself close to Paul, the young Communist I had met in Lokawei Prison. He had been released before me and believed at the time that he was going home.

On seeing me, Paul nodded his head and I nodded back to him. A guard must have spotted us and, before we could communicate any further, I was moved to the end of the group to await instructions. Suddenly a warder ordered me back to my cell without explanation. I was locked in alone and given a meagre breakfast, while the other prisoners were marched up the stairs onto the roof to get fresh air and exercise.

One redeeming feature of this new prison was that the interrogations had ceased, at least for now. I was left alone with my thoughts and fears.

Some time later, and without notice, my cell door opened and I was told by a guard to roll up my sleeping mat and bundle my blankets together. In silence I was brought out and led upstairs to the second floor where I was placed in cell No. 2146, a similar cubicle to the one downstairs.

The new surroundings were no improvement. Air entered only through the metal grille of the tiny window. The floor was not of solid construction and was home to a myriad of crawling creatures. These, as I would soon discover, were to be my constant company and used to cause me such distress at night time that I used to wake in a cold sweat shaking them from my head and swiping them from every part of my body. I cleaned up the cell as much as was in my power - floor, walls and everything in sight - but it made little impression on my co-residents.

After a few days, two men dressed in white coats came from the prison dispensary and pumped D.D.T.[55] all over the cubicle. I was so glad of the wholesome smell of that anti-bug powder. It did not however succeed in exterminating the problem. The agony went on, night after night and there was little hope for a sound sleep.

During my three months in that cell I was allowed ten minutes for exercise two or three days each week with other prisoners. The exercise, walking or running in line, took place either on the roof or in the garden, under the vigilant eyes of the guards. Constant supervision was in place. Even in the cells, prisoners were not allowed freedom of movement to sit, stand or lie down as they pleased. Like other detainees, I experienced the humiliation and aggravation of being ordered to stand up and to sit down at frequent intervals. I had done my apprenticeship at this of course in Lokawei Prison, but here there was a new intensity about the discipline. The apparent object of this treatment was to inflict the maximum psychological and physical punishment on prisoners by depriving them of relaxation and keeping them continually on the alert.

While the overcrowded cell in Lokawei had its drawbacks, this new location had its own horrors. I felt miserable from the start, wondering how I would ever endure the conditions. Silence was the norm. Though each cell around me caged prisoners, I seldom heard human voices. Rarely did anyone speak out loud. Each breach of the silence rule was punished in various ways, e.g., intensified discipline, long interrogation sessions and threats. Looking out through the grille, I could see some small windows opposite and nothing else except a slab of grey wall. When the sun went down I could not read anything, even if I had any reading material. There was no light in the cell save the

---

[55] Dichloro Diphenyl Trichloroethane, banned from use in U.S.A. since 1973.

211

occasional flashing of the guards' torch scanning the cubicle. I could not even see the prison rules, which were written on the cell wall.

One providential consolation was granted to me here however, and that was the visit to my cell every now and again of a tiny bird. This bird was a source of much relief amidst my weary existence. The sudden chirping of my feathered friend upon the approach of the prison guard proved to be an added benefit. I used some of the long quiet hours to compose a simple poem in his honour:

The Sparrow

I.

I have one little friend within this jail,
Who comes each day to visit without fail.
And which he loves, just me, or what I give,
I should not like to be too positive.

2.

He flies in through the outer window bars,
And nears my cell with eyes like twinkling stars.
He whispers 'Chirrup, Chirrup' from his heart,
And promptly do I cheer up for my part.

3.

His appetite for rice that has been dried,
And which must swell on reaching his inside,
Did quite alarm me when I saw it first,
In dreading that my little friend might burst.

4.

And when there is no rice, not e'en a bit,
I therefore do not move from where I sit.
He tries his best to make his presence felt,
With antics that would cause your heart to melt.

5.

He visits other friends along the line,
In case you think the privilege was mine.
But still I think he comes to me the most,
Without intending to deceive or boast.

6.

One day, I know not what gave him a fright,
For I could not see anything in sight.
He came rushing in, his body all aquake,
And stood beside me for protection's sake.

7.

I often wonder what he thinks of me,
He must know I'm en-caged and not too free.
For he comes very close beside my cell,
And yet he feels that everything is well.

8.

I know what I shall always think of him,
So free, so cheery and so full of vim.
Recalling Jesus and His words about,
The birds and man's solicitude and doubt.

9.

'They do not sow and neither do they reap,
Nor gather into barns, a stock to keep.'
And yet they fare so well, just to and fro,
Without a single care, God loves them so.

10.

Ah ye of little faith, Christ's words were due,
For truly trusting souls are still so few.
Ah! Here's the bird again, how he trusts me,
Dear God, please teach me how to trust in Thee.

After three months in cell 2146, I was moved to the fourth floor of an adjoining block to another isolated cell. Again, I was only occasionally allowed out for exercise. It seems that priests were put in solitary confinement, while foreign lay prisoners were housed mostly two, three or four to a cell. Of course by rule none of us were allowed to speak, but this certainly didn't stop us from communicating. I gradually learned that adjacent cells were occupied by

Russians, Koreans, Yugoslavs and Japanese, with more than one to a cell. Americans prisoners were also kept in solitary. You can imagine how pleased I was to find out that one of my neighbours on this fourth floor was Fr. Carascal, a Spanish Jesuit.

As time went on, I realised that the guards in this prison block appeared to be less vigilant than in other sections. Prisoners managed to talk to each other frequently, even though they were in different cells. When I got to know the movements of the guards, I secretly borrowed a pencil and on some toilet paper I wrote a note in Latin to Fr. Carascal and sent it across the corridor to him through one of the Yugoslav's who was in prison for pick-pocketing. I might mention that under the previous Government, this category of prisoner would have been treated more leniently. By contrast with the former rulers of China, the Communists regarded a five to ten-year prison term as normal for any crime. The death sentence, or life imprisonment was also common.

My note introduced myself as a Catholic priest. I asked the Spanish Jesuit to write out some hymns for me. Within a few days I received a reply, supplying me with words of the many plainchant favourites that I love, including *Lauda Sion, Stabat Mater, Veni Sancte Spiritus* and *Victimae Paschali Laudes* as well as the *Te Deum*. The only exception was the *Benedicite* after Mass, which he could not fully remember. I was able to add a couple of verses to his words of the *Lauda Sion*, and sent it back to him for checking. When he had completed this task, he attempted to throw the little bundle across the corridor and into my cell. On striking one of the bars, it fell back onto the floor. Fortunately the guard had not seen it and I was able, by swinging a towel out through the bars, to drag the bundle into my cell.

It was not long before I succeeded in learning them by heart and would sing them quietly to myself when the coast was clear, to the occasional musical accompaniment of my small winged visitor, the sparrow.

Soon after I received these notes, a guard found them in my cell. He was angry and reported the matter at once to the Governor. I was called up before the prison committee and asked for an explanation. I said that I had written the hymns to amuse myself. After a severe warning, I was taken back to my cell realising that I could not risk further correspondence with Fr. Carascal. Soon after this incident, he was released from Ward Road Jail and expelled from China. Later I heard that another prisoner had concealed a very different set of notes in the lining of the this priests jacket in an effort to alert the outside world about conditions in the prison. On Fr. Carascal's way out of China, the notes were discovered in a search by police at the border and he was jailed for a further year.

While in custody, I got to know bits and pieces about the background of various prisoners. Some case-histories stand out more than others, but I must share a story with you about an American detainee named Dill Kennedy, a young Texan whom I met in Ward Road Jail.

In happier times with Dill Kennedy

This young Texan's mother was Irish and indeed, he used to regard himself as Irish. He had been involved in the cotton business in Shanghai, and apparently was implicated in a $25,000 black-market deal, which the Communists found distasteful. After some time in prison, he began losing his sanity. Dill just kept breaking the rules and he was forever being caught by the guards. The last time I saw him was when I was isolated up on the fourth floor. Dill was walking on a lower level and shouted up: "Cheer up, Father, I'm Irish too!" When I finally arrived in Hong Kong, I was told that he was still in prison, a raving lunatic.

During my time on the fourth floor of this fortress, a group of Yugoslavian gypsies began complaining to the guards "Why are the Chinese allowed out to work (it was a concession to be allowed out to work within the prison) while we are always confined?" A White Russian prisoner named Ivan was among those who opposed this supposed favouritism. The authorities relented and extended to him certain privileges. Ivan even received permission to read books in his cell. He must have given the impression of being a model prisoner. I knew the opposite to be the case: One of his new duties included, coming to the cells with rice at mealtime. I made friends with him and he obliged my by delivering my scribbled notes to other prisoners on the block. It was in this way, I had the privilege of being able to instruct some of the inmates in the tenets of the Catholic Faith.

One of these was a Japanese dentist who had murdered his parents. He claimed to have committed the crime while in a rage and then gave himself up to the police. According to law he should have been condemned and shot. But the authorities decided otherwise. They just kept him languishing in prison. One morning he gave the White Russian a note for me asking: "Father, please say a prayer for my soul. I believe and I still have hope of salvation." At once I began instructing him in the faith with the help of notes smuggled to his cell. Whether the prison guards got wind of what was going on, I do not know; but before long he was shifted to another cell, where he was out of my reach.

One day at exercise, a Christian and an American, named Arnold Khiem whispered to me, "Father, can you recall the Sermon on the Mount?" I said: "I shall try." I went back to my cell and took my toilet paper and wrote all I could recall. He remembered bits here and there too and, between us, we wrote out a substantial amount of Matthew's Gospel, chapters 5 to 7. We were delighted! Again prison life was giving Arnold and myself, a chance to reflect more deeply on the Word of God. Though professing to have faith, he had not been particular about religion. He claimed that he had been quite rebellious in his youth. The day came when he meekly asked me: "Can you give me a few prayers?"

"Any prayers I give will have the name of Our Lady and that's not the kind of prayer a Protestant usually likes," I told him.

"But I believe in the Immaculate Conception," he replied.

So, back in my cell I started to write out prayers, all of which contained a reference to Our Lady. I gave them to him, plus a little memo of the way Jesus treated his Mother, and how Our Lord asked for her consent before coming on earth and lived in absolute obedience to her for many years, and how at Cana, though it was not yet time for working miracles, he performed a striking one because his mother asked him. At the end of my notes I included how Jesus gave us his mother on the Cross. Arnold wrote back: "Yes, Father; from what you say, it could not be otherwise, and even today Jesus must have a terrific respect for His mother."

Arnold continued asking many questions about the Catholic Church. In the end he wrote back saying he was most grateful. "I now always pray through Our Lady," he said, "And, Father," he continued, "you know what it's like? It's like putting aviation gasoline into a jeep!"

The risk of getting caught in these exchanges was great. One of the ways the prison authorities incited the prisoners was to reward those who reported on transgressions of the prison rule. Officially, everyone was expected to inform on everyone else on the basis that this offered the prospect of a lighter sentence. Psychologically, this was a torture in itself. We never knew for certain who to trust.

I was thus inevitably reported for my written exchanges. I was hauled before a panel of judges and asked to explain my behaviour. I started off by saying that I had done nothing wrong and went on to explain that the notes were harmless and in no way breached prison rules. During the interrogations, documents were produced portraying my involvement with the Legion of Mary. The old accusations resurfaced: the Legion was reactionary, anti-Communist and so on. At the end of a lengthy grilling, one of my questioners addressed me: "All these documents report facts about you and your activities. What have you to say?" I offered my usual response: "The Legion of Mary is neither reactionary nor secret." I was reprimanded with a series of strong warnings and ordered back to my cell.

From *The Catholic Herald*, 5th September 1952

'SING-MO-MALAY'

It is very remarkable the way Our Lady holds to her position as Queen of China. Even the storm which has arisen over the Legion of Mary and its condemnation by the Government has had the result that Our Lady is being talked of all over China. "Who is this woman," the Communists say, "who dares to reign over the hearts of the Chinese people in defiance of the almighty Government of China?" The answer is: "She is 'Sing-Mo-Malay', the Mother of God who will reign eternally in heaven and on earth."

CHAPTER THIRTY ONE

INTERNUNCIO BERATES ATHEISTIC COMMUNISM

Wherefore I write these things while absent, that when present
I may not act more severely, according to the power that the Lord
has given me for upbuilding and not for destruction. (Corinthians 13:10)

T he following address was delivered in Hong Kong by Archbishop
Riberi,[56] on the occasion of the Legion Acies at the Cathedral in
September 1952:

The unusual circumstances under which the Acies of the Legion of Mary
is being held in Hong Kong this year cannot but be significant and impressive.
The organisation born in Dublin thirty years ago and initiated in Hong Kong
only a short three years ago, is today the victim of a fierce persecution.

---

[56] The Inter-nuncio was expelled from mainland China at the time Fr. McGrath was arrested,
September 1951.

218

The spectacle of persecution, tragic though it is, has a simple explanation: On the one hand there is a highly-developed and materially powerful political machinery which professes as its basic purpose the liquidation of religious beliefs from the human mind. It controls and directs, through compulsion and terror, an administration that pretends to permit freedom of worship, but uses its every energy to suppress it. On the other hand there is the Legion of Mary, an organisation totally religious in essence and activity, dedicated to fostering a deep devotion to the Blessed Mother of God. It aims at inculcating a fundamental religious outlook on life in its members and in those among whom it works. Its zealous endeavours may, in a general yet accurate way, be described as a participation in the pastoral obligation of the Church: visiting the sick, imparting religious instructions through personal contacts, books and pamphlets; bringing back the strayed sheep to the one sheepfold; winning converts; shirking no menial tasks that enable others to perform their religious duties.

But surely such a dedication of lay people cannot be construed, except purposefully and maliciously, as secret and malevolent, much less as subversive or counter-revolutionary. Only by a novel interpretation of the word 'revolution' to signify suppression of free worship of the Almighty and the most fundamental freedom, to acknowledge the very essence of God, can such a religious organisation be termed 'counter-revolutionary'. When that is the case, then every priest must be considered an enemy of the State. Twenty-one Bishops and over three hundred priests imprisoned in China today bear witness to the accuracy of this statement.

...That they may remain one

Yet, since the [Communist] party has levelled its vicious attack against the Legion, it is fair to review the basis for this enmity. The system, while still professing an undying hatred for Almighty God, suddenly came forward as a loving guardian and protector of the Catholic Church. Under this guise of solicitude for the churches, it promoted a programme, which they called the 'three independence movement'. Their intention, so they claimed, was to force the churches to grow to maturity overnight. This they would do by pulling the churches, like tiny plants from the soil that nurtured their roots. They alleged that the fishes growing and multiplying in the pond would grow and multiply faster if the water of the pond was drained off. They would rush the blossoming of the grapes by cutting the branches from the vine.

The Legionaries, to their eternal credit, were quick to see the true underlying purpose of such solicitude on the part of the enemies of God. Their unpardonable sin in the eyes of the materialist state was to affront its authority by refusing to join a movement that spelled destruction for their own souls. They refused to be dismembered from the Mystical Body. "That they may be one", was the prayer of Christ. That they may remain one was the "crime" the Legion committed against materialistic Communism.

At the same moment, a terrific campaign of materialistic indoctrination was launched and forced on all inhabitants of the country. Since materialism denies the existence of a spiritual principle in life, the indoctrination in this philosophy attempted to wash from the brain of the people the very idea of God, of a spiritual soul, of a life beyond this earthly sphere, in a word, all the principles fundamental to religious truths. The Legionaries could not fail to see the mortal danger of this to themselves and their brothers and sisters in Christ. On the grounds of religious freedom, ostentatiously and officially guaranteed by the state, they strove to safeguard themselves and other Catholics from destructive propaganda. Relying exclusively on the spiritual means at their disposal, they went about their work with a quiet persistence. They advocated earnest prayer to the Blessed Mother, good example and reliance on the grace of God.

A spiritual resistance

The degree of their success, of their intense adherence to their faith, can be gauged by the ferocity of the denunciation of those methods by their adversaries. It was clear to all that the materialistic concept of life, even promoted by force had little chance to establish itself against such a spiritual resistance. It was not defeat of the programme of materialistic indoctrination alone, nor envy of the success of the spiritual revival that sparked the outburst against the Legion of Mary.

...The subterfuge of persecuting the Legion on the basis of forced confessions simply proves beyond doubt that even pretexts for persecuting the Legion were not to be found.

The Legion grossly misrepresented

So they were persecuted. And even in the very act the State uncovered the extraordinary heroism of young boys and girls. The sight of these youngsters appearing at the police bureau prepared to suffer imprisonment rather than act counter to their conscience was a stumbling block for the authority that knew only force to enact its will. We have learned too, that the police themselves found the procedure so revolting that they objected to the campaign against the Legion that was forced on them by another department...

Religious observance throughout the countryside has been practically suppressed under various pretexts. The priests are prevented from working among the people by divers means. The Church's charitable and educational institutions have been liquidated under the most odious and libelous charges. The material church, its buildings, chapels, residences have been by and large confiscated. Missionaries are expelled or imprisoned daily; native priests are subjected to constant pressure to force them to act against their religious conscience. For their refusal they are thrown into jails and kept there under intolerable conditions of segregation and hardship. In many instances their deaths are discovered through sheer accident. Their fate as prisoners is shrouded in secrecy, perhaps to hide the tragic end of many of them from the people. Under such a regime of terror, the term "religious freedom" has become a mockery to the entire world. Each priest who remains faithful to his priestly vocation, does so in the shadow of the gallows, or the gibbet.

Sheep without a Shepherd

The faithful have been forced to submit to indoctrination courses, aimed at the destruction of their faith. Deprived of the spiritual nourishment of the Sacraments and of the religious guidance of their pastors, their lot is the tragic story of the sheep without a shepherd. An almost irresistible pressure exercised with threats and deceit is exerted against them. They are lectured for days on end; they are embroiled in wearisome discussions conducted in an atmosphere of hostility and deceit: they are cajoled on the obligations of patriotism and confused with the exploitation of emotional issues. They are ridiculed, menaced, and beaten into a state of mental submission. They require a heroic degree of faith to withstand the techniques scientifically perfected by masters of psychology.

Concurrently, Catholics are daily faced with the public denunciations of their erstwhile esteemed pastors of their souls. They are herded to cleverly prepared and rehearsed "accusation meetings", to hear re-enacted the trumped-up charges that run the gamut of the capital sins. They are forced to witness the maligning of the religious, who are led silent before the mobs of their detractors. Not a single voice is raised to stem the tide of injustice, falsehood and hatred.

...The essence of Communism is its absolute denial of the existence of God. It purports to rebuild the world on man alone. In this sense we are witnessing the most fateful, far-reaching and destructive revolution of all times. It can only be compared to the revolt of Lucifer, who faced his creator with the cry: "I will not serve." The fixed moral code inscribed by God is, as a result trampled down. Each day brings with more clarity the portrayal of the overthrow of reason by the rule of convenience and opportunism. Mass murder is the morality of the hour. The code of ethics is overflowing prisons; the law is demeaned to the monstrous policing of the family circle and the individual's convictions. The magnitude of this enslavement of liberty has never before been experienced in the history of mankind. Communism leads inevitably to its final end where the individual is less than a beast, a mere cog in the godless and soulless machine.

...Patroness of China

By happy choice, the Fathers of the First Council of China proclaimed Mary, Mediatrix of all graces, as the special Patroness of their country. Through such a dedication, the Bishops of China signified their understanding of Mary's role in China. All graces would flow through her hands to that great country, including the greatest of all, the winning of the hundreds of millions of souls to Christ.

Today we are faced with the unprecedented need of preserving the supernatural life of the faithful exposed to the snares and violence of the enemies of God. In our hour of distress, we turn naturally to Our Blessed Mother. We have prayed in the past and we pray today, with greatest confidence, nay, with the certainty of success.

Through our Act of Consecration, which we renew individually and collectively this night, we re-dedicate our fealty to Mary, Queen of the Legion and our Queen. We beg the strength and blessing for yet another year's struggle with the forces of sin and evil. That these gather more darkly each hour about us should only deepen the fervour of our conviction that through Mary alone we can come to divine life. We close our ranks about her, to work with her in constant endeavors, following the precept of the Handbook: "to imitate her profound humility, her perfect obedience, her angelic sweetness, her continual prayer, her universal mortification, her altogether spotless purity, her heroic patience, her heavenly wisdom, her self-sacrificing courageous love of God and above all her faith, that virtue which has alone in her been found in its utmost extent and unequalled.

CHAPTER THIRTY TWO

CHRISTMAS 1952

I am the true vine, and my Father is the vine-dresser.
Every branch in me that bears no fruit He will take away;
and every branch that bears fruit He will prune,
that it may bear more fruit. (John 15:1-2)

In a prison cell continued ... Not long after after the departure of Fr. Carascal from Ward Road Jail, I was taken downstairs one day with several other prisoners. Our possessions were handed back to us. After fingerprinting a receipt for them, we were placed in a "Black Maria" and driven, under a strong escort and with sirens blowing, through the streets of Shanghai. It was during this journey that I again met my friend from Lokawei Prison, Leo, whose first request was for an Absolution.

Arriving at another prison, I know not where, our finger-prints were taken. We handed over our possessions and were all herded into one room where we were allowed to talk freely for three or four hours. During this time I chatted with among others, a German Jew named Wolfgang Gruen. Realising that he was thirsting for knowledge of God, I gave him there and then his first instruction on the faith.

While we were all wondering what form our interrogation might take, or if indeed we were about to be set free, a policeman announced that there had been a change of plan. No explanation was given. Whether this change of tactic was meant as part of the mental torture, simply to keep us guessing, we had no idea. At any rate, we were all glad of the temporary break from normal prison routine. Then, as suddenly as we had arrived we were again brought out, our watches and other possessions handed back and we were driven through the streets with shrieking sirens and returned to our cells in Ward Road Jail. For this puzzling journey we never got any explanation.

I settled down once more to life in my prison home and managed to communicate secretly with Wolfgang Gruen. I actually gave a complete course of religious instruction to him. He told me that he was in prison on a trumped-up charge of espionage. The prison authorities must have guessed that something was afoot as I was soon strictly rationed on toilet paper.

In a letter to one prisoner I had mentioned that every time Bing Crosby went to Mass in Beverly Hills, Hollywood, the priest celebrant would always knew he had been in the congregation because there would be a $50 bill in the collection plate. This prisoner wrote to me and sent a little parcel with a note saying: "This is not a $50 bill but at least it can be used in God's work." In the parcel were fifty sheets of toilet paper, so that coming near Christmas I had a plentiful supply. I decided to make Christmas cards and send them to my fellow-prisoners.

Incidentally, while I was instructing Wolfgang, he showed me how to make wooden needles as well as thread, an art which had enabled him to sew his clothes. He also gave me a pencil with which I wrote many notes for him on the teachings of the Catholic Church. So eagerly did he receive my instructions that he expressed a desire to enter a monastery, after his release, and to study the monastic way of life for a year or two. I assured him that this would be possible.

Of course, as prisoners, we couldn't see one another, except at exercise in the prison yard and we were certainly not allowed to talk to one another. However, we couldn't let Christmas pass without celebrating it, and celebrate it we did in style!

The Christmas cards I made were not, I fear, a work of art but I was very pleased with them. They had a star pencilled in one corner and the rays from the star shone down on a crib in the opposite corner. Then on the top I wrote: "Glory to God in the highest and on earth peace to men of good will" and on the bottom: "Mary brought forth her first-born Son and wrapped Him in swaddling clothes and laid Him in a Manger."

I sent out a couple of dozen of these cards and some of the prisoners sent cards to me. Wolfgang Gruen's card to me had a Christmas candle, beautifully drawn, with the wax dripping down onto the holly; and he actually had a little poem on his card expressing his Christmas greetings. Arnold Khiem, sent a card showing a Christmas tree decorated with lights and toys. Another prisoner's card was quite ingenious. It had two sheets of paper stuck together with soap. On the first sheet a window was cut and when you opened the window you could see on the second sheet a little Church covered and surrounded with snow. We were delighted with our cards and through them our Christmas wishes went round from cell to cell and the Communist guards knew nothing about our postal service.

Then on the 23rd of December I had a great stroke of luck. I was summoned downstairs to an office and given three tins of food plus two bars of chocolate. I learned afterwards that Fr. MacElroy, my superior in Shanghai, had been sending food to me ever since my arrest the year before. This was the first time I had received any of the presents. I brought the tins back to my cell and found that they contained beautiful pork, beef and peaches. Other prisoners had been receiving food parcels occasionally and they used to send me morsels of food. Now I was able to give them something in return. It was not very much when shared out among twenty-five or thirty people, but after rice and tasteless vegetables, which were our normal diet, it was banquet fare, and far more precious than the turkey dinner you get at home. Afterwards, I got notes of thanks. One prisoner wrote: "Oh Father, I have dreamed of peaches and chocolate and who would ever think that at Christmas they would come along."

Another development around this time was the introduction of a jail journal, which Wolfgang Gruen secretly operated and distributed to various prisoners. He wrote it on sheets of toilet paper and filled his journal with little incidents in the prison, which he would play up in a most amusing fashion. Sometimes he invented imaginary happenings in the world of the future in which some of us prisoners were featured as playing prominent parts. In the run up to Christmas, another prisoner decided to bring out a rival jail journal. I cannot divulge the name of the author, but his journal had a wonderful editorial on Christmas. The gist of it went something like this: "We must all get behind this Little Man, the Little Man being the Christ-Child born in Bethlehem. Let's all, every nation here, get behind Him, look at all He has done for us during these years and look at the peace and joy He has brought us inside, just thinking about Him."

To me the editorial was a real thriller and I wrote a note to the author: "You thanked me for the meat and chocolate but your editorial has done more than anything else to make this Christmas a happy one."

To the Communists, Christmas meant nothing: the monotonous routine of prison life would remain unchanged. We rose with the whistle in the mornings, had our rice and vegetables passed in through the bars twice daily and looked at the grey prison walls all day. But with our Christmas cards, our jail journal, our songs and letters we were full of peace and the Christmas spirit. Wolfgang Gruen sent me a note, which expressed the feelings of us all. He said: "Never in my life have I known a Christmas as happy as this. There is so much give and take. We are all suffering, yet there is such good feeling between us." Strange that he would get peace and happiness at Christmas in a Communist jail!

I was particularly glad that he should say this. Only a few weeks before, knowing that he was depressed and unhappy, I had sent him a note in which I said: "May God give you peace of mind." And at that time he replied: "You speak of peace of mind, that Heaven sent gift. I have never known it."

Another diversion for Christmas was the exchanging of songs we knew. Fr. Carascal had previously sent me the complete words of the *Adeste Fideles*. From a German prisoner I got the words of "The Last Rose of Summer" and from an American "When Irish eyes are smiling" and the song which Bing Crosby made famous, "White Christmas." This American asked me to send him the words of "A Little Bit of Heaven," and I obliged. It is a sentimental little song about Ireland.

> *"Have you ever heard the story of how Ireland got its name.*
> *If you listen, Oh I'll tell you from whence old Ireland came.*
> *'Tis the story of the grandest little Isle beyond the sea.*
> *And here's the way my dear old mother sang the song to me.*
> *Sure a little bit of Heaven fell from out the sky one day"* and so on.

A few days before Christmas I got a strange request from Wolfgang Gruen. He wanted my empty toothpaste tube. I sent it to him and on Christmas Eve I received a present from him, a beautiful pencil holder made out of the tube. He had rolled the lead very tight, then wrapped paper around it and covered the paper with a pattern of multi-coloured threads which he pulled from his socks. He gave similar holders as Christmas presents to other prisoners and we were all able to put our little butts of pencil into them.

Alas for our nice pencil holders! A few days after Christmas we were all suddenly brought out of our cells and made to stand facing the wall on the corridor outside. The guards searched every cell, found our pencil holders and crushed them into smithereens.

They didn't find our Christmas cards however. We had destroyed them all after suspecting that a search was imminent.

On Christmas Eve came the highlight of the whole feast. Word was passed around that we must be very quiet at five o'clock, when the guards would be changed. We didn't know why or from whom the message came, but at five o'clock there wasn't a sound from our row of cells. We were all listening intently. Suddenly our young Irish-Texan prisoner Dill Kennedy burst out singing in a beautiful tenor voice. Defying prison rules, he sang "Silent Night." We listened spellbound as the notes of the most famous and perhaps the most beautiful of all Christmas carols pierced the prison gloom.

> *"Silent night, holy night, All is calm, all is bright,*
> *Round yon Virgin Mother and Child. Holy infant so tender and mild.*
> *Sleep in heavenly peace, Sleep in heavenly peace."*

226

There wasn't another sound until he had finished the last note and then there was a terrific burst of clapping from every cell. Immediately we heard guards rushing up the stairs to the singer's cell and of course he was punished. A week or so later we saw him at exercise and he passed the message round: "Boys it was worth it." And indeed it was.

Christmas Day was rather an anti-climax after the excitement of Christmas Eve. We didn't mind. We were happy and we had made even the Communists take note of the feast. But the irrepressible Gruen caused another incident. He was passing my cell after being down in the prison yard for exercise when he whispered: "Happy Christmas, Father."

The guard on the floor below happened to be looking up and he came charging upstairs to my cell. "What did he say?" the warden demanded. "Oh he just said Happy Christmas," I replied. "There is no such thing as Christmas in this prison. You are all criminals. You are not allowed to celebrate Christmas," he said indignantly. I was beginning to feel very brave by this time so I retorted: "You can't stop us celebrating Christmas. My Christmas is in my heart." And in saying that I knew I spoke for all.

On the Epiphany night while in my prison cell, I recalled with gratitude those good friends, men of many nations, who shared the hardships and the joys of that Christmas in prison. My wish for all of them was that it might always be Christmas in their hearts. As a great missionary priest once said: "For those who love God, every day is Christmas Day."

The New Year 1953 heralded a surprise for prisoners: soup was introduced onto the menu in this section of the prison. We were even allowed a little bread to go with this beverage. I found the soup so salty that, after taking it, I was unable to get sufficient water to quench my thirst. Having left my mug behind in Lokawei Prison, I now sorely missed a drinking utensil. The prison guard refused point blank to supply me with another mug and the only substitute I had was a tiny vessel which would hold only a couple of mouthfuls.

Every day I thought about and prayed for the Legionaries and Missionaries I had worked with in the past, having little idea how most of them were at the present time, or if indeed they were alive. Word came to me at this time through a fellow prisoner that my good friend and co-worker, Fr. Joe Sheng, had died some time ago in this very prison. I felt sure that he was now in heaven. He died the death of a martyr.[57]

---

[57] See Appendix V.

CHAPTER THIRTY THREE

PROMOTED TO THE FIFTH FLOOR

But in this manner the Holy Spirit also helps our weakness.
For we do not know what we should pray for as we ought. (Romans 8:26)

I n a prison cell continued ... By this time, I had become a hardened jailbird. Since my captivity began, I had spent seven months in Lokawei Prison; a period on a lower floor of Ward Road Jail; a term in cell 2146 and a stretch on the fourth floor of an adjoining block, where many foreign prisoners - American, English, Russian, Polish, Japanese, Korean, Filipino and Yugoslavian were being "educated" and brain-washed. My time on the fourth floor had lasted four months.

On St. Patrick's Day, 1953, I commenced a Novena to Our Lady for the Feast of the Annunciation, little knowing that I might need every help and grace for the new and terrible ordeal ahead.

The upper floors of Ward Road, because they were more exposed to extremes of climate - stifling heat in the summer and unbearable cold during the winter - offered additional sources of torture. For my "crimes" and my many breaches of discipline, I was transferred to the dreaded fifth floor. This level housed many other foreigners, a good number of these men being priests.

My only hope and that of other prisoners on this floor was to live moment by moment. Recalling again the words of Our Lord "Be not solicitous for tomorrow, for tomorrow will be solicitous for itself; sufficient for the day is the evil thereof", (cf. Matt.6:24ff.) I set myself a strict horarium of discipline, including prayer and meditation. The slightest negative thought of yesterday or worry for tomorrow would upset me and but for the grace of God, ultimately break my spirit.

Unknown to me, other priests, including Monsignor Prevost and Fr. Legrand, suffered on this fifth floor at the same time as myself; but we were all in solitary confinement and given no information on other prisoners. In some instances, empty cells divided us. With a strict order of silence in force, we had little means of getting to know each other. At once, I missed the relative freedom of floor number four. Prisoners here had to maintain a good self-discipline in the struggle to retain sanity. Despite this increased hardship, I was inwardly happy in the knowledge that my imprisonment was serving a purpose. Like numerous members of the Legion of Mary and my fellow religious Missionaries, I was in effect suffering for the sake of Christ, who had suffered and died on the cross of Calvary to save mankind.

From time to time, good days in the past came to mind as in a dream - travelling long distances throughout picturesque China to promote the Legion of Mary, setting up Praesidia, Curiae, meetings with Bishops, priests, receiving all those wonderful copies of *Maria Legionis* and letters from Ireland. These thoughts might be followed by the most depressing images and a sense of not being in control of my situation. The tendency was to turn inwards at this time, to put blame on myself. I understood as never before how easy it might be to go insane in this place, to lose hope and give up the battle. But the grace of God sustained me in my hour of need.

During those long, months of solitary imprisonment on Floor Five, I was not even allowed out to relieve nature or take communal exercise. Several inmates went completely mad. One man would howl and shriek, calling out "Mammy, Mammy; Tommy, Tommy, open the gate, open the gate". All night this would go on. It was very disturbing. During those nights of shrieking and later, when I became physically ill myself and could sleep very little, the hours would drag interminably. Next day, through loss of sleep I would be unable to concentrate on anything. Life became almost unbearable, humanly speaking.

After sleepless nights, days of listlessness and hours of pain, I felt the greatest sympathy for those likewise afflicted. If they could only realise the tremendous spiritual powerhouse they generate, the great value for themselves and others of these terrible sufferings when united to the Passion of Christ, they would be greatly consoled and relieved. Such was my mentality. It gave me a sense of self-worth and much of the time inwardly at peace.

Before my arrest I used to feel a bit of a hypocrite when reciting the words of the Stations of the Cross: "May I die for love of Thee as Thou hast died for love of me". I thought I did not fully mean them. But when I found myself all alone in prison, these words took on new meaning. In the absence of Stations of the Cross, my constant prayer was that of St. Paul: "God forbid that I should glory in anything save in the Cross of Our Lord Jesus Christ... for I exceedingly abound in joy in my tribulations;" (cf. Gal.6:14) and I meant every word. As I stated before in relation to my earlier confinement, I was also greatly sustained by the spirit of De Montfort's *True Devotion to Mary*.

I have dreaded excessive heat all my life. Floor Five, Ward Road Jail was my ultimate nightmare. From May to August of 1953 in that bake-oven right beneath the prison-roof, I sweltered and languished. On several occasions I was close to losing all consciousness. One more summer in that ghastly heat and I surely would have died.

All I wore was a pair of shorts. When they became soaked with sweat I would hang them on a peg to dry and put on others that were stinking with perspiration. When the slightest breeze wafted through the burning bars of my cell, I would start to sneeze, sometimes twenty or thirty times in succession. Sneezing was still forbidden.

To make matters worse, I was on the West Wing of the prison where from noon until sunset the fierce heat of "shi sai" or western sunshine bore down on my cell. The bars themselves became unbearably hot and I could scarcely touch them and I could only lie with my face close to the door to catch a puff of breath.

From five o'clock in the evening, the situation became intolerable beyond words. The temperature in the shade could be up to one hundred degrees Fahrenheit. Despite the dearth of water meted out for drinking I tried sprinkling some around the cell in a vain attempt to keep this oven cool. In the intense humidity perspiration rolled down my body in streams. The cell walls gave off a mouldy smell, which added to my discomfort. There was no escape and no respite except in sleep, though even then, the torture continued.

The jails reeked and crawled with insects and vermin of all kinds. One of the most awful scourges was an insect known by the complimentary name of "Hsiang Guniang" or "Scented Girl" - the Asiatic bedbug. It is a colourful and attractive bug, but when crushed between one's fingers it exudes a frightful odour.

Of all aspects relating to prison life, what upset me most were these pests. Battalions of Hsiang Guniang used to crawl up from under the floor and out of little holes in the wall, even in daytime. Some prisoners spread strips of white cloth on the floor. On waking, they would shake the bugs off onto this cloth, capture them and crack them against the wall, leaving bloody marks in their wake. I tried something similar, squashing them as they ran up the walls, but I found that it only succeeded in adding to the stench in my cell.

One day, I heard from a guard that the Communists were about to make a concerted effort to rid the prison of the bugs. I rejoiced, but my joy was short lived. The authority's first method, to dose all cells with D.D.T., had only limited success. Another attempt followed, this time pulling up the floors. They were just frames of wood, which fitted perfectly into each cell. The guards ordered the prisoners, to carry these floors out on to the flat roof of the prison.

There the timber frames were left to scorch in the summer sun. Meantime, floors, corridors and cells were washed and disinfected.

This enormous task did not however clear the cells of these creepy-crawlies. After a few nights, the bugs have multiplied in the walls would come out as fresh as ever. There was no stopping this army!

A solution did present itself eventually as there was a treatment put in place in the prison for infested bedclothes. It consisted of a room that housed a steam pressure unit. All prisoner's clothes were through this treatment over a period of time. Then the prison authorities decided to put all the floors under this steam pressure procedure too. It was a colossal job, but it was done. All the toilet buckets were also cleansed one by one. This method of combating the infestation met with greater success and brought much needed relief.

If the Communists are worthy of praise for attempting to rid China of banditry, prostitution and other scourges, they surely deserve praise for ridding such detention centres as Ward Road Jail of bugs, notably, the mischievous "Scented Girl".

However, with so many insect bites, I developed frightful 'prickly heat' on my arms and on the backs of my legs. These quickly festered and, in order to ease the pain, I wrapped them with pieces of what rags of clothing I had. This generated even more sweating, though it slightly eased the pain.

I also developed lumbago, and was afflicted with an excruciating earache. Constipation was also a source of constant irritation. Add to this, the presence of shrieking lunatics, insomnia and disgusting food and it would be hard to imagine a situation more miserable.

Occasionally the doctor would pay a visit to prisoners. He always wore a strip of gauze over his nostrils. Due to the absence of proper washing facilities, prisoners stank to high heaven. The doctor would stand at the bars for a few minutes, ask a question or two, hand out a few pills and move on. His pills did little good, yet his presence represented a faint spark of light in a sea of infernal darkness.

One day, my friend the sparrow flew in to visit me. I was delighted to once more see the little creature. From that day forwards, I managed to save a few grains of rice for the chirping angel of comfort. This bird was remarkable. Flying in from the Shanghai rooftops, he would hop around, cocking his head in a friendly fashion. The moment a guard approached from either end of the passageway, he spread his wings, let out a few chirps and flew off. That was my warning to stop praying out loud, or to stop singing and remember the prison rules.

That feathered creature was my only link with the outside world. While human visitors were forbidden to enter the prison, even the Communists could not curtail his freedom. At a critical time, a token consolation can soften the agony of prison life and act as a sign. My flying guest helped to ward off despair at a time when I was oblivious as to what was going on in the outside world. I didn't even know whether my mother was alive or dead.

For a priest or a well-instructed Christian layperson, prison life is, to an extent, endurable. I pitied those who had no religion, especially the Chinese Communists who had fallen into disfavour with the regime and were now prisoners like the rest of us.

I made it a rule for myself to keep occupied all day, making out a schedule following it as closely as I could. It became a good timekeeping device.

The daily prison routine on floor five varied a little, but as usual, the day began with the rising signal: the guard's shrill whistle. I couldn't "jump" out of bed in this cell as I slept on the floor between Chinese quilts. The first task, after dressing, was to roll up these quilts and place them in one corner of the cell.

Next came my morning meditation. I had no books, of course, but I built my reflection on some text of Scripture. That took me up to breakfast time. I was served rice and a little vegetable which came in an oblong tin dish, pushed through the bars at about eight o'clock and accompanied by a meagre drink of water. By this time I had become accustomed to such rations and the use of chopsticks. I had eaten Chinese food in my upcountry Mission House, many Convents, Monasteries and remote outposts all over China and had learned to like it. In prison, therefore, I was far better off than the foreigners who had never eaten anything but foreign-style food in the hotels and guesthouses of cosmopolitan Peking or Shanghai.

After breakfast I 'took a walk', meaning three short steps repeated back and forth innumerable times in my cell. You can't do much by way of exercise in a cell not much wider than a telephone booth. My thoughts at that time were that we should never stop thanking God for fresh air, exercise and freedom of movement; these things can be so easily taken for granted.

During that walk in my cell, I recited the *Te Deum* and the *Magnificat*. Then I sang. I had learned off a significant number of songs and I chose different ones, for entertainment or encouragement. I had to sing in a low voice to myself when the guard was near. If my little friend the sparrow indicated that the coast was clear by remaining quiet, I sang out loud and revelled in it.

After my "walk" I celebrated "Mass". I went through all the prayers of the Mass, as far as I could remember them, in union with Masses going on around the world. On Sunday I made it a High Mass, singing the *Gloria, Credo, Sanctus* and *Pater Noster*. The spiritual communion in every "Mass" was a great consolation.

Then came my study period. In my mind I tried to translate the Gospel passages, as far as I remembered them, into Latin or analysed the Latin of the hymns. I drafted letters on imaginary subjects in Latin or French. I composed poems in English. In all, I composed thirty-five poems, some of them forty stanzas long. I don't know how they would rank as poetry but I do know that making them up was a fine mental exercise.

After study, I recited three Rosaries and the prayers of the Legion of Mary, again walking back and forth. More study came next, followed by a visit in spirit to the Blessed Sacrament. I knew that the Sacred Heart Church in Honkew section of Shanghai was fairly near and I used to pay a mental visit to that Church as part of my morning routine.

Dinner was pushed through the bars about two o'clock in the afternoon. Again the meal consisted of rice and a little vegetable, with hot water for drinking purposes. Soup was occasionally provided. When I was in good health, I was always hungry.

After dinner, I recited the *Miserere* and *Benedictus* and sang more songs. Another study period followed. Then I recited another three Rosaries and Legion prayers.

In the late afternoon I sat down again, this time to practise writing Chinese characters. I gave myself a Scripture text to write out in Chinese. I could not afford to use my little pencil as the point was getting short; so I just drew each character with my finger on my knee.

During the evening I "attended" Benediction of the Blessed Sacrament in spirit. I recited all the Benediction hymns and prayers. This task completed, I prepared my meditation for next morning and made an examination of conscience. My training for the priesthood in Dalgan Park was a great support to me at this crisis time in my life and I thanked God for the discipline and spiritual formation instilled into me at the Seminary.

At eight o'clock the guards whistle sounded for bedtime. There was no lights-out rule on this floor. The light in the passageway burned all night. At the sound of the whistle, I obediently spread out my quilts on the cell-floor, lay down and fell asleep.

CHAPTER THIRTY FOUR

NEWS FROM CHINA

And a great sign appeared in heaven: a woman clothed with the sun,
and the moon was under her feet and upon her head,
a crown of twelve stars. (Apocalypse 12:1)

The following items of correspondence
are from the pen of an unnamed Columban Priest:

Hong Kong
April 9th 1953

A few days ago I came in touch with a gentleman who had recently arrived from Shanghai. He is a German Jew by the name of Mr. Gruen, who in better days had been a business-man in Shanghai. I heard that he had been with Fr. Aedan in prison, so naturally I got in touch with him as soon as possible. However, it is some time since he laid eyes on Fr. McGrath. Mr. Gruen had been incarcerated in another prison for a certain period before his expulsion from China towards the end of March. Still, he is the last person to have seen the Irish priest. He was separated from Fr. Aedan on the 21st of January of this year. They had been together in the same prison he says from October of 1952.

Mr. Gruen is loud in his praises of Fr. Aedan, his cheerfulness, his charity and his spirit of sacrifice and also his ingenuity in preaching the Gospel, in season and out of season. Whenever possible, he instructs inmates, prison guards and all who come in contact with him. This Mr. Gruen is now one of his most fervent and enthusiastic converts. He told me that for more than twenty years (he is now over forty) he had been searching for the truth, but it was only when he met Fr. Aedan and placed himself under his instruction that he really began to understand the doctrines of the Catholic Church. Now he is well along the road and hopefully looking forward to Baptism in the near future.

Since Mr. Gruen was transferred to the Ward Road Prison where Fr. Aedan was in October, his cell adjoined Fr. Aedan's cell. There were no solid doors on the cells, just strong wooden bars; so the two prisoners were able to carry on conversations in low tones while the guard was at the other end of the corridor. In this way Mr. Gruen was able to communicate with Fr. Aedan and tell him, amongst other things of his spiritual difficulties and aspirations. For the most part, Fr. Aedan gave the answers and explanations in writing, using small pieces of toilet paper, measuring six inches by four inches. Speaking was one thing; writing was another. If they were caught speaking, prisoners usually got an angry dressing down; but if a written document were to be found in a cell, or on the corridor, it led to serious and prolonged investigations. To avoid such a misfortune the pair evolved a plan: Fr. Aedan wrote his document, rolled it into a ball and attached it to a piece of fine twine. He then took aim at the door of Mr. Gruen's cell. If it landed within reach of Mr. Gruen's hand, all was well. If not, Fr. Aedan retrieved it and had another throw, and so on until his objective had been achieved. Thus were passed on the truths of the Catholic Church. It was not on Mr. Gruen alone that the plan was carried out. Fr. Aedan had several other prospective converts on his string: On one occasion the string broke and the document remained on the corridor floor until found by a prison guard. There was much questioning and a prisoner who was regarded as trustworthy by the guards was commissioned to translate the correspondence into Chinese. He did this, but the translation he rendered to the authorities was something far removed from any doctrine ever expounded by the Catholic Church! It was in fact some ancient joke that the prisoner conveniently remembered. So, the document was considered harmless and the matter was dropped.

When Mr. Gruen entered Ward Road Prison, there were as many as fifteen to twenty thousand prisoners confined there. Later the Foreigners, about fifty in number, were separated from the Chinese prisoners and confined in one section of the prison. Some such prisoners, e.g., a batch of Yugoslavians, were confined simply for petty theft. There was only a small group of political prisoners, amongst them, Fr. Aedan McGrath, Fr. Carascal, Mr. Gruen and an American named Kennedy. The two latter were in on charges of espionage. Mr. Kennedy had requested Fr. Aedan to instruct him in the doctrine of the Church.

Fr. Carascal was released some time ago. He said that he had specifically questioned Fr. Aedan on his treatment in his earlier jails. Fr. Aedan assured him that though he had been subjected to many periods of interrogation, he had never been physically tortured. Since arriving at Ward Road Prison there had been little questioning on former activities.

On January 21st Mr. Gruen was suddenly taken from Ward Road Prison and transferred to a military prison, where after another period of detention he was tried by a Military Tribunal and sentenced to expulsion. The day he was transferred from Ward Road he was able to say a few words of goodbye to Fr.

235

Aedan before leaving. He asked Fr. Aedan if he had any messages for his friends outside. His response: "Tell them I have no complaints and I am perfectly happy in jail." On that day, in Mr. Gruen's words: "Fr. Aedan was in good spirits, physically fit and spiritually unbreakable."

Mr. Gruen is convinced that Fr. Aedan shall be expelled soon, but then Fr. Carascal thought the same when he came out. It is difficult even to make a guess at it. We can only keep on hoping and praying for his release.

April 11th 1953

Today I got a message from fellow-Columban, Fr. Ted MacElroy through a Portuguese lady who arrived from Shanghai last night. Apparently our letters are being held up - intercepted in other words. Fr. MacElroy said that he had not heard from me for some time. The letters I sent him did not arrive. He managed to bring in some things to Fr. Aedan for Christmas and he received them. Lately he tried to present some light clothing, but the parcel was refused (by the prison authorities) and returned to him.

CHAPTER THIRTY FIVE

A MISSIONARY CONDEMNED TO EXILE

I turned myself to other things, and I saw the oppressions that are done under the sun and the tears of the innocent... (Ecclesiasticus 4:1)

In a Prison Cell continued... The weeks and months dragged on in desperate monotony. Autumn came and went in a whimper. The winter was cold and harsh. My cell was exceptionally cold. Christmas had none of the charm of our experience the previous year. There were no cards or greetings to exchange between prisoners and no hymns; but it was inwardly a time of joy and hope. I had been cut off from my fellow prisoners as much as I had been cut off from the outside world.

It was on or about Easter Sunday 1954 that a young detective from Tientsin came to my fifth floor cell to interrogate me. He asked me questions about various Legionaries, none of whom I could remember. Then he asked me if I recalled a certain lady teacher in Tientsin.

"No", I replied, "I never heard of her".

"Oh, but you must know her, she was a great Legionary and a magnificent pianist, well known all over Tientsin," he said.

"Well", I answered, "I simply don't know her".

"But she knows you and speaks very highly of you" he added.

"It is possible," I replied, "that she knew me but I just can't recall having met her. And if she plays the piano well, I would certainly have asked her to play for me and would not have forgotten her. Therefore I couldn't have known her".

When he asked again, I admitted that I might have heard her name mentioned, but that was all. He didn't press me too hard on any of the questions, but I wondered if he was trying to find evidence to put me away indefinitely. There was no immediate follow up on this particular line of interrogation.

About two weeks later another detective came along and questioned, not only me, but several other prisoners on the fifth floor. When he spoke to me through the bars, the interrogator asked me for what cause was I arrested, and I replied: "I have been accused of promoting the Legion of Mary, which the authorities have banned as a reactionary and secret society. I have always denied these allegations against the Legion, and I deny them to the end for they are simply untrue." He seemed to accept my answer with calm resignation, and then asked: "Well, if you think you have been arrested and held in prison unjustly for thirty-two months, what do you think of our Government?" I tried to evade his question, wondering what was behind it. "All I know is this: that I have done no evil, neither has the Legion of Mary, but in spite of this I have now been detained for nearly three years in prison cut off from the people I love. What sort of treatment is that? How therefore can I have a favourable opinion of your Government?" To my surprise, he made no comment on my statement. After a further short exchange of conversation, he walked away. What was all this about?

I had not long to wait for an answer: Within the hour, along came a guard with one of the prisoners who was allowed to perform chores within the prison. The guard opened my cell, allowing his assistant to enter. My visitor kindly gave me a haircut and trimmed my beard. This done, he went along to other cells occupied by foreigners and apparently repeated this procedure for them. All this set me thinking. Was this a prelude to release or another ruse to get our hopes up only to have them dashed? It was only afterwards that I discovered that the timeframe for this new treatment of foreign prisoners coincided with the approach of the Geneva Conference. The release of some key prisoners represented a good political opportunity.

For the next few days, I felt upset and distracted at prayer. Instead of caring 'just for today' as had been my strict rule of life, I began to dream of tomorrow and tomorrow and tomorrow, and when nothing happened I became restless. "Hope delayed makes the heart sick", as Scripture says. I decided to forget all about my hopes of a transfer from this torturous floor of Ward Road Jail, and instead went back to my hard and fast rule of being concerned only with today and letting tomorrow look after itself. Within a short space of time, peace returned to my soul.

No sooner had I convinced myself that the incidents mentioned were just more Communist capers to deceive and taunt prisoners, the barber came round again. He gave me a second haircut within a week. Reluctant to be optimistic for a second time, I promptly decided to forget about the prospects of release, and go on with my daily schedule regardless of haircuts and interviews. Then, without notice, a guard, accompanied once more by another prisoner came to my cell door and told me: "bundle up your things". Overjoyed at the command, I gladly obeyed his orders. He went away and promised to return in a short time.

Now it happened that some days previously another prison guard had given me a tin of red peppers, which I had since been using sparingly with my meals. These Chinese peppers are quite spicy, and when chopped up into small pieces and mixed with olive oil, are very tasty. After thirty-two months of prison diet I greatly relished this unexpected treat. As a result, I anxiously awaited each meagre portion of rice that constituted our daily diet, smacking my lips when I heard the guard approaching. These peppers I kept in a tiny bowl, and even between meals I would dip my chopsticks in them and taste anew their rich flavour. You might say, I became attached to my little bowl of peppers; and now I feared that they might not be allowed me in a new cell, or indeed, a new prison. So, when the guard returned with another prisoner, I asked: "May I take my red peppers with me?"

"Bring them along", he replied abruptly. Then the guard unlocked my prison cell and swung open the door. The prisoner shook my hand warmly and said: "Congratulations, you are going home." I was flabbergasted and reluctant to allow myself to believe him. The guard ordered this man to help me carry my paltry things.

In a few moments I stood outside my cell for the first time in months. I could hardly walk. All the other prisoners were ordered to turn their backs on me as I struggled to walk forward along the corridor. One of the poor fellows who had gone mad was forcibly held down by a guard while I passed his cell. I was then brought downstairs on what was to be the first leg of my road to freedom.

I was led across the yard and into the police station. Not being used to walking, my muscles were soft and weak and that short journey was quite far enough for me. My fingerprints were taken yet again. I received back my wristwatch, Rosary beads, medals, belt and everything they had taken from me and given back a number of times within the past few years. I was in a daze. Could it be true or was I destined for yet further detention?

After a tense delay of one hour, I was taken out through the prison gate between two armed guards. A fine American car was parked and waiting. The prison authorities apparently used the American car for greater secrecy. The usual means of transport for prisoners was the common "Red Maria" or "Black Maria". Ordered to get in, I sat in the centre of the back seat of this plush car still grasping my red peppers in my lap! How absurd it all seems in hindsight. While in prison, small things take on huge proportions. The driver revved the engine and we were on our way.

We raced across the city at breakneck speed. Like a child holding onto a toy, I still clutched my oily red peppers lest they be spilled. Eventually we reached Lokawei Prison. I was back to where I started! Yet, this time the police did not take away my watch. Strange to say, they took everything else, including my red peppers! I was escorted to a private cell in a part of the station I had never before seen.

Was the entire operation another act of cruelty? Perhaps I was having a nightmare and about to wake up in my cell on Floor Five of Ward Road Jail.

As I entered, I noticed a chair in a corner of the cell. Out of enforced habit, I was about to sit on the floor when the policeman with me said: "Have a chair." This was most irregular treatment. The Communist security personnel always gave the impression of being incapable of kindness.

So I sat in the chair and looked around. The walls were damp. The smell was unpleasant. My police escort locked me in and walked away without explanation. Later, a man brought a little rice to me. It did not taste so good without my red peppers. It was no better than that served in Ward Road Jail.

Hours began to pass, and sitting on that chair became anything but comfortable. Eventually, I heard someone down the prison corridor calling for a policeman. After a few minutes someone came along and said to the prisoner: "By the way, if you are uncomfortable in the chair you may sit on the ground." I had no idea who this prisoner might be; nor did I know at the time that a third priest was locked up in the same section. I was soon to find out however that they were Pastors who had done excellent work in China to spread the Legion of Mary.

During that day, prisoners were escorted individually at intervals to the toilet and to the washing area. After meals, I brought out my bowl and chopsticks to wash them. Not knowing how long I might be detained in this prison, I began my daily routine all over again. I said my Rosary and other usual prayers and tried to resume my studies of the Chinese written language. That night I slept, but only for a short time.

Next morning, rice gruel was served for breakfast. Half an hour later, a guard came into my cell. He asked me to stand up and said: "You are now going to receive the generosity of the Chinese Government. You are going to be expelled from the country. In a few minutes you will be brought upstairs to receive your condemnation sentence. And remember, 'no awkward questions'. When receiving your condemnation stand erect, your hands together, respectfully, and don't move. When leaving, you will be allowed to take whatever you want with you, and whatever you don't need you may send back to your mission."

I listened attentively, not daring to interrupt his flow of words. "Now" he said, "have you got good clothes to wear?"

"I just have the rags you see me wearing," I replied.

He stared at me: "What, no better?"

I stated firmly. "None whatsoever."

"Well, if you wish you can send to your house for them," he intoned.

I soon realised they intended to dress me well, for the admiration of friends in Hong Kong. He ordered me to sit down and write to my superior for clothes. I wrote a note to Fr. MacElroy, though I did not use his real name. My note was delivered by a messenger to the Columban Procuration with a request for my clothes. Several hours later, Fr. MacElroy sent some clothes, a fine overcoat and a pair of shoes. When I tried on the shoes, I found that they were too big for me. I refused to wear them. I told the guard that I would wear instead, what I had on my feet, and send back the other pair. He said: "Take with you what you can carry and return the rest."

In the afternoon, a young Chinese lady came to my cell door and said I must give an exact list of all items I was sending back to the Columban Procuration. So, as instructed, I wrote down what I wished to be returned: old pairs of shoes, an odd sock, even two sleeves from a shirt, minus the shirt and a few more items. It would have been more practical to bin them.

Fr. MacElroy later informed me that when the bundle of unwanted items arrived, he had to examine each item in detail, even the odd sock and pair of shirtless sleeves, sign a document and send it back to the police.

After a tense few minutes, I was led upstairs to receive my condemnation. Two guards with revolvers accompanied me and led me into a hallway. The picture of Mao Tse-tung, adorned with two flags, hung on one of the walls. I faced two male representatives of the Communist Regime, whom I presumed to be judges, and a female secretary. All three sat behind a table. They looked nervous, for what reason I could only guess. One of the judges stood up and very solemnly read a page and a half of my crimes. According to what he said, these crimes were punishable by hanging under the Communist system.

Beginning with Monsignor Riberi, he alleged that the Papal Nuncio had ordered me to China for underground work among the youth. He also said that I was out to destroy their autonomous National Church Movement and that the Legion of Mary had completely opposed the idea of a National Church. He further charged that I had destroyed Minutes Books and lists of Legionaries in order to cover my tracks. He accused me of being an international spy and listed a host of other crimes that I can't now remember.

After reading my indictment very solemnly, he resumed his seat and invited me to examine everything that was written down. This I did over the next few minutes. I then had to sign the condemnation and impress my thumbprint on the paper.

The judge stood up once more and said: "I hereby, in the name of the People of China, expel you from this country, never to return."

On Wednesday 28th April 1954, I walked down the stairs, a missionary condemned to exile.

PART SIX

VICTORY THROUGH MARY

CHAPTER THIRTY SIX

JOURNEY TO FREEDOM

God gives the lonely a home to live in,
leads prisoners out into prosperity. (Psalms 68:6)

Outside the building I met Fr. Legrand, who had apparently gone through the same process as myself. He was the prisoner who had complained to the guard about having to sit for too long on his hard chair. The poor man was looking like a ghost, and I must have made a like impression on him. He stared at me and said: "Oh, you are here, Fr. Aedan! I was told that you had confessed and had gone home to Ireland two years ago."

Monsignor Prevost was with him and the three of us were hurried into a waiting car. We laughed as we shook hands, astonished that we were allowed to talk; but our guard, in the front seat, didn't seem to care any more. His job was to drive us to our destination. We were out of prison and free as the birds!

The guard drove us to the railway station and parked the car. We followed him joyfully across the tracks to the train that was to take us to Hong Kong.

Looking back on it now, that journey had an air of unreality. A few details stand out: the cleanliness of our surroundings, the goodness of the food. We had been given pocket money to spend. Apart from food and light refreshments, there was little that we wanted to buy. I remember Monsignor Prevost waking up after a nap and exclaiming, "My God, this is terrible!" He must have been thinking of the contrast between that train carriage and the prison cell. After so many endless months in the hands of the Communist Regime, being told what to do day after day, I too was pondering on the strangeness of it all. Our imprisonment was suddenly over. Here we were being transported towards Hong Kong after we had come so near to martyrdom. Now our sufferings were ending, not in glorious martyrdom but in ignominious rejection. It seemed as if it were all in vain.

The Reds had no further use for us, so they were setting us free. We could return to our families and friends at home and be comforted and made much of by them. However, the Chinese Catholics, our friends, our people to whom, we thought, our presence and example meant so much, would have to struggle on and continue to suffer without us. We were no longer to be part of the landscape, no longer necessary!

As prisoners, we had done our share of suffering and indeed had been treated with scorn and contempt in our afflictions. Now, as this freedom-train rattled along, we realised that all this was in the past and the thought must have shown in our smiling faces. In the days, weeks and months ahead, instead of being despised we might be honoured perhaps as heroes. Our friends would treat us with awe and respect because of our sufferings for the Faith. We expected also to meet people who would wish to use our individual stories for the purposes of their own propaganda. All these prospects ran through my head as I looked out the train window to witness, perhaps for the last time, glimpses of the picturesque countryside I knew and loved so well. We were leaving one danger to enter another and more subtle one. God forbid that in the exciting times ahead, we should lose whatever little merit we had gained during the hard times spent in Chinese prisons.

Two guards accompanied Fr. Legrand, Monsignor Prevost and myself on the journey. We suspected that some of our fellow travellers might be Communist stooges set to watch us and listen to what we said. But we didn't care. The heady wine of freedom was beginning to affect us although our journey was only commencing. I made the Sign of the Cross as we passed by the first Church that I spotted and Monsignor Prevost cried out: "Look at the little Irishman!" Yes! We were beginning to feel, talk and act like human beings again and to forget the restrictions of captivity.

Our guards left us pretty much to ourselves most of the way, but as we neared the border they began to insist that we spend all the money that had been given to us for the journey. They told us the amount that we were allowed to take with us to Hong Kong. All the rest must be spent on the way. We wanted to give it to the guards or throw it out of the window but they would not allow that. It was given us to spend on the journey and we must spend it. Eventually we bought some gone-off melons which, fortunately, Fr. Legrand managed to dump out of the window when the guard's back was turned. The rest of the money we spent on cigarettes at the guards' suggestion. We had no intention of smoking. Fr. Legrand had never smoked and Monsignor Prevost and I had learned to do without tobacco in prison. We had no intention of subjecting ourselves to it again. There didn't seem to be much else to buy. The cigarettes were cheap and we got quite a quantity of them for the money we had to spend. This however, made an unwelcome addition to the bundles we had to carry when we got off the train.

At last the restful train journey came to an end and we realised how weak we really were as we struggled along the quarter of a mile or so that we had to walk, carrying our bags. Arriving at the frontier, we were subjected to a thorough search.

First our bags were examined. In mine, the border guards found a bundle of some hundreds of sheets of toilet paper all covered with Chinese writing. This was the fruit of the hours I had spent studying Chinese while in prison. The sheets consisted of pieces I had copied from the printed Communist propaganda we were forced to read. I had studied it only for the sake of the characters or the expression contained in isolated characters. These characters were relatively new to me. Also written on the toilet paper were bits of prayers or doctrine I was writing for practice. The guard examined these stolidly for some time, taking up sheet after sheet. At last he looked up and fixing his eyes on me asked me in a cold voice: "What is this?" I answered him quietly: "I have been in prison for almost three years and I spent much of my time learning your honourable language."

He bundled the papers together in disgust and threw them back into my bag. Later, in Hong Kong I threw those papers away. This action I have since regretted, for the notes represented many hours of hard work and transcribing them had been a great help to me when things were bad in prison.

When our bags were passed by security we were taken separately into a little private room where we were put through a thorough search of our person. Even our shoes were examined. We didn't know then what we might have been suspected of concealing. In prison we had not been allowed to possess anything, so we were not likely to have acquired much on the train journey from Shanghai. But I suppose they were looking for seditious documents! Those who engage in intrigue are always ready to suspect intrigue. I was the first to be put through this search and the operation took so long that Monsignor Prevost and Fr. Legrand, must have thought that I was being returned to Shanghai. I was allowed out of the room at last and my two fellow-priests were put through the same process in turn.

The frontier was marked by a few strands of barbed wire. There was nothing very permanent about it. On the far side stood two or three British Military Police. Their uniforms contrasted strangely with the simplicity of Chinese garb. They looked as ludicrous and out of place as in fact they were, being thousands of miles from their own land. As I looked around, I noticed that the guns of the Chinese soldiers were not pointed towards the foreign enemy who still occupied portion of their land. They pointed instead towards a blank wall so that no offence would be given in the event of their going off accidentally.

The Communists had a last request for us just before we crossed the border. It was for a photograph. I suppose they wished to have it as evidence of our having left the country in case enquiries should later be made. All three of us were allowed to put our luggage in a separate place while we posed for this historic snap. Then we crossed the boundary.

"Welcome Fathers!" said one of the British policemen (who must have heard that we were priests) as we set foot on Hong Kong territory. To us who had been years in captivity, he represented freedom and we gratefully accepted the three glasses of beer which he offered to us. Within minutes we were being greeted and given a royal reception by Fr. Palotti who was in charge of a parish not far from the boundary.

After thirty-two months in a Communist prison, Hong Kong appeared all the more a haven of civilisation. On arrival in the city, we were greeted by Fr. John MacNamara, several Columban Sisters and members of the Legion of Mary. My first enquiry was for my aged mother. I was overjoyed when told that she was hail and hearty and anxiously awaiting my return to Ireland. It was wonderful to be reunited with my many friends in Hong Kong.

Having spent a month in hospital, resting and underoing various medical examinations, I joined my brother Ivar in Formosa on the next leg of my journey back to Ireland.

CHAPTER THIRTY SEVEN

"WE HAVE YOUR HANDWRITING BEFORE US AT LAST"

Let their own table be a snare before them,
and a net for their friends. (Psalms 68:23)

TELEGRAM   3rd May 1954
                                                 8.15pm

Fr. Aedan McGrath,
c/o Maryknoll Procure,
Stanley,
Hong Kong

Joy your release. Sympathy all your sufferings. Gratitude your historic work.

Duff

Chang Road,
North Lane 105,
Formosa
17th May 1954

My dear Frank,

I have been trying to reply to your very thoughtful cable and John Nagle's letter for the past week or so and it is a hopeless job. Please forgive me. I have been quite overwhelmed by all the messages and am beginning to feel that I already received my reward for the privilege of suffering in prison.

The Concilium making me a Laureate member made me blush. I hardly thought I was eligible as a 'Legion Priest,' Frank. I don't know what to say or write, but please convey my most heartfelt gratitude to the Legionaries all over the world whose prayers I felt all the time...I never knew what grace was until I went to prison, and leaving my cell on the Feast of Grignon de Montfort I even felt a pang of regret! This is hard to understand for myself and all who know my cowardice.

Frank, this is just to let you see my handwriting. People are paying me so much attention that I have barely time for my prayers.

I attended a beautiful Acies here yesterday, with Archbishop Kuo attending. All the Spiritual Directors were Chinese except my brother Ivar. It was thrilling! I also attended my brother's Praesidium meeting, which is first class. It is good to see the Legion in motion again.

Fr. Paddy O'Connor flew from Tokyo to see me and also attended the Acies.

Again many thanks for messages and above all, prayers. Hoping to see you soon. I remain, gratefully yours in Jesus and Mary,

Aedan

P.S. I forgot the obvious of course: My first visit was to Msgr. Riberi, who is ever more and more a Legionary.

Frank Duff's reply of 29ᵗʰ May reflects his exuberance at having Fr. McGrath's "handwriting before us at last ..." Frank further intuits that the strength of the script before him provides an indication of the spirit of the scribe - "Your spirit was greater than the ordeal and you have emerged from the latter unimpaired. Truly the Lord and His Mother must have stood beside you to secure that result." He takes as an unlikely coincidence the dates of arrest and release and even goes so far as to suggest that Fr. McGrath has the merit of a martyr.

Fr. Aedan in Taipei shortly after his prison release.

Rome

17th June 1954

My dear Frank,

       Your letter addressed to me in Formosa found me here in Rome on the 14th. Many, many thanks. Again I feel bad over all the nice things you say and can't help feeling uneasy at the attention I am receiving. I need prayers now more than ever I did.

       It was on the 28th April, just when I had finished my Novena, that I realised I was being released. The fact that I did not actually leave until the 29th does not affect my belief that St. Louis was the instrument Our Lady was pleased to use.

       As you know, I was actually arrested on September 6th at 11.30 p.m., but I did not leave my room for the Police Station until 2 a.m. September 7th, a coincidence which was a great joy to me.

       I plan to leave Rome for Paris on Monday 21st, by train. I should reach Paris on Tuesday morning and spend one night there, setting out on the first leg of that journey for London by train on Wednesday morning at 11.45 a.m., arriving at about 8 p.m. I think. I shall stay with my brother in London for two to three days before moving on. So I hope to see you all before very long.

       In any case, I am building up strength so fast that I am ashamed to say I am just out of prison. Again, many thanks.

       Respectfully yours in Jesus and Mary,

Aedan McGrath

CHAPTER THIRTY EIGHT

A HERO RETURNS FROM THE FRAY

24ᵀᴴ JULY 1954

If past experience is an indication,
no branch of the Legion which is worked faithfully
according to rule will fail. (Legion Handbook)

CHURCH AND STATE JOIN WITH THE CONCILIUM IN A RECEPTION FOR FR. AEDAN MCGRATH
(Maria Legionis, Sept. 1954, pp.1-9)

The long-awaited arrival of Fr. Aedan McGrath after almost three years in a Chinese Communist prison, took place on Tuesday, 6ᵗʰ July, 1954 when he was welcomed at Dublin Airport by all the Officers of the Concilium and about a thousand Dublin Legionaries. As a symbolic gesture of the Concilium's gratitude and appreciation for his heroic and fruitful services to the Legion in China, for which he was named a Laureate member, the Concilium President, Mr. Frank Duff, after greeting him, presented Fr. Aedan McGrath with a Legion Vexillum.

Subsequently, on Sunday 25ᵗʰ July, the Concilium held a reception for Fr. Aedan McGrath in the National Stadium, Dublin, at which the heads of the Church and State were present and where three thousand active Legionaries joined in an expression of joyful gratitude for his safe return home and of deep appreciation of his great services to the Church, through the instrumentality of the Legion.

Holding the vexillum presented by Frank Duff

The function began with the singing of the *Ave Maris Stella* followed by the Legion opening prayers. The Concilium President introduced Fr. McGrath, commenting on his glorious accomplishments in China and Fr. McGrath then gave the inspiring account of his travels and travails in China which is recounted below. The Catena was recited and there followed addresses by the distinguished members of the platform - The President of Ireland, Mr. Sean T. O'Kelly; the Taoiseach (Premier); Mr. John Costello; the Papal Nuncio, Archbishop Gerald P. O'Hara; Mr. Eamon de Valera; Archbishop Liston of Auckland, New Zealand and the Lord Mayor of Dublin, Mr. Alfred Byrne. We give below, in full, the introductory address of the Concilium President and the words of Fr. Aedan McGrath; and some extracts from the addresses of the other distinguished persons who had honoured the function by their presence and who spoke so movingly.

Introduction by Mr. Frank Duff:

"We meet together to honour Fr. McGrath and to hear him speak. We are grateful to the eminent personages representing Church and State, who have come to help us in that purpose and to cast lustre on our gathering. On your behalf, I thank them.

My next function is to introduce to you Fr. McGrath. In one sense that is superfluous, but in another it is necessary because I can say things that he is not able to say. I will say them as quickly as possible. Fr. McGrath has done supreme service to the Church. It is a joy to us that he has done this through the Legion. He has provided a chapter of history, which can vie with any that the past contains.

Perhaps the whole course of history is going to be determined by that chapter. The scene has been China, that venerable land which has been of late playing a new and sinister role. A quarter of the world's population lives there and has fallen under the sway of Communism. The military victory through which the Communists gained control was so easy that they thought the intellectual and administrative one would be just as easy; and that then a compact block of Europe and Asia, from the Baltic to the Pacific, containing one third of the population of the world, would be ready for a further step in the destroying of religion and liberty on earth.

In the way of this plan, stood two men. One was Msgr. Riberi, the Internuncio to China; the other was Fr. McGrath. The former made the Legion the policy of the Church. The latter clothed that policy with living flesh. He built up the Legion throughout China. He was selected by the Internuncio for that mission because he was one of the few priests in China who was then operating the Legion. He had two branches, which he was looking after with devotion. And so there descended on him one of the mightiest tasks of all time. To him could be applied those words: "Because thou hast been faithful in small things I will set thee over great things."

Never was a duty better discharged. Moving the whole time, only a day's march ahead of the Communist armies, he showed the Missionaries how the Legion was worked and he helped them to set up branches. His motto during that period might be said to be the same as that of a respected institution among us, Duffy's Circus 'one night only'! And so the Legion grew in ninety Dioceses. So hectic and hurried an organising might be expected to be full of weakness. Surely we have here the proverbial mushroom growth! Would it collapse when pressure would be thrown on it? But no; it did not fail, for the Holy Spirit had been in that mobilising. The sequel is now written down in the ink of the historian and in the Book of Life in the blood and sufferings of the Legionaries. This epic ranks among the greatest in the story of Christendom. Msgr. Riberi declares that its heroes have the stature of the first Christians.

And what of the future? In the early days, the blood of the martyrs was the seed of the Church; spirit prevailed over numbers and always will. In China, the authentic Christian headline has been asserted and all will be inspired by it. Perhaps, indeed, we are at the beginning of the end.

And now the hero of the epic is in our midst. You are about to listen to him. He must be the happiest man on earth. Who among us does not envy him? To his superb achievement of mobilising the Legion, has been added his years in prison. That ordeal has shattered many but it did not master Fr. McGrath. The same High Power that worked with him through the organising period stayed with him in prison and strengthened him. He is now at liberty, but he has the merit of a martyr.

When he stands before you, do not forget that he represents the one thousand Legionaries who have died for their cause, the twenty-thousand who rot in prison, and those other thousands who suffer every sort of tribulation. One might say that he incarnates them all, for they all sprang out of him.

Remember too that the battleground is not China alone but the whole world. The places are different and the settings diverse, but the fight is one and the same: it is Christ or Anti-Christ. And that fight will always be determined by the same things - conviction, indomitable courage, the spirit of the martyr, the presence of Mary. Have we the spirit of our Chinese brethren? We should have, for we were the fountainhead. Let that source remain true, for much depends upon it. The example of Fr. McGrath and his spiritual children will renew our ideals."

Fr. McGrath was then presented to the audience. During the tempest of applause which followed, the "hero of the epic" stood looking around at the great throng, obviously much moved. At last he was permitted to speak.

Fr. Aedan McGrath's Address:

I am overwhelmed by this reception which you have all prepared for me today, and I find it very hard to express my feelings. First, there is a deep feeling of unworthiness, because there must be tens of thousands in China itself who have done and are still doing far more for the Church than anything I have done. Secondly, a deep feeling of gratitude for the warmth in the hearts of the Irish people who came to welcome me home at Dublin Airport, and to all of you who have attended this reception here today. I am glad of this chance to thank everybody present on my own behalf, and on behalf of the priests and people of China; to thank them above all for the prayers which kept me happy in prison and brought me out healthy and sane. Those prayers were and still are a strength to the martyrs of the Chinese Church, keeping a smile on their faces, giving courage to those who are in prison and power to others who continue the fight for the Faith. I am by nature cowardly and full of doubts: I used to be terrified of the Dublin policemen! Yet through these prayers something happened to me in prison, which I shall never understand. The night of my arrest when I was brought to the Police Station in Shanghai, the Communist police left me standing in a corner under armed guard.

They took my Rosary Beads, my spectacles and everything that was in my pockets and then throwing a mat upon the floor, a prison guard ordered me to lie down. In five minutes I was fast asleep. This, my dear people, I can never understand, except that your prayers had obtained for me the great grace of peace of mind. And I might add that from that day I was never worried, and, strange as it may seem, I can honestly say that my three years in prison were the happiest years of my life. I felt all the time greatly privileged to be where I was in the name of Jesus and Mary.

Since my release I have learned that people all over the world had been praying for me and I have longed for an opportunity to thank them. I beg everybody who has so kindly come here today, to help me in this task. I beg of you that you will thank all those whom you know have prayed for me - Adjutorian members, active members, auxiliary members of the Legion and countless other people, for the great graces they obtained for me and mine. I have many further debts of gratitude: one to the Legion of Mary itself. Outside the Faith that I received from my mother, the education I received in Belvedere College and my training for the priesthood in the Society of St. Columban, I have never learned more than I did in my years in the Legion of Mary. Again I wish to thank the Legion of Mary for sending me as an Envoy to China, for in those three or four years I have been thrilled watching Our Blessed Mother working through the most unpromising material; watching old Chinese ladies with small bound feet and as I thought, little ability, leaving the Legion meetings in the name of Mary, and in Her name working miracles of grace.

Once more I wish to thank the Legion for teaching me the True Devotion. I knew my obligation to study the True Devotion of St. Louis Marie de Montfort, but I must admit I have always found that book very difficult reading. I remember walking up O'Connell Street (Dublin) one day in 1947 with a Legion of Mary member.[58] In his own simple language, this man explained to me in five minutes what I had not understood in many years of reading, namely: that the important thing in the True Devotion was life in Mary. And it was this thought and this life that through the grace of God and your prayers, kept me perfectly happy in prison.

There is something else for which I must thank you. On the day of my arrival in Hong Kong, as I sat in the Maryknoll House with the Sisters of St.

---

[58] Seamus McCarthy.

Columban sitting around me asking questions, one Russian lady who had been President of the Slavonic Rite Praesidium in Shanghai said: "Father, don't you know the Concilium in Dublin has made you a Laureate member?" Dear brothers and sisters, at that moment I just felt like crying. I did not know what to say and to this honour I still do not know what to say. I can just thank you.

It would be difficult to over-estimate the part that His Excellency Msgr. Riberi, Papal Internuncio to China, has played in bringing the Legion of Mary to China. I was home in Ireland on holiday in 1947 and wondering if I could ever spread the Legion outside my own Chinese parish, when I received a letter from His Excellency asking me if I would be willing to propagate the Legion throughout China. You can imagine my delight, and, of course, I accepted. Arriving in Shanghai in February, 1948, I began my Legion work in St. Columban's parish and in the Aurora University. Later on, leaving about seven Praesidia established in Shanghai, I went to Central China about six hundred miles away, to Hanyang, Hankow and Wuchang, and there I left a few Praesidia. Later on I went from Shanghai to Peking (about eight hundred miles away) and spent over a month there establishing about fifteen Praesidia.

After that I went to Tientsin and I remained there as long as it was safe, for by this time the Communist armies were closing in. I knew that if I got caught, my work for the Legion would be finished. I returned to Shanghai and commenced the first Curia there, and when Shanghai looked dangerous, I went to Hong Kong, hoping to establish the Legion there, so that through Hong Kong the Legion in South-west China could receive books and have contact with Ireland. From Hong Kong I was able to establish the Legion in Canton where the Irish Jesuits worked. Later I went to the American Maryknoll Bishop in Kweilin and travelled around the country there setting up Legion Praesidia.

In June of 1949, things looked pretty bad down South and I flew the thousand miles from Hong Kong to Chungking over the heads of the Communists. From Chungking I went to Chengtu, then back to Chungking and down to Wanhsien to return to Chungking on November 15th, 1949. In Chungking I decided to wait for the Communists to surround us. Practically all of China had fallen to the Red armies by this time and I knew that if I went to Hong Kong or Formosa, I would never to able to return to Shanghai.

Some time after the entry of the Communists into Chungking, they began to look with suspicion on the Legion. One day, they came to visit me and questioned me for three hours and told me I must stop my Legion activities. I gave them the Legion Handbook to examine and I invited them to any

Praesidium meetings that they wished to attend; but they adhered to their decision and told me all this must cease.

After some time, when they had investigated the Praesidia and had seen that there was nothing going on which they could legitimately condemn, they handed back the book saying: "This is a great organisation, just like Communism." It was the greatest compliment they could pay to the Legion of Mary. Anything that was considered like Communism must at least be efficient. It would appear also that they regarded their initial condemnation of the Legion as tactically premature. Whatever their reasons, they permitted the Legion in Chungking to begin again and they actually gave me a pass to return to Shanghai.

I returned to the Catholic Central Bureau in Shanghai in June 1950, and continued my work, establishing new Praesidia in Shanghai, visiting Praesidia already established, giving Legion retreats, and corresponding with Curia and Praesidia throughout China. During my eighteen months' absence from Shanghai, the affairs of the Legion in Communist-controlled China had been taken care of by Fr. Joseph Sheng. Many of you here today must have met Fr. Joe Sheng when he visited Ireland in 1946 and 1947. He was a brilliant young Chinese priest of Bishop Galvin's Diocese of Hanyang and he was attached to the Catholic Central Bureau in Shanghai. Along with Fr. Chen, who was private secretary to the Internuncio, he had translated the Legion Handbook into Chinese. Even after the Communists took over he had made several trips into the interior of the country, preaching and organising the Legion. He was thrilled by the work the Legion was doing. He himself said to the Legionaries in Shanghai: "This is my life". At that time he did not know that it would also be his death. He was arrested with me in September 1951 and he died in prison in Shanghai in January 1953.

Also in Shanghai at this time were Monsignor Prevost and Monsignor Quint, both of them Bishops, whom the Communists would not allow to return to their dioceses. Monsignor Prevost was Spiritual Director of the Senatus of Shanghai. Monsignor Quint was Spiritual Director of a Curia and of six Praesidia. Both later suffered long terms of imprisonment for their Legion activities. In Peking there were over one hundred Praesidia and Fr. Van Coillie, a Belgian missionary, was Spiritual Director of the Senatus there. He suffered three years of imprisonment for his Legion work. Also in Peking was Fr. Maurice Kavanagh, Irish Vincentian from Wexford, who later suffered fifteen months' torture and imprisonment for his Legion work. In Tientsin there was another Senatus under Fr. Beunen, a Dutch Vincentian. All in all, there were about one thousand Legion Praesidia throughout China. The Legion had spread so fast that the Concilium in Dublin was concerned. Were we going ahead too quickly? I was nervous too, but I wrote back at that time and said: "Our progress is terrific, but the people realise that they must do something in face of this diabolical Communism. Why stop Our Blessed Mother's hand when she feels that it is necessary." The important thing to do was to try to deepen the Legionaries' spirituality and with this end in view, retreats for Legionaries were organised on a big scale. The result was a great movement to study St. Louis Marie de Montfort and great numbers became slaves of Mary and those who did not, at least imbibed de Montfort's real spirit.

At this time Teresa Su, the Legion Envoy who was trained in the Philippine Islands, returned to Shanghai and gave us great help in the administrative work of the Senatus. But as it soon became clear that the Communists were going to target the Legion, we considered it wise that Teresa should leave rather than have the Communists say that we had spies coming from outside. Thus I was forced to order her to leave China, although she wanted to stay.

Shortly afterwards, the Communists started their infamous Triple Independence Movement. This was an organised initiative to try to undermine the Catholic Church in China. The Triple Independence was: (1) Self-support; (2) Self-propagation; (3) Self-rule. With the first two, self-support and self-propagation, we could have no quarrel. That the Catholic Church in China should be supported by its own Catholics and manned by its own clergy was the ultimate objective of all missionary work in China. But the third, Self-Rule, meant that we must separate from Rome. No Catholic could accept this. But because of the cunning way the Communists proposed it, there was a danger that some might consider the Communist formula acceptable. To counter this danger, Fr. Legrand of the Catholic Central Bureau got pamphlets printed defining the position of the Church and had them posted to every part of China. The priests explained the pamphlets to the Legionaries, who then distributed them to the Catholics. The result was the complete failure of this movement to separate the Church from Rome.

The Communists now saw that the Legion of Mary was the most active organisation in the Church of China. Such a perfect organisation, they decided, must first be crushed into submission and then used to run a National Church, independent of Rome. Let no one think for one moment that the Communists made a genuine mistake about the name of the Legion of Mary, which translated into Chinese means "Holy Mother's Army", or that they were genuinely deceived by the military terms such as 'Legion' or 'Praesidium', which we are so proud to

259

use. The Communists knew perfectly well that the Legion was a religious organisation, but they realised that it was far too effective in preaching the Gospel of Christ. In order to discredit it, they decided that they must put a political cap on the movement. So the Legion of Mary was labelled 'Anti-Revolutionary', 'Reactionary' and a 'Secret Organisation'. In preparation for the attack on the Legion, an order went out from the Government asking every church in Shanghai to register all its parish organisations, the Legion of Mary being the only group specifically mentioned. All they asked at this time was the number of persons in each group and the name of the person in charge. Not long afterwards, the Communist police came to the Catholic Central Bureau in Shanghai and closed down all the offices. We priests in the Bureau thought we were going to be arrested on that day, but it was actually three months before this came about.

Three thousand copies of the *True Devotion*, which had just been translated into Chinese, were sealed in the Bureau by this police action. Not long afterwards, there was trouble in Peking and in Tientsin. The newspapers were full of the alleged crimes of the Legion of Mary and we saw very plainly in Shanghai that the Communists were not sincere in their statement that they wished to protect the Legion and the Church. They had said to the Legion in Peking: "In order to protect you we must know who you are. Therefore, we must have the names of all your members, the times and places of all your meetings, your telephone numbers and the minutes of your meetings." When we heard this in Shanghai we decided to stop all Legion meetings and to burn the minutes and the lists of names of all Active and auxiliaries members. I recall mentioning in my last Junior Curia talk in Shanghai, that in the near future we might not be allowed to continue our meetings. But I also said: "Remember, that in the Legion you have learned three things:

(1) You have learned that you must be Apostles.
(2) You have learned that you must do your apostolate through Mary.
(3) You have learned a method for doing that Apostolate. You know the method, now go and put it into practice."

So, we decided to disband. Late that night, I got a telephone call from the President of my Junior Praesidium and later from the President of the Junior Curia, both young girls of about twenty. They said: "Have you heard the good news?" I said: "What news?" They answered: "We have got together the Junior Officers and we have decided to go on." I knew the telephone was being tapped and I told them to come to see me in the morning. It was a grand thing to see that these youngsters, who knew from the daily papers that they faced prison or worse, still wanted to fight to the last. But now it was a matter of obedience. I said to the President of the Junior Praesidium: "Isn't it a pity that the Communists have turned against the Legion."

She replied: "Don't say that, Father. This is glorious."

Since my expulsion I have learned that she, Noelle Wang, has been in prison for the past sixteen months.

At this point, the Legionaries, seeing that Communism was a diabolical force, felt the need of developing even more, their own spiritual life. In Shanghai, not only the Legionaries, but all active Catholics began to attend daily Mass and to receive Holy Communion. They would frequently attend Benediction of the Blessed Sacrament; make a daily meditation, do their spiritual reading, pray the Stations of the Cross, and, studying Grignon de Montfort, great numbers are making the offering and becoming Slaves of Mary.[59] When I arrived in Hong Kong I found this same spirit among Legionaries there. They would ask of the priests: "Father, what are we to do to prepare for Communism?" And the answer always was: "Cultivate a more intense spiritual life."

The next step was a propaganda campaign in the Communist newspapers against the Legion, with specific accusations against Monsignor Riberi, Brother Duff and myself. You probably know that Brother Duff is known to the Communists as Irelands' greatest imperialist! One little girl had accused Monsignor Riberi of being an imperialist and that same girl had written a letter against me saying that my Praesidium was reactionary and secret. A week later Monsignor Riberi was expelled from China and not very long after that, on September 6th, 1951, at half past eleven at night, police entered our St. Columan's Mission in Shanghai and arrested me. On the same night Fr. Legrand of the Catholic Central Bureau, Fr. Sheng, who later died in prison, and Fr. Chen, who is still in prison, were arrested. One month later Bishop Prevost, Bishop Quint, Mr. Francis Seng, the president of the Senatus of Shanghai, and Dr. Chang, the Vice-president, were all arrested.

Later, four of the Maynooth Mission to China Fathers in Huchow were arrested, Frs. Casey, O'Kane, Ronan and Reilly. I believe that they are here today.

The great move against the Legion of Mary had begun. It was organised by the Military Control Committee. This was the most feared and the highest local authority in Shanghai. It was responsible for the register of Chiang Kai-shek's supporters and for the appalling executions, which even now continue.

---

[59] Part of the act of Consecration to Our Blessed Lady as recommended by St. Louis Marie de Montfort.

The Military Control Committee demanded the registration of all Legionaries. In Shanghai, forty centres were set up with about five hundred officials waiting to receive registration. A placard outside each station read: "Registration of Reactionary and Secret Organisation, the Legion of Mary." Clemency was promised for early registration, otherwise punishment, prison and possibly death. The newspapers were full of alleged Legion of Mary crimes. The trams, buses, rickshaws, shops and schools were all covered with cartoons of the Legion of Mary, with my name figuring very prominently. Songs were written so that even the children could sing the crimes of the Legion of Mary.

Under the Communists' cell system, the people are organised into groups and each group has to study the Communist Newspapers. By this method the anti-Legion propaganda reached everyone in China. The photograph the police had taken of me on the night of my arrest was faked. On the table before me were pictures of nude women, knives and guns. This picture was exhibited in Shanghai with the Legion of Mary Standard and Our Lady's Statue and the flags of the Legion all surrounding it. The people, forced to come out and see it, were told: "There is your priest."

Only a relatively small number of the weakest Shanghai Legionaries went freely to register. Many Legion members were beaten by their non-Catholic parents, in efforts to make them comply with the order. Some were even disowned by their parents and put out of their homes. Non-Catholic brothers and sisters dragged their siblings, who were Junior Legionaries, to the police station. But the thirty or forty who were in this manner forced to register returned to the police station at the first opportunity and retracted in a loud voice anything they might have signed. Many even tried to force the police to hand back the documents. The Legion priests and the vast majority of Legionaries decided that they would not register. To register would have been to admit that the Legion was a criminal organisation.

The Chinese Bishop of Shanghai, Bishop Kion, faced quite a problem since many good Catholics and their pastors had decided that a compromise was actually possible and that the Legionaries were far too strict. There was a danger of a split, which would have been disastrous. However, the death of Fr. Bede Chang, SJ in prison settled the question. The Catholics of Shanghai were now really roused. Masses were offered all over the city, not Requiem Masses but Masses said in red vestments to honour a martyr. Then a letter was written by the Legionaries to the Bishop of Shanghai and in it they said: "Monsignor, we will follow you wherever you go. We are proud to live in this age of persecution and there can be no compromise." This of course decided the Bishop and with the death of Fr. Chang, all Catholics were united and the Church in Shanghai presented a united front and a stonewall resistance. No one would register from that day.

After a month or two of waiting, idling in the forty registration stations, the police had to change their tactics. They decided to go to the homes of the Legionaries. They bullied, threatened, flattered and even wept tears to try and make these young boys and girls sign an admission that the Legion was reactionary. In every case they failed. When I arrived in Hong Kong, a young man came to see me one day. "Father, you do not know me," he said, "but you probably know my two sisters who were Legionaries in Shanghai." He told me that he had been a Communist. "I thought Communism was magnificent," he continued. "When the police came to our house, all of us were non-believers except my two sisters. They arrived every day and spoke to my sisters. These two little girls stood out and fought the police, refusing to register. Even my parents begged my sisters for the peace of the family to give in and sign the document, which the police said, was of no consequence. My sisters replied: "We are sorry, we cannot do it." The police returned again and again. In anticipation of their arrest, my sisters cut their hair and made special cotton clothes for prison wear and with their bundles under their arms, they would say to the police: "Take us with you if you like but we will never sign."

The young man said to me: "Father, seeing the bravery of my sisters, I could not resist becoming a Catholic. I was baptised in Shanghai and then came down to Hong Kong." From then on, he served my Mass every morning in that city.

Another young girl got married and during her wedding breakfast the police arrived and took her to the police station. They kept her standing for six hours, playing on her weakest point and saying: "If you sign your name you may return to your home, otherwise we will send you to prison." The girl refused and in the evening, to their shame, they had to let her go.

The wife of Francis Seng, the President of the Shanghai Senatus, was called to the police station and kept standing there a whole day. She was expecting a baby and the Catholics, who were raging that she should be submitted to the strain of interrogation, feared the life of the child might be in danger. However, the Blessed Mother was watching over her. Later, that child was born in perfect condition. The Bishop of Shanghai came to our church (St. Columban's) with mitre and crozier to baptise the baby; many priests surrounded the altar and the church was packed with Legionaries. The child was called

Cecilia, and after the ceremony all sang the *Te Deum* in thanksgiving and the Legion hymn.

The wife of Dr. Chang, Vice-president of the Senatus, who was now in prison, was also called to the police station. The authorities told her: "Your husband has confessed and is ready to come home, but you must confess first." She replied: "I do not believe you. If the only way my husband can receive better treatment is by confessing and denying his Faith, I do not want to see him home; and if he comes, I shall go to prison in his place."

The President of my Junior Curia, who was a University student and who in normal times each week gave twenty-three hours to her Legion work, was never arrested. Part of her work was to instruct children. Even after the Legion was disbanded, she continued to gather the children - between one and two hundred, to the Church of Christ the King and teach them as she had done before. Questioned for entire nights by the police, she almost certainly ended up in prison.

Another demonstration of Catholic resistance took place during the arrest of the American Jesuit Fathers in Christ the King Parish in Shanghai. People and Legionaries knelt in the yard of the Church and made it difficult for the soldiers to proceed. They recited fifteen decades of the Rosary and after that sang the *Totus Tuus*, composed by George Dennis of Dun Laoghaire, Co. Dublin. They sang it over and over again. Only when the people had finished their protest were the police able to proceed. The people in the house opposite the Church, seeing this resistance to an intolerable yoke, cheered with delight.

One final example of Chinese Catholic heroism is that of a twenty-five year old woman and a member of an old Catholic family. She was President of the Curia in Tientsin. During the Red campaign against religion, she travelled around through north, west and east China extending the Legion. In order that she could travel from place to place, she disguised herself by dressing in Communist uniform. When she arrived at her destination she would put on normal dress. Wherever she went she established the Legion. Eventually she was arrested and sentenced to ten years' imprisonment.

It is certain that the officers of all three Legion Senatus' in China are in prison, along with most of the officers of the Curiae of China. How many more Legionaries are in prison we do not know. I do know that there are at least one hundred Catholics in prison in Shanghai and of these over fifty are Legionaries.

I have just heard lately that there was one Spanish priest, a Dominican from Fukien, who was arrested for being in the Legion of Mary and who died on the road as he was being dragged along by his captors.

The Communists, seeing that their tactics had failed hopelessly, actually changed the wording of the registration formula; and when this failed to have any effect, they decided that a verbal statement would be enough if made to the head of each Communist street committee. But the Legionaries still refused to sign or admit anything. As a result of this failure, the leader of the persecution against the Legion was made a scapegoat. He was expelled from the Communist party and put in prison. What happened to him there, nobody knows. To distract the people's attention from this great failure, the Government started a movement against corruption amongst its own officials and this was so vicious that within one month in Shanghai alone, there were ten thousand suicides. Most of these persons threw themselves from windows, causing many deaths in the streets below. All hotels were then ordered to put netting on their windows. But the Communists said to the Legionaries: "We are not finished yet; we will come back again."

I was in prison altogether thirty-two months. In my first prison, I spent seven months sharing a cell at various times with three others, a White Russian and two Chinese. We had no books, we were not allowed to talk, to cough, to sneeze, not even allowed to blink our eyes. We were frequently interrogated not only during the day, but very often during the night. I kept myself busy with my prayers and I was glad to be able to keep my three fellow-prisoners from breaking their heads against the prison bars. After that I was moved to another prison, where for almost one year I was isolated but allowed some exercise.

Then I was brought back to the police station and asked if I was willing to confess that the Legion was reactionary and secret. Because I refused, I was brought back again to absolute isolation in the top storey under the roof of the prison. There I was detained for thirteen months, without leaving my tiny cell except for interrogation sessions and visits to the toilet. This detention period included a summer under the burning heat of this top floor, which was a last attempt to extract a confession from me. Other prisoners were brought to cells on the same floor and after a certain time they confessed or informed on others and were changed to better quarters.

Under these conditions, it was not unusual for prisoners to lose their minds. I could hear them shrieking day and night. I am sure there are hundreds of cases like that, even cases of suicide in that huge prison.

On the wall of my cell were displayed the prison rules. One of them read: "Struggle to win the generosity of the Government by informing on your cell-mate or on anybody who speaks, thinks or does anything which is reactionary. Inform without sympathy." That was the only way to get a reduction in sentence. Not surprisingly there were many informers in Ward Road Jail. As Mao Tse-tung, the Chinese Communist leader, has said: "You are either with me or against me. There is no sitting on the fence." If you are against Communism you go into prison, survive on meagre meals and without wages. If you are with Communism you must enter a Communist organisation and in that organisation your rule is: "Inform on those in your group and on anyone you know to be anti-Communist."

I heard that on one occasion during my imprisonment, certain inmates were brought to the prison roof to hear a reduction of one man's sentence. His life-sentence was being reduced to seventeen years, after which time he would be seventy-five years of age. The reason for the reduction of the sentence was that he had informed on his wife and children. At the end of the proceedings, a Communist official rose and said: "This is the kind of man we want in the new China." It is a diabolical system. The children in China are informing on their parents and the parents are terrified. Chinese children are singing today: "We are the children of Lenin; we wish neither Father nor Mother."

During all my solitary confinement, I had a daily routine. From the whistle in the morning, when I rose from bed, to the whistle at night, I filled my day with various exercises, meditation, going through the words of the Mass, a spiritual Communion, Rosary, study, writing poetry, quietly singing the hymns of Benediction. To preserve my sanity, I dared not leave a space in the day. My particular examination of conscience was this: "I must not think of yesterday, and I must not think of tomorrow." Doubts about yesterday's decisions or the thought of life imprisonment could have unbalanced me in a few hours.

On April 28th of this year I received a haircut and I was told to gather up my things. It was the feast of St. Louis Marie Grignon de Montfort. My novena to St. Louis Marie was just finished and I was wondering what little grace I should receive. Later my cell door was opened and I knew that things were about to happen. But I say here before you in this vast gathering, as I left that cell, I felt a pang of regret. I had felt that I was a moral support to the Legionaries fighting for the Faith in China; at least I was still in the land of my adoption.

The next morning, I was taken to Lokawei Prison and brought before my judges. A Magistrate read my condemnation, which ran to a page and a half in length. This document stated that I had been ordered by Monsignor Riberi to come to China to start the Legion of Mary: that with Monsignor Prevost and Fr. MacElroy (my superior in China), I had tried to turn the people of China against the Government: that I was an international spy sending messages to America:

that I had torn up the Legion minutes and lists of names and letters in order to cover my tracks and endless other accusations.

Then my judge said in a very solemn voice: "In the name of the people of China, I expel you from this country never to return."

Two armed guards led me down the stairs and I was pushed into a motorcar in which Monsignor Prevost and Fr. Legrand were already seated. Until that moment I did not known that they had been in the same prison as myself. Then we were driven to the train and after a three day journey we crossed the Hong Kong border to breathe free air and to hear the first genuine words of kindness spoken to us in three years, those of a British policeman: "Welcome, Fathers."

If you ask me now if there is freedom of religion in China, the answer is most emphatically, 'no'. In many places, the Churches have been confiscated. In other places where churches still remain, there are no priests because nearly all of the foreign missionaries have been expelled. Many Chinese priests are languishing in prison. In the bigger centres, which are Communist show grounds, and where there are churches and a few priests, Catholics can attend Mass and the Sacraments only at the risk of being arrested by the Communists. The more fervent Catholics are, the greater the danger of imprisonment. Such churches are fuller than ever because of the persecution and in spite of those dangers. But, the Communists do not want a repetition of the early history of persecuted Christianity, which drove believers underground. By giving this so-called freedom of religion they easily pick out the most active elements and crush them. Prominent Priests and Christians are slowly being rounded up and thrown into prison. In 1948, Chou En Lai, the Chinese Communist premier, so prominent these days at Geneva, told Fr. Patrick O'Connor, NCWC correspondent, that there was no place for religion in a Communist state. The Chinese Communist State is clearly aiming at that goal.

They think they can finish us, but I would quote a nun who was imprisoned in her convent room for nine months. She was able to look out through a crack in the door and could see into the chapel where there was a beautiful statue of Our Lady. The Communists held their big meetings there every day and did not like the presence of that statue. They attempted to position a portrait of Mao Tse-tung so as to obscure it, but the statue seemed to maintain its presence. This nun tells us that she heard them remark, "that Woman is very hard to hide!" And so she is. They do not realise that they will never hide her.

Dear friends, the Catholic Church is the only answer to Communism, with its people living apostolic lives. We priests and sisters are in a helpless minority; vocations are too few. We can never hope to have sufficient numbers to meet the menace of Communism. Therefore, an apostolic laity is indispensable.

As Brother Duff once wrote to me: "It is sometimes said that the people are the bricks which make up the Church of Christ, sometimes even crumbling bricks. Now, it is not bricks we want but germs of life." To me, there is no better way of making them so than through the Legion of Mary.

"The world belongs to him who loves it most, and who proves that love." These words of the Cure d'Ars, quoted in the Handbook, are very apt. Our apostolate of love must be through Mary, as Christ's apostolate was through her. Mary, Our Mother and Our Queen, is still the spouse of the Holy Ghost, from Whom our Church receives its perpetual guidance and strength.

Reverend Fathers, dear brothers and sisters of the Legion of Mary, I salute the martyrs of China, and I again wish to thank you all for your prayers and for this reception. I receive it all on behalf of Our Lady.

I would ask you once again to remember that there are still great numbers of Bishops, priests, sisters and Catholic laity still in prison in China. I am out and safe. The Chinese can never get out. I beg of you to continue your prayers for them. Nor should you forget those helpless pagans who are in prison also. They have no hope in this life and they know nothing of a life hereafter.

And I would ask that you pray not only for them, but also for me, that this, my second life may not be unfruitful in the service of Our Queen.

268

EPILOGUE

At 48 years of age, Fr. McGrath's life had only just passed its half way stage. His apostolic zeal was to continue to see him traversing the globe, from England to Canada and from the USA to the Philippines, right up to the day of his death on Christmas Day 2000.

The final words of this volume are given to those dignitaries who spoke in the National Stadium, Dublin following Fr. McGrath's testimony. In them, we perceive the unity of mind and spirit among the leading Irish personalities of his day, endorsing the work of the Legion of Mary in the context of proclaiming the Gospel to all nations.

Dignitaries in attendance at the National Stadium Address. From left to right Alfie Byrne, Fr. Aedan, Sean T. O'Ceallaigh, Archbishop Gerald O'Hara, John Costello, Frank Duff, Eamon de Valera, Archbishop Liston of Auckland.

The Papal Nuncio, Archbishop Gerald P. O' Hara:

"Mr. President and my dear friends, it is good for us to be here, good for us to be associated with His Excellency the President and the Taoiseach (Prime Minister) and the many distinguished people in the paying of tribute to a noble and heroic priest, who has done so much for the Church in China. Yet we know that in spite of the honour that he has received here, Fr. McGrath would prefer to be back in the Communist prison suffering with the people whom he was forced to leave against his will. It is good for our souls to receive the inspiration that comes from knowing the remarkable work done by this priest in

269

that distant land; it is good for our faith. So we welcome Fr. McGrath back, but we hope that the Bamboo Curtain will rise again so that he may return with his fellow-missionaries to China.

It is good for us to be here because it gives us an opportunity to speak of that magnificent organisation that was started here in this city, a movement that was destined to grow so much and to do such a vast amount of good. We are happy to pay tribute to the Legionaries everywhere. They are proving to be the leaven of which Our Lord spoke in the Gospel. They are everywhere. They have smiled in the face of grave danger. They have confronted every peril and they are at this moment bringing countless souls to know and serve Our Lord, who without them would never have known Him. Fr. McGrath is a typical Legionary and so I am happy to pay tribute to him and to this splendid organisation, which has spread to the ends of the earth. God has blessed Dublin in making it the centre.

When sometimes we are tempted to tremble as we see Communism threatening the world, let us recall that story of Our Lord crossing the Sea of Galilee with His Apostles. There came a storm; the wind tore away the sails and the vessel was sinking. Through the storm, Our Lord lay sleeping. In the middle of the fury, the Apostles awakened him and asked Him to save them, certain that they were about to perish. Looking at St. Peter and the others, the Master exclaimed: "Oh, ye of little faith; why fear when I was with you? Why be afraid when in my company?" Then with a gesture, He calmed the wind and the sea. Remember dear friends, the Church is never more glorious than when it is suffering, when it is being persecuted. The badge of the Christian is not a carefree life: it is the Cross. Thus our brethren in China give us a great example, with so many of them suffering at this very moment while we are talking about them. But we can be sure that Our Lady, Queen of the Legion gives them a joy of soul that we have never known. We are very fortunate to have this opportunity of hearing an authentic account of the work being done by the Legionaries in China. It will help us towards a greater and deeper love of our Catholic faith."

Sean T O'Kelly, President of Ireland:

"I am happy and proud to be here as President of Ireland to join in welcoming back a man who has suffered and striven for God's Church in foreign lands. I hope that we all bear in mind the appeal he made for prayers for those who are still suffering at the hands of the Communists."

John Costello, Taoiseach (Premier) of Ireland:

"I wish to express on my own behalf and on behalf of my colleagues in the Government our appreciation of the great achievements of Fr. McGrath and to pay tribute to him. Fr. McGrath's spirit and the work he has accomplished in China will live on there and will bear noble fruit."

Eamon de Valera T.D.:

"In my dreams of the past I had thought of Ireland's destiny in the Europe of the future as being similar to what it had accomplished in the evangelisation of the Nations of Europe years ago. Ours would indeed be a glorious destiny if we are to be instrumental in bringing the torch of faith to the countless millions in Asia."

APPENDICES

APPENDIX I

CHINA

SOME OF FR. MC GRATH'S IMPRESSIONS

China, or "The Middle Flower" as it is known in poetic parlance, is a vast subcontinent stretching from the Amur River in Siberia to Hainan in the tropics, a distance of about two thousand two hundred miles, and from Shanghai on the east coast to Yarkand in Chinese Turkistan, a width of about three thousand miles. The eastern, southern and western plains are extremely fertile and in these plains, especially along the valleys of the Yangtse, Yellow and West Rivers, dwell the vast majority of its people - 650,000,000 in the early 1950's. The west and north-west, comprising three-fifths of the total area and embracing the Provinces of Tibet, Chinese Turkistan, Outer and Inner Mongolia, is made up of wide plateaus, barren deserts and towering mountain chains which spread out like gigantic fingers from Mount Everest and the ranges of the Himalayas. Here the population is sparse, consisting mainly of nomadic tribes.

As a nation, the Chinese are classified by ethnologists as mongoloids. With the Japanese, they form the bulk of the yellow race. Their culture, like that of Egypt and Babylon, is extremely ancient. The Chinese were a civilised nation two thousand years before Saint Patrick set foot in Ireland. Their early classics were written fifteen hundred years before Julius Caesar's *De Bello Gallico*. Among their ancient scholars, moralists and philosophers, the names of Confucius, Mencius, and Lao-tze for whom they have supreme reverence and respect, stand out as prominent. The people love learning and books. When the Catholic missionary gave them good schools and trained teachers, they supported the schools in great numbers.

The Chinese are a polite, courteous and intelligent people, with a remarkable capacity for commerce. In the matter of courtesy, I have never met their equals. It is a pleasure to attend a Chinese festive occasion with its many tasty dishes and watch their delightful etiquette and good manners, their graceful bowing and expressions of unworthiness to occupy any but the lowest place. By tradition and customs, the elders, scholars and statesmen occupy the first seats, but they do so with the utmost grace and profuse apologies. No matter how noble or exalted, the speaker will always put himself last and exalt even the humblest of his audience. He will speak of his unworthy name and his lowly profession, even though he is a General, a Statesman or a Professor of Philosophy. Having said that, deep down, the Chinese regard themselves as a superior race and an ancient civilisation.

The Chinese ancient order of precedence or seniority, is as follows: Shih, Nung, Kung, Shang meaning: Scholars, Farmers, Artisans and Merchants. The Communists have changed that order, putting the artisan or proletariat in the first place. They have also changed and ruined the age-old good manner, and have taught the people to speak and write of China in arrogant and haughty tones.

China used to be a land of small farmers; twenty acres would be considered an estate. Yet, with three crops in rotation annually and every rood under cultivation, a farmer can support a large family, even three or four families. They marry young and for each member of the family who brings in a wife, a new wing or annex, consisting of a single mud-walled room or cabin, is added to the existing house. I had a family in my parish who reminded me of Noah and the Ark. There was a great-great grandfather Joe, his two sons and their two wives, their two sons and their two wives and so on down. All apparently got on together in perfect peace and harmony until cooking time, when on occasions they would even fight over the firewood.

The Chinese are a peace-loving nation; yet it is difficult to maintain peace and order in such a vast country with its enormous population. We might therefore expect to find bandits. Like Saint Paul, the missionary is often in peril of robbers, in peril of land, in peril by day and by night. Many of our Columban Missionaries have been captured, robbed and beaten with rods. There is the case of Frs. Laffan, Linehan and Sandes, who spent nearly a whole year in the hands of Communist bandits. Fr. Leonard of Limerick and Fr. Tierney were put to a cruel martyrdom by them.

Fr. Joe Crosson was stripped and sent home by four gunmen. The sequel to his story is typical of how things happen in China: The following night at dusk, the same four men entered the Columban Centre in Hanyang. Two of them held the Priests at gunpoint at the foot of the stairs and two rushed upstairs, entered the offices of our Procurators, Frs. O'Rourke and McPolin. Threatening with their pistols they forced the priests to unlock the safes. They took all the Chinese money they could find and the Bishop's pectoral cross. Then they departed into the night. When they had gone, Fr. O'Rourke telephoned the police. Soon the building was swarming with police and plain-clothes men. They asked questions, took fingerprints and left. For two days nothing happened. On

276

the third day there was a banquet at the police station. During the festivities, one of the lady entertainers said to her police friend: "You're no good; come here and let me show you what my other boyfriend has given me." She led him to her room, opened her handbag and drew out a beautiful gold chain and bejewelled pectoral cross. The policeman's eyes lit up: "Okay," he replied. "I can never hope to beat that." Out he went and rang up the detectives, who duly arrived and arrested the lady, threatening her with the full rigour of the law if she refused to reveal the donor of the cross. She informed without delay. Soon her benefactor was captured and was probably beaten with bamboo rods until he in turn informed on his accomplices, who were promptly arrested, tried by court-martial and condemned to death. The Bishop pleaded for them, but in vain. He was told that they were highway robbers who had terrified many people. The Bishop received back his pectoral cross, but not the money.

The majority of the Chinese, nominally at least, belong to the Buddhist religion; but my impression is that Buddhism doesn't seem to mean a great deal to many of them. I have seldom met a Chinese who could give an intelligent account of the tenets of Buddhism. I asked one monk why he entered a monastery. He replied: "It's because I failed in business." On another occasion, I offered a glass of wine to a Buddhist monk. He asked permission to join the Columban monks! The response he got was: "He would be welcome to come along." Next day he returned and was treated to another glass of wine. The Buddhist reiterated his desire to join the congregation. The third day he came, no wine was offered. He departed in sadness!

Christianity was introduced into China in the 8th century by the heretical Nestorians. This sect seems to have faded out by the 13th century. Under the great Mongol conquerors, Ghengis and Kublai-Khan, Christianity was the re-introduced by Bishop John of Montecorvino and his companions, who were contemporaries of the explorer Marco Polo. The Mongol Empire lasted ninety years before collapsing. The Mongols reverted back to their original nomadic life. Under the succeeding Ming Dynasty, the Catholic religion was persecuted and practically stamped out. In the 16th century, under the last Ming Emperor and the Manchu Emperor, Kang Hai, Catholic Missionaries arrived at the courts of Peking. For a while it seemed, under the influence of Jesuit Missionaries, Frs. Ricci, Schall, Verbiest and their companions, that China would be converted en masse. But once more, persecution prevented much progress. Kang Hai's successor, fearing the aims and influence of foreign Missionaries, banished them and executed the Christians.

Napoleon Bonaparte once remarked: "Whoever conquers China, rules the world." No doubt, he had in mind mighty armies and fleets of unsinkable ships. The missionary 'armies' of the twentieth century had no such forces at their disposal; nor did they seek to conquer in the military sense; but they went forth in Faith to build schools, orphanages and churches, with the genuine motive of spreading the Gospel and helping the people in every possible way.

That Communism is extremely efficient, no one will deny. China has become a powerful nation, disciplined, respected and feared by the other great nations of the world. Much has been done to reduce corruption and crime - bribery, banditry, gambling, opium and prostitution. They have harnessed the great rivers to supply the country with electricity. They have reclaimed vast tracts of desert and wasteland, built or repaired the dykes, promoted education, improved health.

The Communist cure of China's material ills is almost complete; but surely the cure is worse than the disease?

They seem to have shown an extraordinary intelligence; in fact I would say a superhuman intelligence. Their grasp of every situation, their keen insight into all societies, even their astute knowledge of the affairs, methods, principles and dogmas of the Catholic Church, would give one the impression that there is more than mere human knowledge in their minds. It would seem that they are guided by a preternatural spirit opposed in all things to the spirit of God. The examples of hatred that I have seen in Communist jails could scarcely be attributed to mere human beings. Undirected human nature could hardly stoop so low. Hatred is supposed to be the worst sin that a person could commit, for it is opposed to the queen of virtues which is charity. As a Saint once said "Where there is love, there is heaven; where there is hatred there is hell, for in hell there is no love." The animosity displayed by the Communists in China for God - whom they say does not exist - for their enemies, the "Western Imperialists", for the Catholic Church and the Legion of Mary, which is their "Enemy Number One", is so extreme that it seemed to me it could emanate only from one source; the father of lies.

Of special note is the disproportionate Communist hatred of Mary, the Mother of God. They seem to dread her influence and that of her Legion. I believe that in doing so they have unwittingly prepared the ground for the sowing of the Word of God, and for the conversion of the nation. When the time comes, and with the help of God, the Legion of Mary will be at hand to reap a bountiful harvest of souls.

278

APPENDIX II

PERSECUTION REACHES ITS PEAK

BY ELIZABETH REID [60]

1955

The night Fr. McGrath was taken prisoner, the persecution of lay Catholics reached its peak in China. During the days that followed, office-holders of the Legion were taken to police stations throughout the country and interrogated. They were asked to sign "confessions". The form read like this: "I, the undersigned joined the reactionary Legion of Mary ...(date) and conducted secret counter-reactionary and evil activities against the government and the people. I hereby resign from the Legion of Mary and promise never to participate in such activities in the future."

Out of thousands of Legionaries submitted to this treatment, many of whom were imprisoned and a good number killed for their resistance, only 72 signed the confession sheet. This was a magnificent victory for Our Blessed Mother and one in which surely, she played a big part. Even children became fearless in their answers. Teenage Legionaries in Shanghai packed up bundles of prison clothes, ready for when the police would come to arrest them. Truly in those days of crisis, the Church in China came of age. Without exception, in more than 1,000 recorded cases of Junior Legionaries, they stood firm. One Catholic mother remarked: "Soon my daughter will be fat enough to endure the rigours of prison life. We expect her to be taken in any time, so I am giving her extra food." It was the Junior Legionaries in Shanghai who organised their still smaller brothers and sisters, children of no more than eight or nine years old, to act as spotters, because the Communists had been trying to receive Holy Communion with the faithful in the churches. At first the students tried to head them off, but

---

[60] (1915-1974). As a journalist, Elizabeth Reid became a member of the Catholic lay organization The Grail in 1938. She encouraged Catholic laywomen to play a more active role in the work of the community. This Appendix is drawn from her article, The Legion in Chains, *Queen of All Hearts*, Montfort Fathers, Bayshore, New York, September-October, 1958.

they got into trouble and were either arrested or beaten for their actions.

The intention of the Communists was to make Aurora University in Shanghai the centre for the Reformed Church, so every possible pressure was brought to bear on the Catholic students to join the new church controlled by the Communist Regime.

From China, the only place to go was Hong Kong, the small British Colony off the coast of South China. On the mainland, hundreds of thousands were imprisoned or liquidated. The lucky ones got out. The population in Hong Kong skyrocketed from 500,000 to 3 million. Refugees came in hundreds of thousands.

In 1948, the figures for the Catholic Church in China were as follows: 3,276,282 Chinese lay Catholics: 2,698 Chinese Priests and 3,015 foreign Priests of nearly every Western Nation: 7,644 native and foreign Nuns. There were one hundred and forty seven ecclesiastical divisions in China, all operating on an organisational basis - today, none of these survive.

When Fr. McGrath crossed the border back into Hong Kong in April 1954, 400 Chinese Priests were imprisoned, and the remaining 2,298 were for the most part scattered and living apart from their churches. 166 members of the secular clergy and religious orders, male and female, Chinese and foreign had been executed by the government, or had died in prison at the hands of their jailers. The exact figure for the laity has been hard to calculate, but a conservative estimate for Legionaries killed during this time is the round figure of 1,000. At present there are no foreign Missionaries left with the exception of two American Jesuits imprisoned in Shanghai and Bishop Walsh of Maryknoll.

The expelled Missionaries form the spearhead of religious refugees; but beside them are thousands of lay Catholics. Heading these again are members of the Legion of Mary, seeking refuge in Hong Kong - many after years of imprisonment, and all dispossessed of their belongings.

According to many observers, the Catholic Church endured the cruellest persecution of all in the two thousand years of its existence, in China under the Communists. To quote the words of Pope Pius XII: "It is the darkest hour since the deluge."

Since the days of Nero, most or all the persecutors have oppressed the Church and Christ in his Mystical Body; but they did not attack God, or the idea of God. Not so with the Communists. Marx, Engels and Lenin denied the existence of God. Joseph Stalin, dictator of Russia was the constituted head of the anti-God League; and I have no doubt that Mr. Kruschev held the same office.

According to Mr. Mikoyan, Vice Premier of Russia, Mao Tse-tung and Chou-En-Lai, Chairman and Vice-Chairman of the People's Republic of China, all good Communists must be atheists.

St. Louis Marie Grignon de Montfort in his book, *The True Devotion*, predicts that the last age of the world will be known as: "The Age of Mary." In that age, great saints will be raised up by God who will be remarkable for their devotion and consecration to Mary. To the great glory of God and His Church, these saints will become slaves of love to Mary. By so doing, they will excite the jealousy and towering rage of Satan, who will try to tear them asunder. Judging by the signs of the times, his prophesy seems to be coming true. Great people are springing up all around us; we find them in the cloisters and outside. We find them amongst the Hierarchy, clergy and in the ranks of the laity. Such lay Apostles are the Legion of Mary, men and women from every rank in life, working for the salvation of souls.

Appendix III

The Trial of Fr. Robert Greene MM

These extracts from chapter thirteen of *Calvary in China* by Rev. Robert W. Greene MM, who was based in the south east of China, provide further proof of the barbaric treatment meted out to prisoners on trumped-up charges involving the Legion of Mary. The text quoted here describes the Communist trial against him.

Fr. Green's ordination photo

After his ordeal

"...On the front of the manual in large Chinese characters were the words: 'Reactionary Technique of the Catholic Church.' And in smaller characters, it said: 'The Legion of Mary.' Thinking that he was going to say the book had been found in my quarters, I told the judge that it was not mine, that I had never seen the book before. But he said: 'This is our book. It explains in detail this American spy organisation, financed by the American Government.' Then he asked for the tenth time: 'Now do you still deny that you know Mo Ke-sin?'

I still asserted that I did not know him. One of the soldiers at this point walked up to me with a newspaper, on the front page of which was the picture of a man who was definitely not Chinese. I looked closely at it and recognized a man whom I knew: Fr. McGrath, of the Columban Fathers. The picture was obviously a composite photo aimed at making the priest ridiculous. The judge sneered: 'Well, I see you recognized the man Mo Ke-sin after all.' I admitted that Fr. McGrath was known to me, but that I had not recognized him by his Chinese name in the preceding testimony.

Then the judge asked: 'Who is the agent who brings you the instructions that come from this man?' I said: 'As it happens, I have never had correspondence with Fr. McGrath. I have received no instructions from him at any time.'

The judge then began a long dissertation on the espionage activity of the Legion of Mary in China. Each time I would attempt to interrupt him, I would be banged in the ribs or slapped in the face. When the judge pointed to his textbook on the activities of the Legion, I shouted out that the book was a lie. 'Anyone who knows the Legion understands that it is entirely a spiritual organisation, formed to help Catholics in their spiritual lives. We do not even discuss politics at our meetings.'

Angrily, one of the officials on the right of the judge picked up the Communist textbook on the Legion and shouted: 'Listen to this. What is the meaning of this if it has nothing to do with politics and military matters? "Who is she that cometh forth as the morning star, fair as the moon, bright as the sun, terrible as an army set in battle array?" Is that not part of your Legion handbook?'

'Yes,' I said: 'That is an opening prayer, but those words have a spiritual, not a literal meaning.' The man on the judge's left broke in: 'Well, who is this Mary and where is she?' I started to answer him, but the judge waved his Communist book on the Legion and told me not to bother replying. He motioned the official on his left to be quiet. Then he read some more from the book and paused when he came to the words: "Mary gives to her Legion fullness of faith to conquer the world." 'How do you explain that?' he sneered. 'Does that have a spiritual meaning too?'

I said: 'Yes, that also is understood in a spiritual sense and if you read further you will see that we are to conquer the world with love, and by aiding our neighbour.' Then the judge, banging the desk with his fist and looking through me with his eyes of hate, said: ' That is why we must rid our country of this evil spying force in which you are the leader in Southern China. It is because it is spiritual that we must wipe it out. We can fight the bandits with guns and exterminate them, but this spying Legion of yours we must attack with other weapons.'

Puzzled as to how a Communist official could admit to the presence of a "spiritual force", I interrupted him to ask what evil the members of the Legion had ever committed in China. But he made no attempt to answer, except to mutter the worn-out Communist cliché that all religions are the "opium of the people."

It seemed to me that in their eyes the Legion of Mary was worse than a narcotic acting as a opium for the masses; it was a vital force filling these men with terror and hate. I thought why won't they come out bluntly and say that they are accusing me of spreading religion which they hate and fear? But they would not give me that satisfaction.

…At least five or six more times that night I signed my name to something they said I did. What these things were I cannot now remember, and my guess is that I did not then understand. I knew that with the signing of each confession I was allowed to sit down and the tourniquets were taken from my arms. But from somewhere strength always came to me to resist the temptation to sit when the testimony concerned my priesthood. I kept repeating to myself 'You are Father Greene, remember that and you are a priest. Remember also that you cannot get the Legion of Mary in trouble - anything else, admit.' So I would say: 'Chen-jen,' I acknowledge it. Occasionally, coming out of a stupor, I would recall that I had acknowledged or signed my name to something that might involve the Legion, and I would ask to have the acknowledgement changed. They would merely sneer at me and tell me again and again that they understood who this woman Mary was and what the Legion of Mary really did, and they were going to use every means in their power to obliterate both from the face of China.

As they led me back to my cell, I asked myself: Why do these men hate Our Blessed Lady so? And why do they hate her Legion? My real crime seems to be that I allegedly used the Legionaries to foster my spy work here in Tung-an. It was ridiculous, yet it was frightening too. And the intense hatred of the judge and his diabolical dislike for Our Lady scared me as nothing before ever had. I was weak and felt very much alone and I asked myself if this was what Communism really did to people - the things they feared most, they hated most."

APPENDIX IV

OTHER HEROES IN THE FRAY

T his appendix further portrays the heroic Christian witness of Legion-minded missionaries and Legion members alike from Hopeh to Kiangsu to Kwangtung.

THE LEGION OF MARY IN NORTH-EAST CHINA (1948-1951)

Lambertus M. Steenstra CM - 7th October 1952

Father Lambertus M. Steenstra was born at Sneek, Holland and went to China in 1932. He was at first a missionary in the country, but went to Tientsin in 1946 where, among other work, he provided also the spiritual care at a girl's school called Scheng Kung. He remained there until he was expelled from China in February 1951. After spending a year in the Philippines, he arrived in the United States on July 15, 1952.

In the mid 1940's, the Legion of Mary had existed in central China but not in the north. Fr. Steenstra first heard of the Legion at the end of October 1948, after an Irish priest, Fr. McGrath, came from Shanghai to tell the Bishop of Tientsin, His Excellency, Monsignor De Vienne, about it and ask his permission to make a start in his diocese.

Father McGrath gave a talk on the Legion of Mary to many priests and several Praesidia were formed. Fr. Steenstra, not convinced that the Legion was all it claimed to be, asked the Bishop to keep him aloof from that organisation and to appoint a young priest, Fr. Beunen, who was not yet two years in China, as head of this new work. Even when Fr. McGrath invited him to attend the first Praesidium meeting of girls in the school where he was chaplain and asked him to give an allocutio, Father Steenstra agreed, but brought another young Father with him to become the Spiritual Director.

When the meeting was over, Fr. McGrath insisted again and again that Fr. Steenstra become the Spiritual Director; and in the end he gave in, but without enthusiasm. Only after some meetings, when he saw that this organization was so wholly different from every other kind; that here was not much talk, but real work, that pagans were brought into the Church and lukewarm Catholics brought back, he became more than interested. After only a month and a half the legionaries of this Praesidium were already giving instruction in a camp of refugees and three families were, after due instruction given by the Legionaries themselves, received into the Church.

The Legion in Tientsin had begun with seven Praesidia only two or three months before the Communists took the town in January, 1949. By this time it had grown to about ten or twelve Praesidia. The priests were surprised and encouraged because the Catholics stood this test despite personal danger. Only one of these Praesidia stopped meeting, partly because it had not been well established. Seven weeks later, it was reorganized and became much more effective. Because the Catholics remained steadfast, they went on to spread the Legion.

In two years, more than 50 Praesidia were established in Tientsin, and this in a city with an overall population close to 2,000,000 among whom 1% were Catholic. Every Praesidium had a priest as spiritual director but there were only 15 or 20 priests taking care of them all. One priest cared for six Praeisida and another, seven. Fr. Steenstra had four. Tientsin had six Curia, but only about 45 or 50 members would come together because it was too dangerous to have larger gatherings. During their first year of work the legionaries brought more than 500 lukewarm Catholics back to the Church.

The Legion also spread to many other dioceses in northeast China. The most helpful legionary in this extension was a girl about 25 years old. She was put in prison in June of 1951 and may even now be dead.

When Father Beunen had been looking for a girl to help him establish a youth organization, she had been mentioned. Father was told that because of her temperament she would not be easy to handle: "she is sharp and will criticize everything you say. She will destroy everything you try to build." But Father wanted to talk to her himself and perhaps give her a chance anyway. She told him that she went to church every Sunday, but had never done anything to Propagate the Faith. She warned him of her reputation for destroying things, but if he still wanted her for the work, she was willing to try. She proved to be the most courageous and ingenious worker in the propagation of the faith and later became Secretary of the Senatus.

The Bishop of Manchuria, Archbishop Moukden, had asked the Legion in Tientsin to help him establish the Legion in Manchuria. This girl volunteered to do this. She refused a letter of recommendation because she was afraid it might fall into the hands of the Communists. This, she assured them, would be dangerous for her, for the Archbishop, and for the Legion of Tientsin. For greater protection she disguised herself in Communist workman's dress consisting of blue-grey trousers, jacket and cap. When she arrived at the Archbishop's palace, it took her an hour to convince him that she had come from the Legion in Tientsin to help him establish the Legion. He helped her call priests together and also to start the Legion in four or five other dioceses. It wasn't easy for the Catholics in Manchuria to establish the Legion.

In some places they had the meeting in the sacristy with one or two guards outside, so that if a Communist showed up, all would move into the church and appear to be only praying there. They used only the barest essentials on their altar consisting of an image of Our Lady and two candles so that it could be dismantled quickly. These Praesidia got beautiful results. Many Catholics were brought back to their Faith, and many converts were won over. The Senatus was located in Tientsin with Fr. Beunen as Spiritual Director, so the reports of their activities went there.

This girl later went to some dioceses south of Tientsin and established many Praesidia in different towns - about 16 or 20 different Praesidia. One Diocese to which she went before going to Manchuria had about 60 Praesidia before Fr. Steenstra left China. There were 35,000 Catholics in this Diocese but most of them couldn't be reached by priests. One of the towns had only two or three thousand Catholics, and yet they boasted twenty Praesidia.

Before Fr. Steenstra left China there were about 250 Praesidia in the different dioceses. Each Praesidium had engaged in the work of extension to bring this situation about in northeast China.

In the beginning of 1953, the Communists tried to establish an independent Catholic Church, a Nationalistic Church for China alone, free from Rome. They published a manifesto which was predominately a political statement against America, but at the bottom of it was attached a statement which expressed a desire for Church independence. It was deceitfully written.

The Communists asked the Catholics to sign this manifesto. Here the Legion of Mary did a most important work of countering it. The Catholics couldn't be told not to sign it openly in the Church or the Churches would have been closed. But the Bishop told the Legion Spiritual Directors to explain during their allocutios why the Catholics couldn't sign it; Legionaries were to tell every Catholic family in town that they were not allowed to sign the manifesto. The result was that at that time among the 20,000 Catholics in Tientsin, only 200 signed and 100 of those signatures were false.

287

THE LEGION OF MARY IN PEKING

By an SVD Missionary

Towards the end of World War Two, a Divine Word Missionary started a branch of the Legion of Mary among the female students of Peking's Catholic University, Fu-Jen. This was the first Praesidium in the Chinese capital. Wiseacres expressed their misgivings as to the future of this apostolic organisation. In the time of calm before the boding storm, it slowly developed.

Fr. Dries Van Coillie and officers
of the Senatus of Peking

Then in May 1949 the Communist troops entered Peking. Fears for the future and the prospect of bad days to come oppressed the hearts of priests and people alike. Yet it was at this very time that the apparently insignificant organisation lifted itself up like a giant roused form his slumber, and developed with lightning rapidity among the 24,000 Catholics of the capital, especially among the youth, until it became a real peoples' movement.

It was difficult to understand how Praesidium on Praesidium sprang up almost simultaneously in the various Catholic centres of the city without any previous arrangements having been made.

The Legion seemed to grow quite spontaneously of itself. An invisible power seemed to be gathering together an elite in this young mission church and forming them into a spiritual army, which would fight for God and His Church with apostolic generosity and with that unity which results from being animated with the same Spirit.

Within two months of the Communist invasion, the first Legion Curia in Peking was set up. Its task was to unite and direct the various individual Praesidia. As the number of Praesidia grew the formation of a second Curia became necessary, so the first was divided and Fr. Glanemann SVD became spiritual director of the second while Fr. Van Coillie, of the Scheut Missionary

Society remained director of the first. The number of Praesidia continued to grow and still more Curiae became necessary. Fr. Gerhards SVD became director of the fourth which took charge of all the junior Praesidia in the city. When the number of these reached 32 a further division was necessary, and two more followed in quick succession. Finally, the fourth Curia was left with 18 Praesidia composed almost entirely of students from the Catholic University and from the secondary schools attached to it.

The parish of the Divine Word Missionaries, which includes the University, had 15 Praesidia, not including the two Junior Praesidia, at the end of May 1949. Five Praesidia were at work in the University itself under the direction of Fr. Zloch, spiritual director of the students. Many of the students were acting as presidents of other Praesidia in the city. Fifteen Chinese priests studying at the "Sincium", the college for higher studies for native priests, formed a Praesidium among themselves in order to become acquainted with the Legion system. This was to prove of great value to them later.

Fr. Kronthaler, an Austrian Jesuit, did all his mission work along Legion lines, and had 15 Praesidia at work in his parish in the south suburb of Peking, a largely Mohammedan quarter.

At the University, Legionaries strengthened the faith of their fellow-students, made things as clear to them as possible and restrained them from imprudent action. To the pagans they explained the growing campaign of calumny against God and the Church on the part of the Communists. They succeeded in interesting many in the faith, and led them to receive instruction which they often gave themselves. A special work of theirs was to issue regularly large placards in which by means of well-thought-out articles and modern pictures, they fearlessly expressed the mind of the church on the burning questions of the day.

In May 1951, shortly before it was outlawed by the Communists, the Legion in Peking numbered 10 Curiae, with 120 attached Praesidiae comprising 1,500 active members. Two thousand auxiliary members reciting the Rosary every day for Our Lady's intentions gave them valuable spiritual support.

The Legion had been a thorn in the side of the Communists for quite a while, and the blow which was intended to destroy it was carefully prepared.

Towards the end of 1951 the Communist youth organization started a well-planned campaign against the Legion, as a result of which the meetings and external work had to be discontinued. A few weeks later, the Legion was declared to be a reactionary organisation and was forbidden in the whole of China. Its members had to appear before the police to be registered. The spiritual directors were imprisoned, and Frs. Van Coillie, Glanemann, Gerhards, and Zloch along with other members of the Society of the Divine Word were kept in prison for over a year, where they were given "special treatment". Their punishment included being forced by prison guards to stand for days on end without sleep. They were subjected to interminable cross-examination and for months were fastened by hands and feet with heavy iron chains.

The Communists were convinced that the Legion was equipped with secret transmitters and well-hidden weapons, and was organised as a super-organisation of spies. They strove by every means to disrupt the great efficiency of their Public Enemy Number One. All they ever found in Legionaries possession was lists of members, some Legion Handbooks, the Legion standard and the statue of Our Lady. The Reds were bitterly disappointed - and with reason: for what they were unable to find with all their searching was the Spirit, Who, on the first Pentecost, inflamed the Apostles with zeal for God and souls as they were gathered with confidence around the Mother of their Lord.

THE LEGION OF MARY IN SHANGHAI

The following is a letter written by Fr. Valerian Schott OFM to his confreres in the U.S. shortly after his expulsion from China in 1952. He is a member of the Franciscan Fathers, Sacred Heart Province, St. Louis, Missouri.

I have been asked to tell the story of the Legion of Mary in Shanghai: It was the Feast of St. Francis in 1951; zero hour for the Franciscans in Shanghai was twenty minutes past midnight. At that time the Red police made a raid on the Franciscan Procuration. They climbed over the garden wall and forced the gatekeeper to unlock the gate. We were half prepared for this, but we really did not think it would happen. On the night before they had raided the Catholic Central Bureau and had arrested Msgr. Prevost, who was, you might say, second in command of the Legion of Mary in Shanghai. The number one man, Father McGrath of the Columban Mission, had already been arrested. The number three man was our Franciscan, Msgr. Gabriel Quint. So after Msgr. Prevost, was arrested on October 3rd, we figured we were next.

The police said they had come with orders to arrest Msgr. Quint because of his crimes, and as for the rest of our community, we could continue as heretofore. When asked what was the accusation they said the accused knew what crimes he had committed, and that we would find them in the newspapers. Then we were told to go back to our rooms. This was about one o'clock. They searched Msgr. Quint's room and the Procuration office till about two thirty and then left, taking their "criminal" with them. We have not seen him since. For some time after his arrest the local papers carried articles about Monsignor's crimes, his collaboration with Imperialist elements principally through the Legion of Mary.

With this arrest, the three top leaders of the Legion of Mary were taken out of circulation: Father McGrath (Columban), Msgr. Prevost (Canadian Foreign Missions), and Msgr. Quint (Franciscan). Five days later, (October 8th, 1951), there appeared in the local newspapers the Government's official condemnation of the Legion of Mary as an Imperialist agency working against the "People's Government of China." It demanded that all members of the Legion appear at specified Police Stations to sign a confession and a "purpose of amendment." The Legion officers were to bring along several photos for identification. Those who refused to answer the summons would be subject to "severe punishment." Men who knew something about such matters told me that "severe punishment" meant from three years in prison to capital punishment. This brought the Legionaries in Shanghai into direct grips with the Red regime.

During the week the two top lay leaders of the Legion "disappeared." Everybody was so certain that the round-up would go right on down the line: spiritual directors, officers, and then the members, if the summons to report and "confess" were ignored. All Legionaries were now on the spot; they had to make up their minds; it was a question of life and death, of resisting or surrendering.

Two incidents should be narrated here: one that could have broken down the morale of many a Legionary; the other which actually did raise the morale of all.

The first is that of the missionary priest who lost his mental balance and committed suicide. He was under fire on two counts: as a member of the Catholic Central Bureau, and as a spiritual director of a Legion Praesidium. Priests had been attested from both groups. There was no doubt in his mind that his number was up. He got himself into a state of nervous prostration waiting for the call from the police. He could not eat or sleep. A week after the public proclamation condemning the Legion, word got around that he was in the hospital. He had cut both his wrists at the mission house on Sunday morning after Mass and let the blood run into the bathtub. When he left the bathroom he fell unconscious in the corridor. The Fathers found him there and took him to his room. After a while he came to and expressed surprise when he saw what had happened. He is reported to have said over and over again, "Do I have to die?" He was given the last sacraments and taken to the hospital. After twenty-four hours he died. When this news got around among the Legionaries it left them stunned.

The second incident happened perhaps a month later. It was the martyrdom of Father Chang, a Chinese priest of Shanghai who died in prison. He had been picked by the Reds to become the leader of the new independent National Catholic Church. They had taken him into custody, given him fine living quarters and treated him royally in an effort to win his "good will." When this failed they went to the other extreme, threw him in prison and maltreated him until he died. After his death the Reds sent for his superior to come and identify the corpse, and told him to take it away and bury it. But when the news leaked out that the remains of the dead priest would be brought home, the concourse of people was so great, that the police had trouble keeping order. The crowds gathered at the front of the church and waited half a day to pay their respects to the heroic death of the priest. The police reported this, and as a result, the body was not permitted to be moved. Several days after, it was secretly given over to his relatives and buried quietly in the Catholic cemetery. The example of this priest and no doubt, the merit of his sacrifice aided mightily in strengthening the morale of the Shanghai Catholics.

So, as we said above, the Legionaries were on the spot. There's quite a bit of difference between kneeling down and saying a pious prayer in which you offer your life for the Faith (at some improbable future date) and making up your mind "hic et nunc" whether you are going to sign a document (which you don't very well understand) and being arrested. No one, not even recognized saints, can meet with a real and present threat to their lives, without causing their hearts to pound and their knees to quake. And there were many pounding hearts and quaking knees among the Legionaries when they were ordered to the police station.

The siren of the police-wagon was screaming through the streets day and night and keeping everybody on edge, especially the "guilty" ones. Hundreds of people were sleeping dressed for the journey and with their little overnight bag handy. The tension was palpable; it was on men, women and children, lay people and religious, Chinese and foreigners alike.

The peace of many families was often threatened simply because one member belonged to the Legion. Many of these families were not as fervent as the member who was a Legionary; and in some cases the family was pagan, only the Legionary being Catholic. Such Legionaries were under pressure from the family to go and sign anything, just to get this tension lifted.

All heads were busy trying to find a way out. There was question as to whether it was morally wrong to sign the document prepared by the Reds. There was question about signing the formula with corrections. There was question about going to the police station and signing that you were a Legionary, but nothing else. The question was also raised whether it was permissible to go to the police station at all. And there were some fine distinctions even within all of these questions. The Missionary Fathers had to answer these questions for themselves and for their faithful. After a month or so of experience, seeing and hearing what went on at the questionings in the police stations, it was generally accepted that it was morally wrong to go to the police station at all, unless one was personally summoned.

Some people brought their questions to the Fathers, but some solved their own doubts. A few individual cases of how these doubts were solved are of note.

There was a group on a certain hospital's medical staff: a doctor, some nurses and other Hospital staff who had formed a Praesidium. The day after the public condemnation of the Legion they all went to the police station and signed "something." One of the nurses involved told me she did not read what it said on the paper. She took the signing to be an admission that she was a Legionary; and thought it quite heroic to admit this and be willing to take the consequences. The doctor said, "Why not sign? If I don't sign I'll lose my position in the hospital, which means bread and butter to my family. And signing harms no one. I don't believe the accusations made on the paper. I signed; the Reds know I don't believe them; God knows I don't believe them. So where is the harm in signing?" There was only one member of that Praesidium who refused to sign; and she was, perhaps, the least educated of them all, a seamstress. But she was from old Catholic stock; and those quoted above were converts of a year or less. This seamstress had the pressure put on her from every side, from within and without the hospital, by those in the other camp and by some supposedly in her own camp. She was visited by official filibusters, whose object it was to wear a person down by talking. One would talk with her for a couple of hours; and as he went out another one would come in and go over the whole field again; an endurance test. Every time they gave her the works she came out more determined to sign nothing. When they finally summoned her to the police-station, she was convinced she would not comeback. She packed her things together and put them in charge of the director of her section of the hospital, who was a Communist. She told him that his group was responsible for this call, that he must accept responsibility for her belongings, and if she needed something she would write him a note from prison. Then she gave him the key to her room, said good-bye to everybody, took her overnight bag and left. She went over to get the blessing of her spiritual director (in this case, me) and made her lonesome way to the police station on a cold winter afternoon, convinced that she would not come back. Her sacrifice was certainly complete, but God did not accept it at this time.

When she arrived, after all her experiences with them, she was so wary of signing anything that she would not even sign the "visitor's book" demanded at the gatehouse. The gate-man would not let her in without signing, and he could not chase her away because she was summoned; so he went up to the office to report and they sent a man down to usher her in. In the office they offered her tea, which she accepted.

The Officers asked her questions and she answered them. They gave her indoctrination and she listened. They tried being understanding and kind; they tried being rough and threatening. They told her they would put her in prison right away. She answered, "All right, I'm ready." After two hours they told her to go home and think it over and then come back. And they said, "Don't bring that bag the next time." They saw she came prepared for prison; it was a direct challenge, and they did not like it.

She came, dragging herself in, after dark, to tell me the results of her questioning. I asked her how it felt to go through the ordeal. She said when she got the summons she could not steady her knees; she felt weak all over. But, she said, as soon as she arrived at the police station and they began questioning her, she became calm and confident and the answers came with ease. "I even thought my answers were quite good - but they were really not my own answers." God gives special help to those who, for His sake get into special difficulties. What she was driving at was the "*dabitur vobis.*" She experienced it, but did not know how to express it. I found this occurred in ever so many cases. Those who were simple and strong in the Faith, upon being questioned, won a verbal battle with trained Communists. But not being trained in logic, these ordinary people were at times not aware of their own victories. One of them told her tormentor: "I am just as ready to die for my Faith as you are to die for Communism." This remark brought on a short period of thoughtful silence. But she probably did not realise that she had made a direct hit.

A little boy who had answered a Communist tormentor according to his Catholic instruction was asked, "Who told you to answer in that way?" All that he would have had to say was, "Father So-and-so." And Father So-and-so would have been in serious trouble. The boy answered, "I was born smart."

Another Legionary was faced with this accusation: "You say that the accusations on this form you are asked to sign are not true. This form is a Government document. Do you presume to say that the Government made a mistake?" What would you answer? If you say the Government is fallible, that alone is sufficient to make a serious case against you. How would you avoid the snare, yet tell the truth and shut them up? This Legionary said, "I am a private citizen. The Government is a public institution. I mind my business; the Government minds its business. It is not for me to say whether or not the Government has made a mistake; and the Government does not force me to say black is white."

Here is another one: "What do you think of Mao Tse-tung?" This is not an easy question. In the mind of the questioner what he is asking is not, "What do you think of Mao Tse-tung," but "What are you willing to say of Mao Tse-tung without getting yourself into trouble?" Because they know what sensible people think of Mao Tse-tung, they are merely trying to get a condemnation of one's own self from one's own mouth. This Legionary (who did not get beyond the first year of high school) answered, "Mao Tse-tung has made great sacrifices for the people. He has shown great courage in working his way to the top. If his motives are unselfish and he is in good faith, God will reward him. If not, God will punish him." This answer, so to say, jumped off into such deep water immediately that the tormentors could not reach the bottom; so they swam for shore and dropped the question.

It was an experience for me to be in personal contact with so many individuals in whom the workings of grace was so visible. Of those who were summoned to the police station, many had the experience narrated above: first, great fear, consternation, pounding of the heart; then when the zero hour arrived, calm confidence and courage and the "*dabitur vobis*", a seeming inability to cope with the situation on the part of the police; and when it was over, greater courage and new determination.

There was the timid music teacher. She was a strong Legionary, but always afraid of the cost. When the storm broke, her father, who also is a fervent Catholic, appealed to the Ten Commandments. 'The fourth commandment," he said, "tells you to honour your father and your mother. Here you are deliberately bringing calamity upon their aging heads. You must go and sign the 'confession' for the sake of your father and mother." She felt she could not sign. The tension was wearing her down until one day she went to the police station, not to sign, but so that she could not be punished for disobeying the order to report. After much talk - talk that lasted for an hour and a half, she made a footnote - to the document in which she said in effect: "I do not agree with what is printed on this document, but I sign my name as testimony that I am a member of the Legion of Mary." With that she was released and her parents were satisfied.

An outstanding case is that of a partly-crippled young high school student. A month before the real trouble started, she had resigned from the Legion and went into the service of the Reds for a pecuniary consideration. She served as a spy, went to Red meetings and reported what she knew and what they wanted her to say. She continued to come to Holy Mass daily and to Holy Communion. Hers, I think, was a case of inferiority complex. Because of her physical condition, she felt that she was looked down upon. By following the leaders, those who seemed to be getting into power, she felt that she could get into a position of authority. Her father said, "Religion is a matter of one's personal conscience. If she feels she is doing right, no one (including the Church) can tell her she is wrong in receiving Holy Communion." Everybody had an eye on her; she was a public scandal. Finally a group of college boys, Legionaries, decided to do something about it; and if there were consequences, all right, let them come. So one day when she was going to the Communion rail, three of them followed her. When she knelt down they stood immediately behind her. When the priest came to her, one of the boys held a large piece of cardboard in front of her face so she could not receive. The priest passed her up. She looked around, turned red, said nothing, got up and walked back to her pew, the boys following her. Everybody was secretly delighted. This could have brought a concentrated attack of the Reds on the college boys and on the priest.

All were waiting anxiously for the outcome; strange to say, nothing happened. I say "strange to say", because only in a small number of cases did the prompt reaction of the Communists fail to materialise. God has a hand in their works not only more than they know, but also more than we know. He directs everything accordingly to His plans and purpose. Anyway, this person was never seen in that Church again, although some claimed that she went to some other one where she was not known. Later on her father reported, "She is in so deep with the Reds now that she cannot get out"- an indication that either he or she would like to be free of any commitment to the wrong camp. She gave me a few headaches, and so I still pray for her. I hope she is one of those who has recently made a public retraction and being taken back into the fold.

By far the majority of Legionaries remained faithful throughout. They all began the battle in great trepidation; but as time went on they grew more determined. From October till Christmas individuals were constantly being summoned to the police station in an attempt to make them sign. One man put in twenty-one hours of questioning and indoctrination in one week. Most of them, when they refused to conform, were told to go home and think it over and come back. The police also made visits to the homes of individuals. On one such visit a Legionary asked, "If I do not sign, what will you do?" The agent replied, "I'll come and talk to you again." "And then if I do not sign what will you do?" "Then I'll come again." "And then what?" "Then I'll come again." One investigator admitted, "We cannot put everybody in prison."

Six teachers (in a Catholic school that was taken over) were plagued day after day for a couple of months. Then they were fired from their positions, and still have little prospect of finding other occupations. All such characters are put on the black list; and when they try to find work they are always asked whether they have been a Legionary. If so, there's no job.

As mentioned above, the reaction of the police to the answers they got was unpredictable. I will cite three instances:

1. Pang Niu, a high school girl, was one of the most active Legionaries in her school. One night the police came to her home and took her to the police station at nine o'clock. They questioned and threatened all night, but with no success. At five in the morning she said, "You must let me go now; it's time for me to go to Holy Mass." They said, "All right, we'll take you." They drove her to church in the car, let her out and went away.

2. Then there was Theresa Wang of the same school. After much quarrelling over the point at home her brother dragged her to the police station and made her sign. She did. The next day she went back to the police station and protested that she had not signed freely and demanded that they turn over to her the signed paper. They refused of course. She stayed there and raised a howl. She got down on her knees and yelled bloody murder. The men in the office did not know what to do. After a while an officer came out from the inner office and asked what was going on. They told him. He said to the girl, "you go home nice and quietly now, and I promise you that I'll bring the paper myself." She went home. That night, after everybody was in bed, two cars drove up. The whole family expected the worst. In one car was the officer and his aides; in the other were guards. They made a speech to this effect: "This young lady claims that she was forced to sign a document. The one who made her sign did wrong. You must know that we force no one to do anything. If she signs, she must do it freely." And handing the document to the girl he said, "Here is the paper you signed. You can bring it back to the office when you choose to do so." Then

they all left. It's an unusual story, but I got it first hand. Everybody expected something more to happen. She never took the paper back to the police station; and up to the time I was ushered out of the picture, nothing had happened.

3. Then there's Martha E. Sum. She and her aunt and three brothers were all in the Legion and, to the Reds, notorious. Martha was one of those souls in whom Faith is a living thing. She put all her confidence in the Blessed Virgin Mary, and worked for her with all-out intensity, and did not count the cost or reckon the consequences; so much so that her father, who was a fervent Catholic and approved of Martha's activities, nevertheless was always "sitting on needles and pins" knowing that she was going to get in trouble with the Reds.

For a long time before Msgr. Quint was arrested there had been a woman Red spy shadowing him. This spy was pointed out to Martha. One Sunday morning she said to me, "The spy is in church; I'm going after her." I said, "Be careful." When the spy came out of church after Mass, Martha fell in line beside her and opened conversation. The spy became very friendly; she thought she saw an opening to do some propagandising. Suddenly Martha broke in, "I know you; you're the spy who is always coming to church to take notes and report on the Fathers."

The spy replied that it was nice to be recognised. Martha then said: "you have no right to come to church." Spy: "Does the church belong to you?" Martha: "The church does not belong to me; but it is the house of God. And anyone who is playing the part of Judas has no right to enter the church."

After a little more verbal cross-fire, the spy left. The onlookers were glad that the bull had been taken by the horns; but at the same time everyone also knew that the spy would report the incident and Martha would be subject to attack.

This happened on the Sunday before Msgr. Quint was arrested. On the second day after he was arrested Martha got a summons to go to the police station. She came to say goodbye and to ask for my prayers; she knew she was going to prison. She packed her little overnight bag and her mother went with her. What happened she believes to be a miracle to this day; I do too. At the police station they identified her, and then gave her an exit visa for Hong Kong. (She had applied for it several months before, and had now given up hope of ever getting it.) Within twelve hours she had packed her things, bought a ticket and was on the train bound for the other side of the Bamboo Curtain.

The following Sunday the spy came back looking for her; too late. Another week went by and the police were looking for her; also too late. It seems that one Red agency was issuing her the exit Visa, not knowing that another agency was getting ready to pounce on her. The Blessed Mother it seems, was pulling the strings for one who really did heroic things for her and had confidence in her. Some time later, while they were questioning another Legionary, the Reds admitted that Martha had slipped through their fingers. Several months later when they were purging those accused of bribery, etc. Martha's family was investigated to find out if they had bribed some official in order to get her the exit Visa.

We must not omit here the incident of the holy water in the tea. Some time before Martha left Shanghai, she and her aunt (who lived in the same house) had a caller one day at noon. He politely asked whether they had time to talk. They said, "No time." He said, "Then I will come back this evening at seven." This man was known by the Legionaries as a clever operator. He visited from one to the other, always courteous. Claiming to be a Catholic, he showed sympathy with Catholic ideals. But everyone knew him as a Communist whose business it was to draw the Legionaries out, get them talking by seeming to be sympathetic. If he could get them to mention another Legionary's name, he would go to visit this person next. He came to know a lot from persons who were not on to his tricks. Knowing his character, Martha and her aunt prepared tea for him, and before he arrived put holy water in it. He arrived at seven thirty. The conversation must have got rather controversial, because one of Martha's young brothers went for help. He called another aunt who lived nearby. She was not so strong on the spiritual side, and she was not a Legionary, but she was a good talker and quick-witted. Grandma was present too. The conversation went on and on and round and round. At about nine thirty Grandma had enough. She said, "That's enough of this; it's time to say our night prayers." The visitor offered to stay for night prayers. Martha, two aunts, three brothers and Grandma all knelt down before the statue of the Sacred Heart. They recited all the night prayers they knew, including all the "frills" that Grandma added in the course of time; recited the Rosary and added two litanies. The visitor sat through it all, saying nothing. After night prayers he started more conversation. Shortly after ten o'clock Grandma made a few sharp remarks and asked him to leave. He walked out of the house without any new information on the Legion.

To my mind, the Legion of Mary was especially ordained by Divine Providence to get the Church in China over this very dangerous period. I had known the Legion back home in only the most superficial way. When I got into the Legion work in Shanghai, I came to know something of its spirit. I was greatly edified and inspired. Its first objective is personal sanctification; but it is the most effective Catholic Action I have seen in operation. The members get a definite work to do each week, and each week they report on the progress in their assignment. There is no room for unfulfilled good resolutions. If one member is getting no place on his project, the other members gang together and help. There's no such thing as failure; because their motivations are wholly supernatural. To the Spiritual Director, the workings of grace are simply visible. I have known people to join the Legion by being "dragged in", as it were, by some zealous member; and within a short time transformed into its most zealous workers. It may be that God had special work for the Legionaries to do in Shanghai, and therefore gave them special graces. But I am inclined to think that the spirit of the Legion is the same the world over. It was, with us, not the case of the priest pushing the Legionaries, but rather of the Legionaries pulling the priest along with them. They asked for days of Retreat; they helped organise novenas of sermons before the greater feasts. They visited the sick, baptised those in danger of death; catechised the children; brought couples to have their marriage rectified; kept a friendly watch on those who were wavering or being worked on by dangerous influences They explained to those who needed it that religion and patriotism are not the same thing, but are often opposed to each other. They went to listen to talks with a notebook, and carried the messages to others. Their enthusiasm was contagious. They were the leaven wherewith the whole mass became leavened.

According to one pagan in Shanghai, "The only group of people who still dare to stand on their own feet is the Catholics." "Every other group," he noted, "immediately backed down when pressure was put on them by the Red Regime." This was true not only of civilian groups, but also of other religious groups; for instance, the Protestants. They preached what they were told to preach. Not to do so was to risk your life; the Catholics took the risk, and the churches were crowded. Most of the instances which brought the courage of the Catholics to the notice of the public, were cases of persecuted Legionaries. Nothing did so much good for the Legion as the propaganda given it by Communist posters displayed all over the city and articles in the newspapers condemning the organisation's crimes.

The people saw and admired the courage of those who dared to hold their heads up in the face of such ridicule and threats. All watched closely the progress and outcome of the battle. They passed the stories around of how the Legionaries went to the Police Station with their little bag, prepared to stay, but not to yield; of how some of them sat there fingering their Rosaries while the police talked, threatened and indoctrinated for hours; of how one after the other went through the same ordeal (and some many times), never yielding, always

300

coming out with a moral victory. People who never before gave a second thought to the Catholic Church, now became greatly interested not only in the Church, but also in the Legion. They were fellow travellers now: all were being persecuted; and they admired those who dared resist.

The Communist effort to start a schism in the Church by getting the Catholics of Shanghai to sign the "Three Independencies Movement" was fermenting all during the spring of 1951; but it was getting no place. The Legionaries were quietly leavening the unleavened. Nothing serious happened until the first day of the novena in preparation for Pentecost. On that night and the following night, extensive raids were made in the city. It was said that 10,000 people were arrested on those two nights.

From the time of Msgr. Quint's arrest on 3ʳᵈ October 1951 until after Christmas, when the vast majority failed to show up at the police station to sign their 'confession', individuals were summoned for questioning. What they were asked to sign was morally wrong on two counts. 1. It was libellous; it contained lies about the Legion and about the characters of the leaders of the Legion 2. The signatory promised to make up for his past "mistakes" by working in the interest of Communism.

The Communists seemed to think that by first arresting the leaders and putting the fear of prison into all the members, a little more pressure would bring enough signatures to make good headline reading in the newspapers. They would thus discredit the Legion, and make the members afraid to oppose the "Three Independencies." To put everybody in jail would arouse the populace in favour of the persecuted, so when the Reds met with real persevering passive resistance, what could they do? After three months of putting on pressure and getting no place, people were laughing at them up their sleeves; and the Legionaries grew more confident and an impetus was given to all Catholics and their sympathisers.

In February 1952 the Reds became all absorbed in a purge of so-called corruption in business, which resulted in thousands of suicides. They did not have much time to bother Legionaries during this time. It started on St. Valentine's Day and carried on for perhaps two months. When this distraction had passed, they seem to have remembered that the Legion question was not yet closed. What to do? From what we can see, it seems they determined to expel the foreigners and gradually to imprison or indoctrinate the rest.

In June, agents of the new Regime called me to the police station. And this time there were no questions; this time they had only the answers. To wit: 'You have been ordered to come and sign your confession. You have had plenty

of time to make up your mind. You persist in ignoring the orders of the Peoples'
Government. You have done much harm to the people of China. You are,
therefore, hereby declared expelled from the country.'

Indoctrination is insidious. I left China wondering what the future had
in store for the Catholics of Shanghai. And so I find great consolation in the
following quotation of what may be considered the latest out of China. It is from
the *China Missionary Bulletin* published in Hong Kong: the most recent issue,
January, 1953. And with this quote I close for the present. I hope to live long
enough to witness and tell the story of the final victory of the Catholics of
Shanghai. It will be an edifying page in the history of the Legion of Mary, and
one more facet in the gem that is the Age of Mary.

> Last year as we looked forward to 1952, it did not look very promising,
> but now that it has passed, we may say that it was far better than we
> expected. The Catholic Church was by no means crushed out of existence
> (as was to be feared). It has rallied and come back stronger than before - it
> is more vigorous than it has been for centuries.

PERSECUTION OF THE LEGION OF MARY IN CANTON
by an anonymous Jesuit

Since the Communists came to Canton, they have done the Legion of
Mary the signal honour of special attention. During recent months this has
increased and on August 5th 1953, it took the very definite form of planned
persecution. It is hardly necessary to say that the Legion had ceased to hold
meetings and no longer existed in Canton: it had stopped operating as long ago
as the month of April 1951, after a short existence of two years. This did not
suffice for the Reds. On the date mentioned (5th August) hundreds of police and
soldiers were sent out all over the city to announce to each member of the Legion
that the government declared the organisation to be imperialistic, reactionary and
engaged in spying. All Legionaries were to sign a document admitting that they
had belonged to this traitorous society; former officials were to give up all
records, Handbooks, flags, etc. Those who conformed would be granted a full
pardon: those who did anything to oppose the carrying out of the decree, were to
be severely punished: three bureaus would be opened in the city for the
convenience of those who wished to sign.

Three foreign Fathers who had been Spiritual Directors were called at 5a.m. and whisked off to the Central Police Station where the proclamation was read to them and they were asked to sign. When they refused they were given some time for reflection and sent back to their own residences where they found a dozen or so police busy examining their property. Each was told that he was confined to his room under care of these guards. The priests were Fr. E. Limat, Swiss, of the Paris Foreign Mission Society, parish priest of Shameen; Fr. C. Egan SJ, Superior of the Irish Jesuits in Canton; Fr. J. O'Meara SJ, parish priest of Tunghsan. Their trials were brief and light: they had two more trips to the Police Station where they were condemned for all the evil they had done through the Legion and ordered to leave the country immediately. Thus after nearly two days of house arrest they found themselves on the train for Hong Kong, where they arrived about midday on 7th August.

For the Chinese clergy and laity, the easy road of expulsion to Hong Kong is closed. They have to stay behind and face the music; and they have shown courage of the type that is the glory of the Church and the witness to the power of God's grace down the ages. Chinese priests were at the altars of the three Churches the day following the arrest of the foreigners: the Holy Hour in preparation for the First Friday was carried out in the presence of Communist guards, the hymns being chosen and sung in a way calculated to show that the faithful defied their enemies. After the Holy Hour, the congregation remained for a time under the windows of the Father's rooms shouting farewell and good wishes. It was for this reason that the Reds chose the night train for the Father's exit: they feared a demonstration at the railway if they waited for the regular morning train.

Punishment of the Chinese had already begun: Fr. Francis Tam, a very active and zealous priest, was arrested on the evening of the 6th. He had been connected with the Legion but would certainly have gone round exhorting the timid to stand firm. The laity were being told lies, tricked, threatened, and subjected to family pressure to force them to sign the document condemning the Legion.

About a dozen did sign, but of these all but two rushed off to the priests as soon as they had got rid of their visitors. They were advised that as the Communists wanted both a signature and a photo from each, they must now refuse the photo which they had not yet been able to provide: they were also given a penance according to the circumstances of each: some were even deprived of Holy Communion for some weeks in order to let them and all know that while a battle is on, there can be no tolerance of weakness such as imperils the safety of all.

News has come through of young Catholic men being interrogated for long periods of time. Five were arrested and kept in gaol for ten days. One of the five, a teacher is to report twice weekly to the local Police Station and to give an account of all his doings and probably of his thoughts as well. Another has been told that he may not continue his University studies unless he gives in to the Communist demands. The other three will find it impossible to get a job. There have been no arrests of young women, but they are subjected to continuous visiting, one "comrade" taking up when his predecessor is weary. Pagan fathers threaten their daughters with expulsion from their homes and subject them to day-long nagging together with rather comical and over-dramatised appeals. One good man pretended that he was so overcome that he dropped down as if dead. Another started a funeral service for his daughter outside the door of the house.

These brave and faithful souls do not fear death or imprisonment, but they do fear their own weakness. For them death would be a short and easy way out. But they will not be offered this privilege. The long slow painful torture of unemployment with absolutely every door closed to them, the horrible, insidious methods of 'brain-washing' - these are the dangers which fill them with fear. Some are inclined to smile when they hear this strange term, 'brain-washing', but it is far from being a laughing matter. It is a skilfully planned form of psychological torture designed to break down one's manhood, to humiliate, degrade and terrify so that a man will be afraid not only to speak against the government but even to harbour any thoughts against its alleged omnipotence.

The Catholic Church in Canton is a small flock and the Legionaries are only a handful. They are suffering no more than many pagans, for it is not only Catholicism that has to be destroyed. Man himself, as God made him, does not please the Communists and he has to be torn apart in spirit and put together again, if anything remains after the destructive process. The Catholics and among them Mary's soldiers are in the front line of battle for humanity. They need and deserve the help of our sacrifices and prayers.

COMMUNISM AND THE LEGION OF MARY

Rev. Albert V. Fedders, MM
Published in *Pagan Missions* June 1953,
by courtesy of the *Sunday Examiner*, Hong Kong

Father Fedders belongs to the Catholic Foreign Mission Society of America
(Maryknoll Society), which was founded in 1911.

I was accused of being a criminal by the Communist government in China. For fifteen months, the Red authorities of the little village of Taai Wan kept me under surveillance because of "my criminal acts against the People's Republic of China." The crime that I had committed, so they often told me, was establishing the Legion of Mary.

In the hinterland of China, the Legion of Mary was the number one enemy of the Government. An official addressing the people in Church one day, while I was held prisoner in the sanctuary, my "home" for fifteen months, ranted at them, "It is more dangerous than an army of wild bandits. We can see the bandits, chase them, tie them up, shoot them. The Legion is a spiritual force. We can't see it to shoot it!"

Yet they were unable to answer just why the Legion was their enemy. What they shouted and propagated was only that which they had read in their newspapers. They had their orders, to be sure, to root out this "Spiritual force" because it was their deadly foe, but they did not know how the Legion came to be such a hateful object to Communism. It was only after I had been released that I discovered for myself the true extent of the campaign against the Legion throughout the country. Taai Wan was such a small village, one of the thousand of such villages that formed the chain of mission stations that made up the Church in China. The local officials obeyed their instructions to the letter, like automatons, without knowing the wherefore.

Enter Communism

The Communist armies reached the mountains of Taai Wan on December 3, 1949. There was no resistance from the people, and no thought of resistance. When the army took Pingnam, the county seat, the fall of Taai Wan, only a village headquarters, was taken for granted. The Mission of Taai Wan counted some nine hundred Catholics, half of them scattered through twenty-three outlying smaller hamlets or Mission Stations. Most of the Taai Wan village population of 500 people were Catholics. The Church, and the Christianity, dated back to 1923, when Father Thomas McRae, a Maryknoll priest, began working in the district.

The changes that Communism brought to the area came slowly. In the early months Father John Curran, MM, of Butte, Montana and myself were free to visit the country stations. It was customary to spend days on the road, going from one Catholic home to another, saying Mass and administering the sacraments to small groups.

Then we began to be questioned by the Communists when we were away from home. On one occasion Father Curran was arrested while on a mission trip, and forced to walk through the dead of night to the riverbank, a distance of eight miles, where he was kept in a Chinese inn. The following day he was escorted down river on a Chinese junk and handed over to the Magistrate. He was only released when a Chinese priest gave a guarantee for him.

Not long after this, we opened a Catechumenate for doctrine in a village about four miles from our Church. One Sunday morning after Father Curran had celebrated Mass at the Catechumenate, the Mayor told him that the house we used was needed for a village school, and told Father to take all his equipment and his Catechists out of there.

We opened a Catechumenate in another village where, 1,500 pagans had signed up for the course in doctrine. The two native Sisters we sent there lasted only six or seven days. The village leader informed them that if they remained he "could not take the responsibility for their safety." They had to pack up and come home.

The Reds increased their restrictions on the people, and on their movements. The officials told us to apply for "permits" when we desired to leave Taai Wan. We complied, but found it more and more difficult to get such permission. We were interrogated about our business, our destination, the purpose for the visits, etc. Finally in July, our requests were refused outright. We never left Taai Wan again to visit the country Catholics.

Communist "Campaigns"

The restrictions affected not only ourselves, but the Chinese as well. The campaign to eliminate the "bandit remnants," as the Communists called the guerrilla forces who resisted from mountain strongholds, was followed by another campaign to eradicate "reactionaries," and yet another campaign to liquidate "Landlords." The Reds imposed their will by mass arrests, executions and terror. Whatever opposition remained to the new Regime petered out.

Mail was still reaching us regularly although we were otherwise cut off from communications. Just before Christmas, 1950, we received word that our Bishop had been arrested on December 19th. Two other priests and one of the Sisters had also been taken off to gaol in the See city. It wasn't difficult to read the signs of the times. Father Curran and I packed a little bag of clothes and toilet articles and made whatever other preparations we thought necessary for prison.

Christmas passed peacefully in the sense of freedom from outside interference. We enjoyed one of the greatest feast day celebrations in our memory. The attendance for Mass was larger than usual. The Christians shot off firecrackers as usual in honour of the birthday of their Saviour. The following morning we solemnised a triple wedding by celebrating a High Mass, with all the outward splendour we could command in such an outpost. With all the external manifestations of joy, however, went the conscious, though unspoken thought that it was for the last time.

Arrest

The following morning a big procession of officials entered the mission compound. Soldiers surrounded the chapel and our house with drawn guns. Everyone was herded out into the open, our catechists, workmen, the native Sisters and the people who were there studying the doctrine. We stood in a ragged circle on the basketball court surrounded by the soldiers.

It was Father Curran's suggestion that we follow the government officials when they entered our house for a search. We pushed through the soldiers and insisted on being present when they went through our effects. Our demands were founded on solid reason. We had heard why the Bishop, priests and Sister had been carted off to gaol in the See city. During the search the police planted the evidence, then tied up the 'criminals' and marched them off. It wasn't brilliant police work, but it was effective.

We had our way. We opened the doors to the various rooms and stood by while soldiers made a poor disguise of the "investigation" They lifted the corner of the blankets on the beds, opened cupboards and pulled out drawers. Whenever one of the searchers took off from the group, we hurried after him. It was apparent that it was not a real investigation but a search for an opportunity.

When they finished our house they went to the Sisters' dwelling. We stayed right behind them. There was much opening of rattan baskets or suitcases, but never once when we weren't in sight. They covered all the rooms in the house, peering under beds, in corners and behind doors.

By the time we got back to the basketball court, the two Chinese Sisters were kneeling on the ground being tied with ropes. A Catholic woman and a young man were also being forced to their knees. The four of them were roped and tied together. We demanded to know why these people were being bound but got no answer. The soldiers shoved them rudely to their feet and marched them out of the compound.

Terrorising the People

The authorities never revealed why they took these people off. A woman who was a prisoner at the Mayor's office where the Sisters were held overnight revealed that she had heard the entire plan discussed by the officials the night before the search. Their intention was simply to terrify the Catholics. Next noon, the four prisoners returned to the mission. The Sisters were instructed to remove their religious habits and return to their own villages. The woman and young man were given court commands to "go home."

The Mayor's plan worked well enough. The unwarranted search and arrest threw a fright into those who were living at the Mission. They knew well what it meant to be carried off to prison and never heard from again. Our Catechists, workmen and those who were studying the Catechism, left us and returned to their homes. By remaining, serious trouble would be in store for them.

The school children were not permitted to leave the compound. The Mayor's office had made it clear that the school was no longer a part of the Mission and that the children were to continue their studies. A few days later, under the Communist teachers' instructions, the school children in a body turned over their prayer books and catechisms to us. The officials wanted it to appear that the children were doing this of their own volition because they no longer believed in the Catholic doctrine.

The Communists from the first had preached the freedom of religion while at the same time ridiculing and deriding belief in anything supernatural. Cartoons and caricatures painted or pasted on the walls of the town lampooned American Imperialists. Red propagandists on street corners and in meetings mocked those who prayed or went to church. In spite of this, close to three thousand pagans in different hamlets surrounding Taai Wan had given in their names as a proof of their intention to study Catholic doctrine. We had organised three Praesidia of the Legion of Mary in the parish. The most promising group was composed of eighteen students who exercised a powerful influence over their non-Christian fellows (about half of the 100 student-body). These ardent members had almost all the pagan students coming for morning and evening prayers and attending Mass. Propaganda was simply not enough to discourage the people from being attracted to the Catholic Church, so the officials were warning them off by an exhibition of Communist terrorist methods.

Two days after the search and arrest of the Chinese Sisters two soldiers appeared at our gate. They were to be our "escort," so they said, to the county seat some six miles away. We can be forgiven the thought that immediately jumped into our minds. "This is arrest!" We implied as much to the soldiers and they assured us immediately that they had not come to take us off to prison. Yet six other missionaries in our diocese were in Communist prisons already and we had no reason to doubt that their summons to gaol was also under the pretext of "registration." Father Curran and I walked upstairs, rather slowly I suspect, each keeping his thoughts to himself. We picked up the two bags we had packed a week or so earlier and presented ourselves again to the soldiers "to be escorted."

Taai Wan, the village seat, was ruled over by a Mayor. The place to which we were going had a Magistrate as head of the country area, who in turn was under the Governor of the province. As we walked along the road carrying our bags, Father Curran said to me, "If they would only take us out and shoot us now, and end all this nonsense, we'll be all set. Today is the feast of a political martyr (St. Thomas More - Dec. 29th). This should be a nice day to be executed."

Our registration involved more than simply filling out a prepared form. I sat in a straight back chair for four hours answering questions after I had put down in writing where I was born, how many brothers and sisters I had, where and what I had studied, when I had come to China and all the places I had visited in those fourteen years, when Maryknoll had been founded and why, how many priests were in the society and where, who my superiors were, and so on and on. The written interrogation was routine. The Communists picked up all this information from every foreigner in China and painstakingly filed it away for reference, and later condemnations. The files of the security police must be enormous!

The verbal questioning was much more enlightening. There was one single avenue of interest - the Legion of Mary. We went over the nature of this lay organisation, its purpose and the type of work the members did. I was given instructions to write to each pastor in the diocese to collect the names of the members throughout the area. I listened to the instruction but never carried it out.

"You will go back to your Mission," they said, "under guard, and give the soldiers two copies of the Handbook of the Legion of Mary in English and two copies in Chinese." I agreed to this. And so we went home. The dust seemed to settle down after the investigation and the "registration." We lived at home, confined only to the crooked alleys of the village. Mass was offered regularly and the people, at least those in the immediate vicinity, were fairly faithful at fulfilling their Sunday obligation.

Propaganda against the "American imperialists" was at white heat. Missionaries were being branded by the newspapers as "imperialist aggressors hiding under the cloak of religion." Priests and Sisters were being arrested all over the country for deliberately killing orphan babies and horrible pictures of dead waifs appeared under the titles "Christian Charity in Action," and "The Imperialists' Hell on Earth." Children in schools were being fed this propaganda for hours on end. Their libraries were filled with new picture books, depicting – cleverly, if diabolically - the crimes of the imperialists, and most especially of the Missionaries. It was little wonder that "Imperialist devil" and "American devil" became the password among youngsters who knew nothing about either.

Outside of Mass, people kept well away from us. The laws for the restriction of counter-revolutionaries and reactionaries made the Chinese liable to imprisonment and even the death penalty for "relations" with either of these classes. No one wanted his actions misinterpreted.

At home, the banging on the door was a signal for only one thing, another visit for Red officialdom with its interminable interrogations carried on with dogged determination to make the victims speak "tan pak" (truthfully). On April 3rd we expected only another such lengthy quiz when the knock was heard.

Eviction

It was the Mayor himself. He couldn't be accused of verbosity. We were ordered out of our house. Confiscation is just that easy under Communism. We were instructed to leave immediately to make room for the Mayor himself, who would use the place for his office and home. There was one point he wanted to make however: "You are not being evicted," be said, "on the grounds of being teachers of a foreign religion." The Communists did not want anyone to get the idea that their "enemies" were suffering for an ideal. They didn't want 'martyrdom.' "You will move out of here because the American system of government is opposed to the People's system of government." This was a neat ruse. Our nationality, which we couldn't shed, was being used as the pretext for every encroachment on the religion we came to preach. As priests, we were free as

310

the birds of the air. For being Americans, we were moved from our house to the church.

We set up our household in the sacristy and the sanctuary. The sacristy was barely twelve feet long by five feet, enough room to vest before Mass. We "annexed" the sanctuary in order to stand guard over the Blessed Sacrament. It would be a new life, with soldiers rambling over the property and officials living in our former quarters. One thing we wanted more than anything else was to preserve the presence of the Blessed Sacrament as long as we could. At first we had the chapel completely to ourselves. Several days later the Mayor appeared again with another "demand." The chapel was to be used as a meeting hall, and we were "advised" to partition off the sanctuary from the rest of the building. We clashed when we came to a definition of the sanctuary. He wanted the partition at the foot of the altar steps. We argued till we had the altar rail within our own precincts. It was still a novelty each morning to awaken with one's feet already on the altar steps...

...Months went by. One got the feeling of living outside the world, totally apart from it. Our sphere was four walls, a few books and the companionship of the altar. On April 25, 1952, Father Curran was given orders to leave. At the office of Security Police, he was grilled and interrogated about the Legion of Mary once more before his departure. They tried again to force him to reveal the names of members of the Legion; they threatened to lock him in solitary confinement in a dungeon until he admitted everything; they called him a liar because his information didn't coincide with the confessions they had forced from the Chinese.

Legion Under Fire

The Legion was under attack throughout the diocese during these fifteen months while we lived in our "sanctuary." Catholics were being pestered on every occasion, brought in to the police for questioning. But the real investigation, with all the Communist wit and talent expended to its limit, began on May 9 at Taai Wan.

For two weeks the members of the Legion of the surrounding missions were called into the Mayor's office. Seven or eight officials of the Public Security Bureau questioned them all day and part of the night. Each member was detailed to disclose five crimes against me.

Some of these poor people were held at the Government Headquarters for days at a time, and interrogated every day. Others were questioned and released, then called back and interrogated once more, five, six and seven times.

Each Legionary was given strict orders not to reveal to me that an investigation was going on.

The Security Police forced the members of the Legion to surrender their Rosary Beads, Miraculous Medals and the prayer cards of the Legion. They couldn't plead that their beads had been broken and discarded. They were made to hunt up the pieces and turn them in. They couldn't excuse themselves for having discarded the prayer leaflets; out they must go to find them. One lad claimed that he had thrown his away in a rubbish heap. I saw him bring it back, crumpled, smeared, tattered. The 'evidence' against the Legion!

Then there was a demoniac frenzy among the officials to track down each and every Handbook of the Legion throughout the Diocese. They had found out how many books had been circulated, and they set on their trail like baying hounds. Anyone who was reported as having a Legion of Mary Handbook was in for a very rough time.

In like manner they sniffed out the presence of the Legion Standards and any articles used at a Praesidium meeting. Candles, pictures, statues, tablecloths had to be turned in. Even burnt-down candle stubs became a big issue when they were not handed over.

It is hard to picture the rabid energy and distraught animosity that any and every item connected with the Legion evinced, or wherein lay the reason for this fanatical implacability. One young man, treated to endless questions by the Security Bureau, his fear overcome by a thorough loathing of the persecution, sneaked in one night to see me and exclaimed:"The Legion! That's all they harp on! What did we do in the Legion but pray and propagate the faith!"

Legionaries in China

The situation spawning the hounding of Legion members had its origins months before and many thousands of miles away. The Communists conceived a plan for the liquidation of the Church that was both uncanny and insidious. They would not legislate the Church out of existence, or forbid people to participate in services for the worship of God. They would take over the Church, or the external structure of the Church, and make it another tool for Communism. The plan went under the name of an "autonomous programme for the Christian Churches."

Through craft and outright deceit they attempted to get the people to sign a "manifesto" demanding such a reform in the Catholic Church. They forced the people to attend meetings at which the programme was discussed by the Communists themselves, and had each participant upon entrance sign his name as a testimony of his attendance. The list appeared later as that of signatories of the "manifesto."

Throughout it all, the Communists professed that it was not a movement against religion. They claimed that the Catholics had a patriotic duty to sweep out the imperialists from the Church by making their organisation, "self-ruled, self-supported and self-propagated." In itself, the purpose was exactly what the Catholic Church had aimed at in its missionary programme. One day the Chinese were to be ruled by Chinese Bishops, supported by the Chinese people and propagated by the Chinese priests. As an earnest of this final aim, China already had a Cardinal, 24 native Bishops, 2,700 native priests and more than 5,000 native Sisters. The Communists, however, planned the self-rule to be a complete separation from the spiritual supremacy of the Holy Father.

This, of course, was not immediately perceptible when the "three-autonomies movement" began. The seeds of schism were present in the Communist scheme and it became clearer and clearer as the leaders of the Protestant reform, after which the Catholics were told to model their movement, spoke of "a new theology, a new liturgy and a new Canon Law" for the Chinese. When the Catholic Church issued its stand on the question of "independence," the official newspaper of the Peking government, *The People's Daily*, excoriated the "position" as "an imperialist plot to sabotage the Government's wishes."

The Legion in the larger cities of the north, particularly in Tientsin, Peking and Shanghai, was a strong element in the resistance to this imposed "reform." The lay people overturned many of the Communist ruses to obtain signatures; they also strengthened the faith of others, where priests were not able to directly contact the Chinese. In Tientsin and Shanghai particularly, Legionaries wholeheartedly opposed the Communists.

So the Government "outlawed" the Legion … They made much of the "secret" of the Legion, claiming it was a "secret organisation" of the imperialists. Fantastic as the charges were, that was the government's decree. No mention of religion was made in long and bitter propaganda against the Legion. Instead, the Regime brought accusations of issuing threats, of misuse of spiritual powers by excommunication of those who followed the Independent Church, of interfering in the internal affairs of the Government.

Along with the suppression of the Legion went the order for all Legionaries to register and sign confessions, prepared by the Communists themselves. The Legionaries refused. Spiritual directors and Legion members were thrown into prison. The newspapers printed pictures of the "evidence" against them: the Legion Handbook, the Legion standards, holy pictures, prayer cards, etc. In each accusation, however, they listed a long catalogue of "crimes," imaginary evil acts of the imprisoned, to substantiate the demand for punishment.

Interrogations

In Taai Wan the natives had read of the "Criminal acts against the Government" of the Legion, had seen the "evidence." Undoubtedly the Communists had their orders to suppress the Legion and punish the directors. Red agents were zealots on a crusade of hatred.

One of the tirades against the Legion that was preached at one of the meetings, held in church, had to do with the prayer recited by the Legionaries daily: "Confer, O Lord, on us," the prayer went, "that fullness of faith in Thee and trust in her, to which it is given to conquer the world." The speaker harped on about the military nature of the Legion as a force to conquer the world. During these two weeks of intensive "investigation" of the Legion, I got my full share of questionings, too. Questions and answers were all written down by two secretaries, who accompanied the official questioner.

"Are you responsible for the founding of the Legion of Mary in this mission of Taai Wan?" was the first question.

"I am responsible," I answered, "for the founding of the Legion of Mary, not only here in this mission of Taai Wan, but in every mission where it exists in this diocese."

"Answer the question that was asked," my interrogator shouted back. "Are you responsible for the founding of the Legion of Mary in Sz Wong (another mission)?"

"I am," I answered again, "responsible not only for the founding of the Legion of Mary in Sz Wong, but in every Mission where it exists in the diocese."

The official pounded on the table. "I asked you were you responsible for the founding of the Legion of Mary in Sz Wong? Answer only that," he thundered.

It was apparent that the examiner had set out to fill a definite and not meagre number of pages of detailed information to send in to his superiors. He didn't want any short cuts. He stuck closely to the question of responsibility for establishing the Legion, convinced, I suppose, that a confession on that score alone was enough to condemn a person to punishment. That, and accusations from Legion members of what I had said against Communism as an enemy of religion, were the backbone of the Government's case against me.

314

"Did you write a Chinese letter to members of the Legion in the diocese?" I was asked. "Yes," I replied. "How many such letters did you write?" was the next query. "Two," I answered.

"Who wrote the Chinese characters in the letters?" was thundered at me. I became as angry as I could force myself to become. "You have no right to ask such a question," I shouted back to him.

I knew what the next question would be as soon as I gave the names of the manuensis. He would want to know who received the letters. "Listen, Mister, get this clear. If you think you are going to get any names out of me, you're wrong. If you keep me here until I rot, or throw me into prison, or take off my head, you will get no names from me. You people proclaim that there is freedom of religion; if there is, you have no more right to ask who is a member of the Legion than you have to ask who is a Catholic."

I wasn't bluffing, but I was quaking. My knees were knocking together because I thought the interrogator had no other alternative but to take drastic action for my refusal. Instead, however, I was merely lectured on my impolite behaviour towards a representative of the People's Government. The session slowed down to desultory questions and then an end. The two secretaries then had to recopy all the information that had been received during the interview. While they were doing so, I reached back to the Communion rail for my breviary and recited the Litany of the Blessed Virgin and other prayers to Our Blessed Mother. I am not sure today whether they were for help or in thanksgiving.

Reactions

A strange phenomenon took place during these days of the investigation. It dawned on me that there was a decided change in the attitude towards me on the part of the teachers and also among the students, even those who were non-Catholic. The ridicule and abuse with which they amused themselves at my expense suddenly came to an end. They began to speak to me as I passed through the yard. Some of the older pagan boys sneaked in at night for a chat, although they were doing so at a tremendous risk to themselves.

A Catholic lad who usually cut my hair became talkative after this and told me that the officials had stated that one may be a Christian, but not a Christian who practised devotion to the Mother of God, that is, a member of the Legion of Mary.

I also learned from one of the students that Communist officials were applying pressure on the boys in the junior Praesidium, trying to get them to admit that they joined the Legion of Mary to become exempt from tuition fees.

The boys answered: "How can we admit such a thing; none of the Catholic boys pay for tuition."

One of the Catholic teachers was more demonstrative and a much more striking example. Months ago he had been appointed by the Mayor of Taai Wan to represent the village at a county meeting for the "Independent Church." At this gathering he had proclaimed that he no longer believed any of the doctrine of the Catholic Church. We will let God judge his motives and his actions. As a non-believer, he extricated himself from any entanglements over the "reform" movement. When he returned, he avoided me and never spoke when we couldn't help but meet. He came to see me one day in a contrite mood, his disgust evident over the fact that the government was trying to destroy the Legion.

There was nothing the Communists did that made the people so hate Communism as their campaign against the Legion and the manner in which it was conducted. Those who were always on the borderline of doubt whether Communism was a persecutor of religion, or merely a persecutor of imperialism, were no longer doubtful at the close of investigations.

It was unbelievable and inconceivable the way the officials confined their activities to the Legion of Mary investigation. They questioned the people about nothing else. They announced from the very beginning that there would be a great public trial and promised that the date of this event would be given later. Frankly, I experienced a very definite spiritual joy, such as I never knew before, in the anticipation of being the representative of all the priests in Wuchow to be publicly ridiculed in honour of the Mother of God. To my cook, who was giving me the details of the coming meeting and how I was to be treated, I promised: "I will try to keep the ropes they tie me with as a memento of the great favour bestowed on me by Our Blessed Mother."

The days of the investigation were filled with a special calm and joy for me. There was nothing to do but wait for the trial. Two weeks passed. The meetings in the chapel under the direction of the Communist officials went on. Then the tenor of the speeches changed. Lying beyond the thin board partition I heard the people were no longer being incited against me. The climatic preparations for the meeting didn't materialise. The talks drifted off to other matters. I began to think that some strange change must have taken place.

One night around midnight, as I was preparing to move my chair to the bed alongside it, hoping to sleep in spite of the fact that a meeting was still in progress in the chapel, I heard the Mayor say: "now, just to show how this American imperialism makes use of perverse methods, take the Legion of Mary. This Legion of Mary is more dangerous to our country than an army of wild bandits. If an army comes after us, we can see them; we can take our guns and shoot them. But this Legion of Mary is a spiritual force. We can't see it. We can't shoot something spiritual."

I listened further. There was nothing more about the Legion. The name was not even mentioned again. Yet, the single phrase lifted up my hopes again that the public trial would soon be held.

Another visitor came to see me. He was the cook for a neighbouring Chinese priest some twenty miles away, home for a visit. He came into the kitchen furtively after I had finished cooking my supper. I invited him to sit down and share my pot of rice, though I thought he'd never dare risk staying that long lest he be caught. He surprised me with, "Sure, Father, I'll be glad to be arrested."

While we were eating, he told me how all the members of the Legion were interrogated in his district. Then he made an observation. "Well, Father, if these stupid officials think that they are going to have a public trial to ridicule Our Blessed Mother, it won't work. Our Lady will certainly defeat them."

It was a different viewpoint, all right. It dawned on me then that perhaps I should be praying that there wouldn't be a public demonstration at which Our Blessed Mother would be subjected to abuse and derision. I honestly had been thinking of myself all along and the honour attached to suffering for the cause. I hadn't taken Our Blessed Mother into consideration very much, except to ask her help and strength.

Expulsion

On July 12 the Mayor called on me. He was terse and direct. He ordered me to appear at the Magistrate's Office in the county seat the following day. All along the twenty-mile walk I prepared myself for the reception I was to get. I could only imagine being met by soldiers, tied up and dragged before a public tribunal.

I walked into the Magistrate's Office unattended. Not one word was said to me about the Legion of Mary. I was given simple instructions to leave the country; and the date of my departure was given with finality.

What were my reactions? They came slowly at first. There was disappointment, of course; but I was filled with joy over the triumph of Our Blessed Mother and the defeat of Satan, whose head was crushed again by the great Mother of God. The pride that lay deep within me kept the twinges of regret alive that I had not been found worthy to suffer. Honoured are those who are subjected in China to the public ridicule of fanatical mobs for the sake of the Blessed Virgin.

The story of Taai Wan is a mere episode in. the great epic of persecution of the Legion of Mary in Communist China. Since my expulsion from the country, I have heard from fellow-priests and read about the furious and diabolical hatred of the Communists towards Our Lady. In all the persecution that rages in China today, it is the dominant note. It would be pathetic if the great lesson to be learned here was not broadcast to the peoples of the world.

The Communist's insidious and satanic hatred for the Mother of God should fill the hearts of all those interested in the salvation of souls, with an invincible confidence that the mission efforts in the world will quickly come into a flourishing and fruitful period. The Reds have chosen the worst target - for their own good - when they singled out the Mother of God as their deadly enemy. Perhaps though, it was not they who chose to hate the Blessed Virgin. They have merely recognised an enemy of old: "I will put enmities between thee and the woman and thy seed and her seed: she shall crush thy head, and thou shall lie in wait for her heel."

The Communists could not have done us Catholics, Missionaries especially, a greater favour than being duped by Satan to start a widespread persecution against the Mother of God. We can flash across the darkened picture of a tormented Church in China, the glorious antiphon of the Feast of Our Blessed Mother: "Rejoice, O Virgin Mary, for you alone have destroyed all heresies throughout the whole world."

APPENDIX V

HEROIC LEGIONARIES

As told by Fr. Aedan McGrath SSC

FELLOW-PRISONER, FR. JOE SHENG

You will have come up against the name Joe Sheng, otherwise known as 'Uncle Joe' many times in the account of my life in China. Among his achievements was the translation, with Fr. Chen, of the Legion Handbook into Chinese. This man was a fellow-prisoner of mine in Ward Road Jail, though not incarcerated in the same section.

When I first came to China as a missionary priest, I was stationed in Hanyang for one or two years. Because of banditry up country, the Seminary had been removed from Huangchiasan to Hanyang, and here for the first time I laid my eyes on little Joe Sheng. He was then a mere boy of fifteen years, small and neat, with his head shaved in Chinese fashion. He had a rather striking appearance, which I never really forgot. I used to take photographs of Joe and his companions playing football, snowball and shuttlecock with the priests.

After Joe had finished his studies in Hanyang, he and Peter Chen were sent by Bishop Galvin to complete their studies for the priesthood in Rome. They were both very clever, perhaps the brightest in the Seminary, and were therefore chosen to go to Rome to do post-graduate studies in theology and Canon Law. Ten years later they both received a doctorate in these subjects after which they returned to China as missionary priests.

While in Rome, Joe made his first acquaintance with the Legion of Mary. There he attended some Praesidia meetings of the Legion with his future confrere in the work of the Apostolate, and Monsignor Riberi's secretary, Fr. Chen. He would also become an ardent promoter of the Legion of Mary.

During holidays Fr. Sheng visited Ireland and Scotland and to fill up his spare time there, and in Rome, he made his first translation of the Legion Handbook into Chinese. This manuscript was posted to China, through the General Post Office in Rome. Unfortunately the Post Office was destroyed by fire and Fr. Sheng's only copy of the Legion Handbook with it. During his next visit to Ireland he managed to make a second translation which did survive. While in Ireland he visited many friends, Legion authorities, including Frank Duff, and he attended meetings of the Concilium in Dublin.

My return to Shanghai in 1948, found Fr. Sheng in charge of the Pontifical Work for the Propagation of the Faith. At this time he had not yet engaged in the work of the Legion in that city. Later on, after a visit to Peking and Tientsin, I returned to Central China, and as I was preparing to leave for Hong Kong I met Fr. Sheng in Hankow. Seeing he had little to do I tried to reawaken his interest in the Legion of Mary, and to engage his services. I succeeded in connecting him with the Curia. I asked the Jesuits, who were in charge, to appoint a Spiritual Director for the first Curia which we were forming in Shanghai. They requested that I nominate a particular priest who did not belong to the Diocese and who had superior knowledge of the Legion. Immediately, they appointed Fr. Joe Sheng.

In December 1949 I departed for Hong Kong, which became my headquarters in the South until June 1950. During that period I had one letter from Fr. Sheng telling me that they had decided to retain the name for the Legion, "Seng Mung Chun" or "Holy Mother's Army". I had tried to get this name changed. I considered that it might provoke too much Communist attention.

While I was in Hong Kong, Fr. Sheng developed the Legion very efficiently in central China. He travelled to Tientsin to find the Legion spreading out its branches very rapidly. He spoke at the Acies meetings there, and remarked how the Communists had been keeping a close eye on him. In fact he seemed surprised that the Communists did not arrest him, but at that time there was no question of imprisoning Missionaries and members of the Legion of Mary. It was too soon yet, but the new regime's plans were certainly in the making at that stage. They wanted everything ready before they should pounce down life a wolf on an unsuspecting flock.

Fr. Sheng endeared himself to the Catholics of Tientsin. The Legionaries used to address him affectionately as "Uncle Joe," which appellation also served as a camouflage.

Uncle Joe returned to Hankow and Wuhan where he approached the Bishops in the disguise of a bare-footed beggar in tattered clothes, concerning the Legion of Mary. The Bishop of Wuchang, an American, and later Bishop Galvin were arrested, questioned and condemned, for, among other reasons, the work of the Legion.

While he was Spiritual Director, first of a Curia, and later of a Senatus, Fr. Sheng was never actually in charge of a Praesidium. After setting up a Senatus in Shanghai, he was forced to resign through sheer pressure of work. Monsignor Prevost was chosen to fill his place. At this time Fr. Sheng used to give many lectures to University students and to the Mothers of the Sacred Heart Convent, who greatly esteemed him. I shall always remember his Triduum on the Sacred Heart which he once gave, both in English and Chinese, for he was fluent in both languages.

Fr. Sheng was very speedy in his work of translation. He would have several people working on different translations, and as was the custom in the Catholic Central Bureau, he would say he had learned his expertise from Fr. Legrand. He certainly wasted no time in what he wrote himself or in what he got others to translate. It was a matter of racing with time, if we were to save the Church. Fr. Sheng was an ideal assistant to Fr. Legrand.

"The Legion of Mary is my life," Fr. Sheng used to say. He was therefore a marked man with the Communists. Soon after my own arrest he too was cast into prison in Ward Road. Frail by nature and weakened from his endless round of duties, consumed with zeal for the salvation of souls, the spread of Catholic Action and especially of the Legion of Mary, he stood a poor chance of weathering the tortures and privations of a Communist jail.

Before long he developed symptoms of bronchial and pulmonary diseases. A fellow prisoner, Fr. Billot SJ, a nephew of the great theologian Cardinal Billot, while passing in silence by a cell, heard the whispered remark "*Sacerdos sum*", "I am a priest". He discovered that Joe Sheng was in that cell, lying on the floor being attended by a doctor. Fr. Joe seemed to be nearing his death as pleurisy had set in.

Later, he received absolution secretly from Fr. Billot, after which he remarked in Latin, "We are all martyrs of Christ", referring to the five priests who had been jailed with him. A short time later, the end came. Fr. Sheng spread out his arms in the form of a Cross and gave up the ghost. He was thirty-six years of age.

NOELLE WANG

One of the best Christians and most zealous and intrepid workers for the Legion of Mary I have ever met was a young Shanghai girl named Noelle Wang,

President of our junior Praesidium of Legionaries. Noelle had graduated in Sociology in the Junior Aurora University and had begun her first year's medicine in the big Aurora University. She was determined to become a Carmelite Nun when she was finished her studies. It was she who made one of those telephone calls to me on the night we decided to discontinue the Legion: she said that the Junior Legionaries had got together and wanted to go on fighting. On meeting her later on I said: "Oh, Noelle, what a great pity the Communists have come down against the Legion!"

In reply she stamped her foot, and said: "Father, don't say that, this is glorious."

And indeed she meant it. Noelle was amazingly courageous. Together with the Catholic students in the Aurora University, she was always in the midst of the tussle against the Communists.

Her best friend, who was a Legionary and a great worker in the University, was arrested a good while before myself; but that did not frighten Noelle. The more accusations she read against the Legion in the Newspapers, the more she rejoiced while continuing to train her little Legionaries, even though there were no meetings. She provided those under her care with copies of the Gospel according to St. Matthew and brought them frequently to an Austrian Jesuit for instruction in the texts. From one of those Scripture classes, they came out shouting: "Matthew: Five - eleven." which indicates the verse: "Blessed are ye when they shall revile you, and persecute you, and speak all that is evil against you, untruly, for My sake; be glad and rejoice for your reward is very great in Heaven."

A former member of my Senior Praesidium, who was not very strong in the Faith, was apparently persuaded by the Communists to publish a letter in the Newspaper, accusing me of various things. On the day following its publication, the children all came to congratulate me, saying it was glorious, and what a wonderfully glorious thing it was to suffer for the name of Christ. While they were brave like this, their Spiritual Director - myself - was knocking at the knees! What must be particularly emphasised about this is that they knew that if I was arrested, it was probable that I would be expelled; while if they were arrested, there would be no such thing as expulsion, but imprisonment, the prospect of torture and also persecution for their families.

Noelle Wang, with some other University students, regularly attended the Sunday Mass said by Fr. Ch'en Che-ming (Chen), who was the secretary of Monsignor Riberi.

Even after the trouble had begun, Fr. Chen insisted on preaching against the Communists during Mass, saying how unjust they were in treating the Legion of Mary as a political society when it was in fact only a religious organisation. He preached strongly and with great courage. Sitting beside the students in the front seat at many of the Masses was a Communist girl, whom we all knew perfectly well. She had sought to be baptised, but her purpose in doing so was to be able to initiate herself into the practices of the Legion in order to discover in what ways she might bring charges against the priests. She would write down everything in Fr. Chen's sermon. After Mass she would bless herself, genuflect, walk out of the Church, cross the road over to the Communist Bureau and hand in what she had written. Fr. Chen was aware of the situation, but yet he continued. Noelle knew what was going on and was certain that she would be accused by that girl; but she did not mind.

According to latest reports, April 1959, Noelle is still languishing in a Communist dungeon where she has suffered a living martyrdom for seven years. Dear readers, please let us not forget in our prayers this heroine Noelle Wang and the countless other people, who have suffered and are still suffering for the faith in China.

SELECT BIBLIOGRAPHY

The selection of books referred to below bear out the facts narrated in this present work. These titles are not intended to be exhaustive but are particularly offered as they reveal the courage under persecution of so many members of the Legion of Mary. The stories of untold numbers of others who suffered for the faith in Communist China resonate in every page of these outstanding testimonies.

Barrett, William E., *The Red Lacquered Gate*, Sheed and Ward, New York, 1967

Cheng, Nien, *Life and death in Shanghai*, Grafton Books, London, 1986

De Jaegher, Raymond J. and Kuhn, Irene Corbally, *The Enemy Within*, Doubleday, New York, 1952.

Devaux, Claudia and Wong, SJ, George Bernard, *Bamboo Swaying in the Wind, A Survivor's Story of Faith and Imprisonment in Communist China*, Loyola Press, Chicago, 2000

Fischer, Edward, *Maybe a Second Spring - The Story of Missionary Sisters of St. Coumban in China*, Crossroad Publications, New York, 1983

Forristal, Desmond, *The Bridge at Lo Wu*, A Life of Sister Eamonn O' Sullivan, Veritas Publications, Dublin, 1987

Greene, Rev. Robert W., *Calvary in China*, G. P. Putman, New York, 1953

Ho, Catherine, *The Lark and the Dragon, A Survivor of the Chinese Gulag*, Printed in Hong Kong, 1996. Originally published as *Many Waters* by Wang Xiaoling, 1988.

Hseih, Philomena, *The Bright Cloud, Faith*, "September 8th" Editorial Board, Taiwan, 2003

Monsterleet, SJ, Jean, *Martyrs in China*, Longmans, Green and Co., London, 1956

Myers, James, T., *Enemies Without Guns, The Catholic Church in China*, Paragon House, New York, 1991

O'Reilly, Luke, *The Laughter and the Weeping – An Old China Hand Remembers*, Columba Press, Dublin 1991

Roberts, Leo, *Mary in their midst*, Clonmore and Reynolds, Dublin, 1960

Van Coillie, Dries, *Brainwashed in Peking, Three years in the prison of Mao Tse-tung*, printed in 's-Hertogenbosch, Netherlands, 1969

Wu, John C. H., *Beyond East and West*, Sheed & Ward, 1952

Scripture quotations are drawn from *The Holy Family Bible,*
Imprimatur - Samuel Cardinal Stritch, Archbishop, Chicago, 1950